The Grieving Child in the Classroom

The Grieving Child in the Classroom integrates the latest research on children's bereavement and adapts it for use in the classroom.

Chapters tackle the neurological, cognitive, emotional, and social effects of childhood grief and demonstrate the ways in which those reactions can manifest in the classroom. By recognizing individual differences in coping styles and considering variables such as developmental stage, nature of the loss, and availability of support, teachers and staff can become better equipped to respond to the bereaved child's needs. The book incorporates theoretical explanations of grief responses as well as practical suggestions for supporting bereaved children in real-world settings.

Whether the loss affects one child or the entire student body, educators can turn to this comprehensive guidebook for ways to support grieving students in their classrooms.

Sue Trace Lawrence, MEd, MA, has worked extensively with children and currently teaches psychology while conducting research on childhood grief.

"*The Grieving Child in the Classroom* is a crucial read in today's world. Lawrence imparts her own comprehensive research as well as the research of many top experts in the field of childhood bereavement to make this book an essential text for teachers, counselors, and school administrators attentive to helping grieving students in their classrooms. This book is truly needed in a society where children are the forgotten grievers. Kudos to Lawrence for writing on this important topic."

—**Dana Hahn**, director of the Friendly Hearts Club Grief Support Program and founder/director of the Luke William Hahn Foundation

"I am grateful to this book's respectful acknowledgement of children's acute attunement to loss and to its recognition of developmental differences in children's experiences and expressions of this grief. This is an invaluable resource for family members, educators, and mentors as they support grieving children with sensitivity and compassion."

—**Kristen English**, PsyD, licensed psychologist and clinical director for the Traces of Love Association

"Sue Trace Lawrence compellingly captures the common challenges children face following loss. This book broadly examines bereavement and its legacy by effectively integrating neurological, cognitive, socioemotional, and psychological perspectives. She offers useful guidance about how educators can best respond in order to facilitate students' recovery and help them thrive. This book is an extremely valuable resource for anyone who cares about children."

—**Catherine Chambliss**, PhD, professor of psychology at Ursinus College and author of *Empathy Rules*

The Grieving Child in the Classroom

A Guide for School-Based Professionals

Sue Trace Lawrence

NEW YORK AND LONDON

First published 2020
by Routledge
52 Vanderbilt Avenue, New York, NY 10017

and by Routledge
2 Park Square, Milton Park, Abingdon, Oxon, OX14 4RN

Routledge is an imprint of the Taylor & Francis Group, an informa business

© 2020 Sue Trace Lawrence

The right of Sue Trace Lawrence to be identified as author of this work has been asserted by her in accordance with sections 77 and 78 of the Copyright, Designs and Patents Act 1988.

All rights reserved. The purchase of this copyright material confers the right on the purchasing institution to photocopy pages which bear the photocopy icon and copyright line at the bottom of the page. No other part of this publication may be reproduced, stored in a retrieval system, or transmitted in any form or by any means, electronic, mechanical, photocopying, recording or otherwise, without prior permission in writing from the publisher.

Trademark notice: Product or corporate names may be trademarks or registered trademarks, and are used only for identification and explanation without intent to infringe.

Library of Congress Cataloging-in-Publication Data
A catalog record for this book has been requested

ISBN: 978-0-367-14554-5 (hbk)
ISBN: 978-0-367-14555-2 (pbk)
ISBN: 978-0-429-05551-5 (ebk)

Typeset in Bembo
by Apex CoVantage, LLC

To Rob and Tim: There are no words to describe your influence on me now, then, and forever.

To Alex: Disenfranchised grief does not hurt any less as the years go by.

To M.: Unconditional love never dies.

I love you all.

Contents

Preface	xi
Acknowledgments	xiii
Author Biography	xv

Introduction: Why Educators Should Be Knowledgeable About Grief	1

SECTION 1
Defining Grief Within a Developmental Context   7

1	Neuronal Pathways in the Brain	9
2	The Role of Memory	18
3	Cognitive Development and Understanding Death	25
4	Children's Psychological, Social, and Emotional Development	31
5	Attachment and Relationships	39
6	Loss as Potential Trauma	43
7	Definitions of Grief	50

SECTION 2
Reactions to Grief and Loss During Early and Middle Childhood   55

8	General Principles of Childhood Grief	57
9	Patterns of Grief Reactions	62
10	Emotions of Grief—Sadness	68
11	Emotions of Grief—Anger	72

viii   Contents

12 Emotions of Grief—Fear	76
13 Emotions of Grief—Guilt	82
14 Learned Helplessness After a Loss	90
15 Effects in the Classroom	93
16 Diagnosable Issues	97

SECTION 3
How to Help Grieving Students   109

17 What to Say to a Grieving Child	111
18 What Not to Say to a Grieving Child	117
19 What to Do for the Grieving Child	121
20 Sublimation, Catharsis, and Finding Meaning	128
21 Starting a Grief Support Group	131
22 Founding a Nonprofit Organization	135
23 When Grief and Loss Hits the Community	138
24 When the Deceased Is a Pet	144
25 Grief During the Holidays	147
26 The Need for Grief Education, Planning, and Training	150
27 Resilience	154
28 A Few Final Thoughts	158

Appendices   159

Appendix A: Statistical Results of Childhood Traumatic Loss Survey Study, Ursinus College (2016)	161
Appendix B: Childhood Traumatic Loss Survey, Ursinus College (2016)	162
Appendix C: Comments From College Students Obtained Via Interviews and Online Surveys, Ursinus College (2016–2019)	166
Appendix D: Online Sources of Support and Advice	167
Appendix E: Annotated Bibliography of Children's Books That Deal With Death, Loss, and Grief	169
Appendix F: Family Movies That Depict Loss Sensitively and Honestly	174

Appendix G: Lesson Plans and Ideas for a Grief Support Group   176
Appendix H: Sample Nonprofit Outreach Letter   182
Appendix I: Sample Nonprofit Information Sheet for Stakeholders   184
Appendix J: Sample Nonprofit Mission Statement   185
Appendix K: Tips and Guidelines for Group Facilitators   187
Appendix L: Sample Letter to Send to Parents and Guardians   188
Appendix M: Sample Application and Consent Form   189
Appendix N: Sample Confidentiality Pledge for Group Members   191
Appendix O: Information Sheet on the Stages of Grief   192
Appendix P: Handout on Coping During the Holidays   194
Appendix Q: Project Ideas for Grief Support Groups   196
Appendix R: Activities to Be Used With a Grief Support Group   197
Appendix S: Suggestions for Activities to Help Kids Cope With Grief   199
Appendix T: Grief Experiences Worksheet   201
Appendix U: Grief Definitions Worksheet   202
Appendix V: Coping Strategies Worksheet   203
Appendix W: My Loved One Worksheet   204
Appendix X: Dead or Alive Worksheet   205
Appendix Y: Grief Scenarios Worksheet   206
Appendix Z: Scavenger Hunt Worksheet   208
References   209
Index   225

Preface

On Tuesday, March 14, 1967, I attended kindergarten at my local elementary school, six blocks from my house. Fifty years ago, most kindergarteners were first-timers in elementary school, and our half-day program was our first experience away from home. None of us had attended daycare or preschool, and a mere two-and-a-half hours of playtime, a recess, a snack, a story, and a rest period comprised our daily schedule. Although a far cry from today's academic classrooms, my kindergarten class proved to be a fun, new adventure. From the first day of school in September until this second week of March, I was a normal student, an average little girl with few distinguishing characteristics. But on the 14th, I became something different— a grieving sibling who lost her little brother.

My brother, Tim, was 3 years old at the time of his death from leukemia. In 1967, leukemia was an automatic death sentence. My brother's journey through illness was a short one. After contracting the mumps virus in February, Tim became sicker and sicker until he was diagnosed with the fatal blood disorder. Although an experimental treatment technically forced the disease into remission, his body had weak immune responses, and he succumbed to an invasive infection. He remained in the hospital for only 12 days before he died, days in which I never had the chance to see him. Hospitals in the 1960s rarely permitted children to visit. Tim's death will haunt and influence me for the rest of my life. For when I went back to my kindergarten class after several days off for bereavement, I had transformed. I was not an innocent little girl anymore. I was different from my classmates. And to be honest, despite their best intentions, school personnel had few ideas about how to help me.

My memories are hazy from the noxious effects of youth tinged with trauma, but I seem to recall my teacher being especially nice to me when I returned. The next year, in the springtime, I was honored with the title of "Princess for a Day" when my new little brother was born, and my first-grade teacher made certain I had the chance to spread the news to other staff. I am sure that the news of a sibling's birth was not typically cause for such celebration; clearly the staff knew my back story. But this was all the special attention I received after Tim's death. The district employed no guidance counselors or school psychologists or any other professional available to help me through my grief. The teachers and principal relied on their own instincts. Sibling loss did not happen every day, so my being thrust into this unenviable role was challenging for everyone. My educators did the best they could under the circumstances. Fifty years ago, childhood grief was not a hot-button issue.

xii Preface

I can only wonder how more effectively I could have coped if the educators in my inner circle had been privy to supportive information.

Fast-forward 38 years later, to a fall day in November. On the tenth of that month I learned that my other little brother, the one whose birth made me first-grade royalty, was found dead in his home, supposedly from natural causes related to diabetes. My two sons were in college at the time, while my daughter was a high school freshman. Although my sons came home from their college classes for a few days, my daughter chose to attend school the next day in a quest for some form of normalcy. That hope was shattered when one of her teachers refused to believe her when she tried to explain the reasons for her incomplete homework assignment. Even when this instructor reluctantly acknowledged the truth of her story, he challenged her level of anguish about the situation. "It was only your uncle," he declared. "There is no reason why *that* would make you so upset." Never mind that this uncle, my beloved brother, was exceptionally close to my family. Uncle Rob was a favorite relative to my children; their loss was deep, and their grief was real. This teacher's lack of compassion and understanding made my daughter's attempts to cope just that much more difficult.

The desire to help other children who today walk in my ancient moccasins, and those of my daughter's, was the incentive for this book. I hope that by teaching the teachers and other school personnel, I can provide insight and practical ideas that will help ease the grieving child's pain. I know firsthand what is lacking and why it is so important for educators to understand the effects and manifestations of childhood loss. I would like to help provide the support my daughter and I never had those years ago. To serve the same purpose, I founded Traces of Love Association, a nonprofit that provides support to grieving children and their educators. Through offerings of grief support group services in the schools to presentations to teachers and staff, Traces of Love Association seeks to provide direct services for those who can benefit.

The sad truth is that when a child is mourning a loss, that situation pervades all aspects of that child's life, leading to limitless consequences, including anxiety, hypochondria, pessimism, and loss of perceived control. These losses can manifest emotionally and physically, both in the home and outside of it (Rosen & Cohen, 1981). A child in grief is a child who desperately needs support, empathy, and understanding. We owe it to these students to be well-versed in how grief and loss affect not only them but ourselves as helpers. We must recognize that the effects of grief can take many forms, some not always obvious, and there are clear distinctions in coping styles among children, adolescents, and adults. It is the purpose of this book to suggest how young kids and preteens process loss, and its implications for the classroom. Learning about this topic may not be a fun journey, but it is a trip we need to take. Our capacity to love means that grief can be right around the corner.

One of my favorite psychologists was Carl Jung, whose unique blend of mysticism and philosophy made him one of the foremost psychoanalytical thinkers of his time. He once wrote, "*I am not what happened to me, I am what I choose to become*" (Jung, 1963). I try to keep this in mind as I walk through my life, and I hope we, as educators, can hold the hands of grieving children and show them they, too, can not only overcome the losses in their lives but learn from grief's lessons.

Acknowledgments

This book has been a pleasure to write and research, but it was challenging all the same. Without the support of the following people, I would have had a much harder row to hoe. I am also appreciative of the moral support and diversions that helped enormously when the heaviness of this topic weighed me down too much.

Special thanks to:

The Ursinus College Psychology Department, especially Dr. Cathy Chambliss, for allowing me time and space to conduct my research.

Dr. Kristen English in the Ursinus College Wellness Center, for supporting my research, providing training and advice to my students, and graciously offering assistance with Traces of Love Association.

The Ursinus College students who have been involved in all aspects of my research over the last 5 years. I have the best helpers ever!

Rachel Allison, Alexandria Birnbrauer, Zachery Brink, Anna Budny, Shelby Carmichael, Mikayla Cimino, Katherine Damato, Natasha Dartey, Gianna Dombray, Naomi Epstein, Lauren Feldman, Thalia Garcia, Carly Gartenberg, Dayna Honyrch, Abigail Jean, Lydia Jerman, Indira Joell, Katelyn King, Megan Keenan, Maureen Lannon, Ria Malones, Alexandra Mastrangelo, Sophie May, Jessica McFall, Sarah Moss, Nicole Pacera, Amber Peiffer, Karla Pisarcik, Taylor Pyle, Kayla Quinn, Coraima Ramirez, Drew Roesch, Kailey Ryan, Jade Schmidt, Alexandra Senger, Salone Singh, Janice Uricchio, Ryan Vega, William Wells, Nikki Wu.

Traces of Love Association board members and directors: Frankie Bohn, Danielle Lawrence, Ian Lawrence, Jill Lawrence, Seth Lawrence, Amy Myers, Nicolette Pennington, Taylor Pyle, Kim Reidnauer, Alma Smith, and Jessica Winebrenner.

My friends, students, and colleagues at Montgomery County Community College's West Campus, Ursinus College and Chestnut Hill College.

My friends and sisters-in-grief: Suzanne Nelson and Dana Hahn.

My family, current and past, human and animal, especially my dad, Robert Trace, and husband, Sam Lawrence, for putting up with me.

My children: Ian, Seth, and Jill. You have become my friends and advisors in my work, in TOLA, and in my life. I could not be prouder or admire you more. You've grown into amazing people, despite having a psychologist for a mother. Thanks for the love and support!

Author Biography

Sue Trace Lawrence is an educator with degrees in psychology, school counseling, and educational psychology, along with certifications in trauma awareness, neuro-psychology, and grief counseling. She has been involved in the early childhood field for over 30 years. She is currently employed as a professor of psychology at several colleges and universities. Her research interests relate to childhood grief and trauma. She is the author of two previous books, *Sob Stories* and *Turning the Page: Helping a Child Cope with the Loss of a Sibling*. Sue also founded Traces of Love Association, a 501(c)(3) nonprofit that provides grief support services to local schools. In addition to working with bereaved students, Sue also trains educators on the topics of grief, development, and mental health issues.

Introduction

Why Educators Should Be Knowledgeable About Grief

Why do you, as a teacher, administrator, or other educational staff member, need to learn more about grief in a classroom setting? This is a good question—one many of you probably are asking right now. Many teachers assume that they know their children's family situations well, and they may seem confident that death is not an issue affecting many of their students. Experts who work in the bereavement field might respectfully disagree. According to the results of several descriptive studies, teachers may underestimate the number of grieving students in their classrooms. Any eye-opening statistic provided on the data sheet, "Did You Know? Children and Grief Statistics" on the website, www.ChildrensGriefAwarenessday.com (n.d.) stated that one in five children will lose a familiar relative or friend by the age of 18. If we extend the definition of a "loved one" beyond family, the number is even higher; 90% of a polled group of high schoolers reported experiencing a loss. Another survey of a similarly aged sample found that 78% reported a loss of a close relative or acquaintance (Harrison & Harrington, 2001). One in 20 children will lose at least one parent, while many others lose a parental figure such as a grandparent or guardian (Owens, 2008). When we consider how many people are raising children later in life than did earlier generations, these numbers will likely rise in future years. Losses do not always refer to adults. One study estimated that 73,000 children die every year in the United States, and approximately 83% of these children have one or more surviving siblings (Torbic, 2011). Regardless of the actual numbers, the takeaway from these facts and figures is that the number of children who are dealing with grief is significant. Whether or not a teacher knows of the loss, we can assume at least a few of her students are missing a loved one.

Since bereavement periods can be lengthy, the number of affected children suffering at any one time gets even larger. As we will see, grief often hits home for children after a delay. Most of us are painfully aware of how grief never completely dissipates. Losses may create a chain reaction of hair-trigger emotions that persist for years, if not for a lifetime. Studies have suggested that for children, the pain of loss may even *increase* over time (Schwarz & Perry, 1994). No matter how we look at it, as students travel through their school years, many of them will be familiar with death and loss on some level. Any strong emotion pervades an individual's life and therefore merges into the school day. Even when the death was unrelated to the educational setting, bereavement will know no boundaries. A grieving child may be suffering wherever she goes.

2 Introduction

Modern society has altered the way we approach death and dying. Before the age of vaccines, sterilization, and antibiotics, large numbers of people passed away in the first decades of life. Death of a family member was a routine occurrence, and most children had several experiences with loss. Often, the loved one's body was on display in the home, so youngsters were familiar with the event. Families were larger and extended, allowing for available support systems. Illnesses were usually brief, while today's medical advancements prolong life, and death, sometimes for significant periods of time. People were less vocal about their problems, having little time to sit idly by and ruminate. Bereavement time was short, whether the mourners were ready to get on with their lives or not. Although holding in painful emotions was not the healthiest coping style, the psychological milieu was one of stoicism and interdependence. Today, an elementary school-aged child is unlikely to have such intimate experiences with death and dying. He may have a small family, removed from grandparents, aunts, and uncles. If a loved one in his close circle dies, he will have inadequate coping skills and perhaps few people at home to help him navigate his grief (Rando, 1991). At the same time, greater public awareness about child development means that at least a few of the adults in his life may be paying close attention to his responses, scrutinizing his every action. This child is likely to vacillate between feeling ignored and being scrutinized. While concerned adults may be observant, they, too, may be poorly prepared to help. In many cases, these grown-ups interact with these kids in the education environment. They are close enough to be concerned, yet distant enough to remain objective. They are you—school personnel.

The New York Life Foundation has been a leader in helping with children's grief and bereavement issues. In a survey conducted in 2012 in cooperation with the American Federation of Teachers, the Foundation found a host of interesting data on the effects of loss on pupils in the classroom. For example, educators reported that students who had lost a parent or guardian exhibited many problems in a classroom. These students had higher absenteeism rates, exhibited lower quality of work, struggled to pay attention, submitted late assignments, and participated less in class. These effects are not vague or abstract; the students acknowledge that they are hurting emotionally (New York Life Foundation, 2017; Supporting the Grieving Student, n.d.). In a 2009 study conducted by Comfort Zone Camps, bereaved campers reported heartbreaking feelings, even years after a loss. For instance, 69% of those who had lost a parent "frequently" think of their Mom or Dad, while 72% say their lives would have been a great deal better if they had not experienced the death. A whopping 56% reported that they would willingly trade a year of their life for just one more *day* with their beloved parent (Life with Grief Research, n.d). Pain that runs deep does not miraculously evaporate when a child enters the school building. Doors to grief do not shut as easily as the ones of a classroom; grief doesn't wait outside for the school bell to ring at the end of the school day. It takes a seat right next to a hurting student.

Many studies show the profound ways loss can wreak havoc on a young person which can spill over into school and beyond. Grief can contribute to externalized behaviors, such as aggression, conduct disorders, and substance abuse, or internalized consequences such as depression and low self-esteem (Allender, 2015;

Bendiksen, 1975; Granot, 2005; Kaplow, Saunders, Angold, & Costello, 2010; Roberts & Gotlib, 1997). Signs of PTSD in children and teens are common after a loss (Boelen & Spuij, 2013). Other studies from the past few decades have emphasized the longitudinal effects of early loss, including psychiatric disorders (Archibald, Bell, Miller, & Tuddenham, 1962; Birtchnell, 1969; Breier et al., 1988; Ellis, Dowrick, & Lloyd-Williams, 2013; Jacobs & Bovasso, 2009; McLeod, 1991; Tennant, Bebbington, & Hurry, 1980). Other research has discovered a link between childhood grief experiences and physical health (Goodwin & Stein, 2004; Perkins & Harris, 1990). Bereavement can affect development, which can lead to future difficulties at work, in educational pursuits, and with personal relationships (Brent, Melhem, Masten, Porta, & Payne, 2012). Despite what may be obvious to those of us who have experienced both the short and long-range repercussions of losing a loved one so early in development, this topic has been largely ignored but clearly warrants greater attention.

Research has suggested that grief reactions may persist well past the actual event that triggered them. Losing a parent often correlates with negative behaviors such as alcohol abuse, drug use, and engaging in violent crimes during adolescence (Tennant & Bernardi, 1988; Wilcox et al., 2010). Bereaved individuals often show increased vulnerability to mental health issues such as depression and suicidal ideation, sometimes occurring years after the loss (Brent, Melhem, Donohoe, & Walker, 2009; Cerniglia, Cimino, Ballarotto, & Monniello, 2014; Elizur & Kaffman, 1983; Melhem, 2011; Raveis, Siegel, & Karus, 1999). Death of a sibling has been linked to behavioral and emotional issues in the surviving brother or sister (Eilegard, Steineck, Nyberg, & Kreicbergs, 2013; Mash, Fullerton, & Ursano, 2013; McCown & Davies, 1995). When suicide was the cause of death, the potential for poor adjustment in survivors is even greater (Kaplow, Howell, & Layne, 2014; Melhem et al., 2004). Biank and Werner-Lin (2011) reported that early exposure to mourning can contribute to coping issues later in life, perhaps well into adulthood. Recognizing the potential impact of grief on newly bereaved youth is essential. Adults who connect with young people would benefit from a deeper understanding of the grief experience. Teachers and other school personnel form strong bonds through their interactions with pupils, which can provide the foundation for a solid support system. However, we could speculate that today's educators are ill-equipped to handle issues of grief with their students, even though this common occurrence has the potential to impact the classroom setting.

The personal nature and significance of this topic has encouraged me to complete research in this field. At the time of this writing, I am beginning my fifth year studying the effects of childhood loss on college students. Certain information in this book comes from this continuing work at Ursinus College, a small liberal arts college located in the suburbs of Philadelphia, Pennsylvania. Over the past four years, this research has taken several forms over the years, but the goal is to determine effects of an early loss years later in development, when the mourner has become a young adult. Data was retrieved from online anonymous surveys, asking students about their experiences with losing a loved one during their childhoods or adolescence. We gathered other data via face-to-face interviews with volunteer subjects willing to discuss their dealings with grief. In doing these studies, we found

4 Introduction

that many of the respondents were dissatisfied with the support within their school settings. This information was direct evidence that our educational system is not adequately addressing students' grief. The school environment may be an excellent setting to address the issues related to bereavement. In addition, we surveyed educators on the east U.S. coast, primarily in Pennsylvania, New Jersey, and Delaware. Although many respondents claimed they have adequate skills to aid grieving students, others admitted poor training. Moreover, the disconnection between the confident educators' positive appraisal of their readiness and the students' reports of inadequate support led us to conclude that our society needs to make grief support a priority. We should find better ways to inform and guide our school personnel in this area.

Many of our findings were fascinating. (Statistical data can be found in Appendix A.) Regardless of the relationship to the deceased, (parent, sibling, friend, grandparent, etc.), students who rated the loss as highly traumatic (6 or 7 on a Likert scale) showed statistically significant lower GPAs, higher levels of anxiety and hypochondria, and external loci of control when compared with students who had not experienced a traumatic loss. We found a significant negative correlation between reported trauma level and overall health score. This last finding is perplexing. Despite higher levels of hypochondria, which included preoccupation and worry about illness, students with higher levels of subjective trauma related to the loss reported poorer health. We based the health score on actual behaviors, such as eating healthy and exercising regularly. The implication is that although the possibility of illness concerned our grievers, they were not necessarily enacting positive behaviors to stay healthy.

The majority of respondents to both the surveys and the interviews reported the loss of a grandparent. This was not unexpected. Grandparents are older and more likely to become sick and die. What was surprising, however, was the intensity of the reactions. Even when the grandparent succumbed from a lengthy illness, was elderly, or had little contact with the subject, many respondents reported that they struggled with the loss. This level of stress was again indicated by assigning a high subjective trauma rating to their feelings. When pressed for details, however, many of the responses implied that the intense nature of the reactions was not necessarily because of the loss itself. Rather, the sense of trauma came from related factors such as anxiety generated from seeing a dead body, attending a funeral for the first time, and most commonly, watching the emotional reactions of their parents. The conclusion is that a child's interpretation of a death comprises many aspects, some of which may not apply to the reactions of adults. Therefore, grownups should know that kids' perceptions are qualitatively different from those of older individuals.

We found discrepancies between students' and educators' perceptions of support in schools. While most reported that assistance would have been beneficial, the majority did not speak to school staff about their loss. Two-thirds (67%) attended public schools, while another 24% attended private institutions. Over half (51%) attended schools in Pennsylvania; 18% went to New Jersey schools, and 27% attended schools in a variety of other states. While only 24% reported that school personnel were unaware of the loss, 61% reported that they did not speak with anyone at school about the death. The average number of days absent for bereavement purposes was 2.56 (*S.D.* = 1.61), with 30% indicating they did not take any time off. When asked to rate the helpfulness of staff on a Likert score from 1 to 7, with 1 indicating "not at all helpful" and 7 indicating "very helpful," equal numbers of respondents (18%) rated staff 1 and 7 (*M* = 4.02, *S.D.* = 2.13). On a similar Likert scale in which 1 indicated "did not understand at all" and 7 indicated "completely understood," respondents were asked to rate staff. Half (50%) rated staff below a 4. Although 21% reported that school was a "safe place" for handling their grief, another 49% rated their school below average in terms of being a safe space. Regarding peers, 32% indicated that they "had many friends and peers who supported them in an empathetic manner"; however, another 14% reported that they "were bullied by peers about my grief." Respondents were then asked to state their perception of the school's preparedness level in dealing with grief, on a Likert scale from 1 (not prepared at all) to 7 (very prepared), over 50% ranked their school below 4. Only 12% rated their school staff a 7.

Responses on the staff survey indicated that 70% reported that their school district had specific grief services in place. Over a third (38%) stated that they directly encounter five or fewer grief-impacted students, while 44% postulated they dealt with five to ten. However, 47% admitted that there were another one to five students who had suffered losses, but personnel were unaware of the situation. Another 30% guessed there were more than ten during the year who fell into this "silent" category. Almost 62% reported that their district had no bereavement policy in place. When questioned on their level of training, 60% claimed to have engaged in grief-specific instruction, while another 36% said they were given instruction that was "very limited in scope." In terms of the entire district, 25% reported that their school system was "extremely prepared" to help grieving children and adolescents, while 53% felt they were "somewhat prepared." Another 19% thought their school was "somewhat unprepared," and a mere 3% admitted their district was "extremely unprepared." On a question asking what type of service or support would best prepare their school staff, 41% suggested that presentations and in-service trainings would be most helpful. Other options included adding more qualified staff (22%), collaboration with outside services (16%), offering support groups (13%), and being provided with additional written information (9%).

As we can see, many subjects admitted that school personnel were not trained or equipped to handle grief and loss positively. This contrasts with the educators' responses; most claimed to have had training and felt confident in their ability to address these issues. Students suggested that educators often were inflexible and insensitive to their losses, not realizing how much time it might take to cope with a death. As one student remarked, "Grief is not linear, and school personnel should stop thinking it is." The responses reflected that, in the view of many students, schools are not acting in their best interest when supporting them in bereavement.

Through the pages of this book, I will take the reader on a journey through loss, as experienced through a young child's eyes. As educators, most readers know of the basic tenets of child development. But grief is a unique roadblock; not only can it send the traveler in odd directions, but no path fits all. Armed with a strong foundation of knowledge about how children think and feel, we can superimpose grief onto these concepts. Then it becomes easier to understand how to communicate

6 Introduction

with a grieving child and assist them in their coping. Knowledge also enables educators to recognize the signs of unhealthy bereavement and provides suggestions for more advanced help.

Several sections comprise the format of this book. The first will present background material on the neurological, cognitive, socioemotional, and psychological development of children. Although this may be a review for many readers, it is important to describe childhood bereavement within the framework of developmental maturation. This section will also summarize the grief processes along with current research, most conducted on adults. Again, this foundation of knowledge can create the context in which we can learn about grief in young people.

The second section delves into how the loss of a loved one by death can influence children of various ages. I will describe common psychological, behavioral, and emotional effects. Specific manifestations of a grief response into a classroom setting will be emphasized, along with the concomitant feelings and thoughts that create these behaviors. I will also outline severe reactions.

The third section provides practical suggestions for educators working with bereaved children. I will offer advice on what to say, do, and avoid when dealing with this issue in the school setting. Suggestions on handling specific situations, such as the death of someone in the school, will be covered, along with the current trends to provide death education in the schools. I will also share my firsthand experience with founding a nonprofit and organizing in-school support groups.

The appendices comprise the last section of the book. I will offer examples of sample handouts, lesson plans, and other relevant information relevant to school settings or grief support organization, along with results from my Ursinus College research.

Throughout *The Grieving Child in the Classroom*, I will be illustrating points through the brief descriptions of children who are experiencing loss. Most of these cases are based on real people, but they are amalgams of actual children, not representative of a specific individual. Some information presented in this book originates from my previous work, *Turning the Page: Helping a Child Cope with the Loss of a Sibling*, which I published in 2015. This work focuses on parents who are coping with surviving children after the death of a child. The books share a common research foundation, and basic tenets are the same. This current book takes the perspective of school personnel who already have a solid foundation in child development.

Both practical and theoretical, the material in this book can serve as guideposts along the way when working with grieving children in the classroom. School is a major part of every child's life, so it is not surprising that loss will affect them there. By increasing awareness, educators can better prepare themselves to work with these children. Grieving children exist in every classroom; there is no escaping this truth. These children are everywhere, and they desperately need help from a caring, sensitive, and well-informed educator—like you. Taking the time to read this book and learn about this topic is proof positive of that fact.

Section 1

Defining Grief Within a Developmental Context

Chapter 1

Neuronal Pathways in the Brain

Neuropsychology, the field that is ostensibly a marriage between traditional psychology and neuroscience, has been growing in recent years. The focus of neuropsychology is on explaining established psychological ideas in neurological terms. Concepts that had been abstract are now connected to the workings of the brain and nervous system. For instance, today's behaviorist understands that while experience molds behaviors, it does so via neural pathways. Every time we learn something new, we change our brains. We use this mechanism in direct instruction and indirect learning. Researchers have studied how early experiences, especially negative ones, influence neural development (DeBellis, Hooper, & Sapia, 2005; Perry & Pollard, 1998). Today, educators take courses in brain-based learning, and with that instruction comes a basic understanding of how the immature nervous system works and matures. Although teachers and other staff may be familiar with the neuroscience of learning, technical jargon and nuances of this information are easily forgotten. While educators can apply these concepts to learning in a classroom, integrating anatomical and physiological knowledge with the grief response may be unexplored territory.

When a baby is born, most of the body's systems are mature enough to operate as they will into adulthood. One major exception is the nervous system. An analogy is the comparison of the immature brain to a new computer. A buyer travels to the neighborhood electronics store and purchases the essential parts, including the hardware and software, but has yet to connect these components. Another perspective is to envision constructing a new town or housing development on open land. Although the blueprints and raw materials may be in place, nothing is yet built. At birth, a human baby has the raw materials he or she needs for a functional nervous system: brain, spinal cord, and neurons. Yet much is unconnected. Throughout life, primarily in the first seven years, an individual's neurons form communication pathways. Nerve cells do not touch each other, but they align in such a way as to allow quick and efficient communication. This takes place when chemical messengers, or neurotransmitters, release from the end of one cell (the axon terminals) and flow into the space, or synapse, between this cell and the next. That cell then picks up the neurotransmitter's message via receptors located in the dendrites. Dendrites are branch-like structures of the neuron, and receptors are designed to receive messages from specific neurotransmitters. This message then gets passed along the receiving cell and then moves ahead to subsequent cells. Through learning and maturation, neurons that perform specific physical and mental tasks connect in this way. Neurons necessary for desired actions become more intricately "wired," while those synapses unnecessary for the tasks are pruned away. Pruning allows for more efficient workings of the remaining pathways, while the ability to accomplish unessential or underutilized tasks lessens (Schwartz & Begley, 2002). One excellent example of this process involves learning language skills. A newborn has the neurons it needs to produce sounds of any dialect, but its brain will become wired to make only the sounds for the language it routinely hears. This explains why a child raised to speak English has trouble trilling Rs when studying a foreign language as a teenager. The neuronal pathways that control moving the mouth and tongue to make that sound were pruned away, making this a difficult task. Although speaking French is awkward, this teen can produce English sounds with ease because of the powerful connections formed within the brain while learning English, the native language (Lawrence, 2015). Pruning of unneeded neuronal connections is an essential mechanism that allows those skills we need to become more ingrained in our brain, while unnecessary skills fade into the background.

Certainly, we can acquire new skills and ideas later in life. Normal human brains remain plastic throughout the lifetime, so they can always learn new information and actions. If this were not the case, there would be no reason for any of us to attend school or read this book. As we age, learning might just need more conscious effort. Teachers understand how young kids' brains resemble sponges by soaking up the variety of information to which the environment supplies. For us adults, learning takes extra concentration and focus. If we draw once again on the computer analogy, it may require additional energy to reprogram an old computer. Erasing and overriding programs require more effort than installing them. Likewise, constructing a grid of roads and highways in an open desert is simpler than rerouting established streets within a city. While a blank slate may take time to fill with information, erasing and revising is a greater chore. We may tap into greater amounts of energy because the past must be purposefully ignored. If you are trying to trill the letter R but can only remember how to produce this sound in English, the task becomes a high hurdle to overcome (Lawrence, 2015).

The brain develops from the bottom upward, with lower-level areas maturing faster than the complex cerebral hemispheres. Physical maturation originates in the zygote stage when the rudimentary organ is forming (Kolb & Whislaw, 2003; Santrock, 2017). We often refer the brain to as the "triune brain" because we can observe and describe three primary levels. The first and lower most part is the brainstem which controls life-sustaining functions. This part maintains heart and lung physiology and plays roles in the control of arousal, sleep/wake cycles, and focused attention. We refer to this as the "reptilian" brain, a reference to our scaly, cold-blooded ancestors who possessed brains that are commonly believed to conduct similar primitive functions. We sometimes refer the higher-level middle brain area to as the "mammalian brain" in a nod to our similarity to other mammals. Much of the middle brain landscape serves as a relay station, collecting signals from elsewhere in the body and directing them to the upper levels of cerebral cortex for more intensive processing. The hypothalamus regulates our endocrine system, which is comprised of glands that secrete hormones into the bloodstream. The master endocrine gland, the pituitary, is nestled near the brain and responds from directions generated by the hypothalamus in response to bodily stimuli. The limbic system makes up most of the midbrain real estate, which includes the amygdala and hippocampus. Our amygdala is primarily responsible for basic emotions, especially primal ones such as fear and anger, and is crucial for storing our implicit memory. Our hippocampus plays a role in the formation, processing, and storage of explicit memories. The midbrain area serves as the connection between the upper and lower brains, which is why we can voluntarily control our breathing, and indirectly our heart rates, to a certain extent (consider yoga, mindfulness, and meditation). We refer to the uppermost area of the brain as the cerebrum, with the outer layer described as the cortex. This is the part we refer to as our higher brain, in that is more developed than the analogous structures in other animals. Four functional lobes, on two distinct sides of the cortex known as hemispheres, comprise this level. The temporal lobes are situated on the sides above the ears, and they play a role in interpreting information gathered from auditory stimuli. The back lobes are the occipital, and they receive information coming in from vision. Top middle lobes are the parietal, and these collect data from nerve cells responsible for touch and muscular movement. At the front of the brain are the two large frontal lobes. These are the primary association areas, responsible for logical thought, analysis, problem solving, and decision making. The corpus callosum, a dense collection of neuronal fibers, connects the right and left cerebral hemispheres. In general, the left hemisphere communicates with the right side of the body, while the right hemisphere is wired to the left side. This explains why a person suffering a stroke in the right hemisphere may have impairments in use of the left hand. We must keep in mind that this description is a simplistic view of brain anatomy and physiology, but it is enough to help us understand how children's brains form and how negative experiences can impact a maturing central nervous system (Kolb & Whislaw, 2003; Lawrence, 2015; Santrock, 2017).

The cerebral cortex is the least mature of the three layers at birth. The brain stem functions by necessity; infants have a heartbeat, respiration, and sleep/wake cycles. Neonates primarily react on impulse. They do not yet think rationally by activating the highly advanced parts of their brains. One way to illustrate this phenomenon is by considering infant reflexes. Newborn infants have a set of specific, innate reflexes such as rooting, grasping, startling, and sucking. Babies and young toddlers react to stimuli by enlisting the lower parts of the brain. These primitive reflexes secure survival by allowing for food and safety. These reactions are not consciously controlled; they are automatic. As the child gets older, the brain and nervous connections mature, and the upper levels of the brain take over and allow for decision making (Kolb & Whislaw, 2003). As a result, the reflexes cease. An older child doesn't automatically suck or grab onto things; he first considers what he is doing. This implies higher-order analysis. As we mature, we get better at solving our problems and contemplating our actions. This is the cerebral cortex at work.

When we are first confronted with threatening or traumatic circumstances, we react unconsciously by using our lower- and middle-level brain areas. When we reflect on a major stressor in our lives, we are familiar with the fight-or-flight response originated by an autonomic nervous system. In times of stress, the sympathetic

12 Defining Grief Within a Developmental Context

nervous system activates, creating an excitatory reaction. Our pulse races, blood pressure increases, respiration rate rises, sweating accelerates, muscles tense, and eyes dilate in acknowledgment of something we find dangerous. This quick response to an external threat requires little conscious thought, as it is the body's way of preparing for danger. When we hear an unexpected loud noise, for example, we jump in anticipation of the fight-or-flight mode. In other cases, conscious ideas can stimulate the perception of jeopardy, such as when our pre-sleep awareness drifts to the concern that the IRS may be examining our tax returns. Although animals exhibit signs of sympathetic nervous system activation primarily, if not exclusively, to external threats, humans trigger similar responses to mere stressful thoughts originating in our frontal lobes. In other words, we not only prepare to fight true dangers, but our bodies are primed to combat imaginary and potential threats, too. Since there is no immediate resolution in these situations, our sympathetic nervous system remains activated for long periods of time. When we are not in danger, the parasympathetic branch of the autonomic nervous system dominates, creating a sense of physiological calm. Our heart rate is slow and steady, our breathing regulates, our muscles relax, and sweating ceases. When our frontal lobes are working overtime and generating worrisome thoughts, the parasympathetic system is overridden by the activation of the fight-or-flight response. The result is chronic anxiety.

This stress reaction is part of the hypothalamic pituitary adrenal (HPA) axis. A threatening stimulus evokes an emotional reaction in our amygdala, which signals our hypothalamus to let the pituitary gland know that we are potentially under attack and stress hormones are required. The pituitary then signals the adrenal glands, located on top of each kidney, to crank out stress hormones into our blood stream. The primary hormones involved in this response are short-acting adrenalin and cortisol, a longer-acting chemical messenger. These hormones circulate through the body, stimulating the physiological responses we associate with fear and anxiety (Cozolino, 2006). A few of these responses, like pulse and breathing rates, are under the primary control of the brainstem. Higher in the midbrain, the amygdala continues to process the threat and perpetuates the corresponding emotional response. The hippocampus becomes involved in the formation and storage of long-term memories. The intense emotionality triggers the amygdala to dominate the response, which can lead to powerful, exaggerated emotional reactions that are frequently irrational. The amygdala may become permanently hyper-responsive to anxiety-producing triggers. Likewise, evidence suggests that increased stimulation of the amygdala, such as what occurs during a crisis, may inhibit formation of memory (Jenkins & Oatley, 1998; Perry & Pollard, 1998). The hippocampus may become less efficient in controlling the influx of elevated levels of stress hormones, particularly cortisol, further impairing memory storage (Cozolino, 2006; Shonkoff et al., 2012). Sometimes, memory consolidation is inhibited, while in other cases, recall may be problematic. Anxiety and other negative emotions may color the memories (Jenkins & Oatley, 1998). Context may be fuzzy, further contributing to biased recall and irrational interpretations (Shonkoff et al., 2012). This mechanism can explain everything from test anxiety, in which stress may block memorized knowledge, to episodes of dissociative amnesia, in which a person remembers little to nothing about a specific traumatic event. Since the hippocampus and amygdala are linked, emotions can affect memory and vice versa. Theoretically, as we increase in age and developmental maturity, our ability to think logically should improve. However, when confronting a stressor, adults, too, may respond on an emotional or instinctual level.

Researchers have studied the response to traumatic experiences, discovering that individuals exposed to extreme and chronic stress react viscerally to triggers. Moreover, this learned response becomes imprinted within the neurological network as neurons create corresponding connections with their neighbors. In other words, a person, especially a young one whose brain is highly plastic, becomes accustomed to tension and learns to react accordingly, even when the sources of the stress are no longer present. An individual becomes primed, or predisposed, to anxiety. This tension generates anticipation of negative outcomes at every turn as the HPA axis is caught up in a feedback loop and stress hormones are secreted abnormally (Cozolino, 2006). Weiss, Longhurst, and Mazure (1999) collected data from numerous studies that suggest that early childhood stressors not only trigger the HPA axis in the short term but also chronically. Stressors cause the release of corticotropin-releasing hormones (CRH), which in turn, initiates the HPA reaction. When these stress responses occur in childhood, they may create a biological vulnerability to depression or anxiety later in life. In fact, elevated levels of CRH are found in depressed patients, and the evidence suggests that early experiences can increase production of CRH and subsequently, generate a hyperactive HPA axis (Coplan et al., 1996; Nemeroff et al., 1984; Heim, Newport, Mletzko, Miller, & Nemeroff, 2008; Weiss et al., 1999). These stressful reactions can become hard-wired in the brain, perhaps increasing the susceptibility to depressive and anxiety disorders in adulthood (Ladd, Owens, & Nemeroff, 1996; Nemeroff, 1996; Perry & Rosenfelt, 2013). Research demonstrated that the earlier in development an impactful event occurs, the more devastating the potential effects (Hambrick et al., 2018).

Studies have indicated that chronic and extreme stress reactions can affect the brain's structure as well as its neurochemical functioning, especially in a young person's brain. Imaging has shown that parts of the amygdala, hippocampus, and prefrontal cortex can decrease in size and neuronal complexity after exposure to traumatic stress (O'Doherty, Chitty, Saddiqui, Bennett, & Lagopoulus, 2015; Shonkoff & Garner, 2012). The prefrontal cortex is the foremost section of the brain. In this area, executive functions such as decision making, problem solving, goal setting, and self-control take place. If a person's prefrontal cortex is damaged, he may demonstrate impulsive behaviors and immature responses to complex situations (Kolb & Whislaw, 2003; Shonkoff & Garner, 2012). The decreased hippocampal volume indicates the potential for memory dysfunction (O'Doherty et al., 2015; Shonkoff & Garner, 2012). Reacting to a traumatic stressor requires making reasonable choices, rational planning, and recalling past experiences. If these areas are negatively affected by chronic activation of the fight-or-flight response, the consequences may not be conducive to effective coping.

There is evidence that early trauma can specifically influence the right hemisphere's maturation, with dramatic results. This side of the cerebral cortex rarely engages in language tasks, responding on a nonverbal, guttural level. This side may be dominant in creativity and emotional intelligence. Studies have suggested that early trauma may impact this hemisphere, leading to weaker attachments, difficulty with emotional regulation, and higher rates of mental illness (Schore, 2001). Details aside, we can assume that experiences in infancy and early childhood can become ingrained in the plastic brain, programming the nervous system for a lifetime if adaptations are not made.

Obvious triggers can stimulate these reactions, but so can anything reminiscent of the original traumatic event. Even when memories appear to have faded or forgotten, impressions may be present on an unconscious level. When the child encounters a triggering stimulus, he may react with fear, anxiety, or panic (Perry & Pollard, 1998). For example, when 5-year-old Brynn learned of her father's death, a song was playing on the radio. The association may not register consciously but occurs somewhere in the unconscious recesses of Brynn's mind. When she once again hears this specific song, she becomes anxious without knowing why. Odors are also common triggers. For instance, we may associate pungent hospital odors with negative events that occurred within its walls and may react with panic at a whiff of the characteristic antiseptic smell. Any sensory experience can trigger emotional reactions. The flood of memory and concurrent emotions from the mid-brain may persist throughout the life span, and it may take patience and a little detective work to uncover the true nature of the associations.

Perry and Rosenfelt (2013) distinguish between our reactions to trauma and grief. They believe that the neurological pathways formed from these two different experiences may lead to two different emotions—sadness in grief and anxiety in trauma. This may be true with adults, but we must remember that children are egocentric and inexperienced. An incident that might cause sadness to a grown-up, such as a grandmother's death after a long-term illness, may create apprehension, fear, and even terror to a young child. A young person's imperfect understanding of such events may generate feelings of anxiety along with sadness. Moreover, certain losses are objectively traumatic, such as when a person dies suddenly, violently, or painfully. Children take losses personally, focusing on the death in egocentric terms. They may worry they are in danger of being the next victim, and this apprehension can magnify to paralyzing fear. When a *young* person dies, the event may drive home the suggestion to a child that he, too, can lose his life. Viewing events through egocentric eyes may lead to phobias or despondency (Brohl, 2007; Lawrence, 2015).

Individuals meeting the criteria for complicated grief, a condition characterized by prolonged, severe reactions to a loss, showed small but significant differences in cognitive functioning and smaller brain volume than controls experiencing normal grief (Perez et al., 2015). Imaging studies, including fMRIs, have demonstrated abnormal neuronal communications in subjects labeled with complicated grief (Arizmendi, Kaszniak, & O'Connor, 2016). While more research is necessary, early indications suggest that severe grief reactions can create biological and neurological changes in the brain. These physiological responses can then present as personality traits, as the developing person's brain is organized around the stress response (Perry, Pollard, Blaicley, Baker, & Vigilante, 1995). Stress that accumulates overtime becomes toxic as the individual's physical and psychological set point is high on the anxiety scale (Toxic Stress, n.d.). The term toxic stress refers specifically to prolonged, repeated, or severe physiological reactions to stress without the buffering effect of a close attachment with another individual (Shonkoff & Garner, 2012). Without the security of a support system, the affected person becomes hypervigilant and quick to jump into action mode at the mere hint of a threat.

If panic, anxiety, fear, and grief can become embedded in the neurological network of the brain, why are a few children more susceptible to this reaction than others? Why do some kids rebound quickly from a traumatic event while others struggle for longer periods of time? While there are a host of reasons for the variety of responses (including social factors, emotional maturity and intensity of attachment), one source of this discrepancy may lie in the brain's genetic composition. In *My Age of Anxiety*, Scott Stossel (2013) describes how a biological predisposition to anxiety may be a contributing factor in a person's ability to handle stress. He writes how research on genetic markers that may indicate susceptibility to anxiety-related disorders, including posttraumatic stress disorder. Research has suggested a link between specific gene sequences and posttraumatic stress disorder (PTSD) (Bharadwaj et al., 2016). Other studies have focused on epigenetics, which involves mechanisms that control a gene's function without altering the actual DNA. These mechanisms vary in detail, but it will suffice to say that environmental factors can potentially influence them. Epigenetics explains why the genes of identical twins, who share the same DNA, may be expressed in different ways. Researchers are still studying the ways in which epigenetic factors influence genes, including ones that dictate responses to severe trauma (Klengel & Binder, 2015). Although Stossel (2013) admits that a few psychologists are skeptical of the importance of genetics on stress responses, the biological nature of our outward responses suggests that a genetic link is at least partly responsible for directing a brain's response. Environmental factors can mitigate or negate a fear reaction, but we cannot ignore or underestimate the role of genes (Lawrence, 2015). Researchers are working diligently to unravel the complex interactions between genes, epigenetic factors, and environment in order to better understand responses to trauma and potentially lessen permanent negative consequences.

Psychotherapist Babette Rothschild focuses on the brain's connection to the body in times of stress and trauma. In her work, *The Body Remembers* (2000), she describes the brain's biological responses to early trauma along with the physiological responses within the body. When the painful experience occurs early in childhood, the young person's body may be programmed, largely unconsciously, to respond to stimuli reminiscent of the original trauma. She discusses how this phenomenon is blatant in some cases, such as the vibrant flashbacks experienced by sufferers of PTSD. The intense emotionality of the event creates a milieu in which the brain behaves uniquely. Structures such as the amygdala and occipital lobe appear highly activated, potentially creating powerful flashes of memory that involuntarily force their way into our awareness at seemingly random times (Bourne, Mackay, & Holmes, 2013). In other cases, the residual effects are more subtle, such as a vague feeling of uneasiness when entering a hospital room and hearing the beeps of the monitors. Rothschild suggests that we can associate positions of the body with previous stressful experiences, triggering a fight-or-flight reaction at nonthreatening stimuli (Rothschild, 2000). The mind–body connection in stress has been garnering attention. The idea that we retain early stress in our bodies, to the detriment of both psychological and physiological health, is gaining popularity (Levine, 2010; Levine & Kline, 2007; Scaer, 2001; van der Kolk, 2014). This concept provides the rationale that explains findings in other research that investigated adverse childhood experiences.

In times of stress, a few organisms may revert to a third option rather than fight or flight. These animals freeze, and this behavior is part of what is known as the defense cascade of reactions (Kozlowska, Walker, McLean, & Carrive, 2015). Possums, for example, display this behavior by "playing dead." Scientists suggest that a physiological response accompanies freezing, too, in that the animal may release endorphins which block pain and, perhaps, consciousness. These reactions offer protection from adversity. As human animals, we may respond similarly when confronted with a threat. This behavior is a type of dissociation, a psychological maneuver to remove oneself from reality (Scaer, 2001). In human beings, freezing may occur at the start of a threatening event to facilitate focusing attention and making decisions. After this brief period of inaction, the person then leaps into fight-or-flight actions. In other cases, the freezing occurs later in the response behavior and may persist for some time. This state, referred to as tonic immobility, occurs in certain animals as a last resort response. When fighting or fleeing is impossible, giving up may be the next best option. Sometimes this reaction scares off the threat, like when a predator chooses to ignore prey it assumes is dead. Other times, tonic immobility leads to unconsciousness, allowing a form of escape for the victim. When it occurs in humans, the freeze response is activated when crime victims find themselves paralyzed with fear or when a patient faints at the sight of blood (Kozlowska et al., 2015). Psychologists have suggested that after a freeze response, the animal will need to expend the energy repressed during the behavior. This explains trembling and shaking that occurs when the danger is past. These counselors suggest that this pent-up energy creates emotional problems in humans and they advocate techniques in therapy designed to expel it (Levine, 1997; Levine, 2010, 2015; Scaer, 2001).

Rothschild remarks on the concept of somatic markers, an idea first researched and described by neurologist Antonio Damasio in the 1990s. Psychologist Louis Cozolino, in his volume *The Neuroscience of Human Relationships* (2006), defines the role of these markers in human responses. He describes them as "visceral-emotional shorthand," which inserts unconscious motives into our decision making. These markers may explain the body's physiological reactions to emotional events suggestive of something shocking, even if that incident occurred long ago. The somatic marker theory may explain how anyone, especially a young child whose nervous system, cognitive functioning, and memory processes are still maturing, may respond to innocuous stimuli in dramatic ways (Cozolino, 2006; Damasio, 1998). On a conscious level, a scared child may be unable to explain her reactions that are odd or exaggerated. But on an unconscious level, the brain perceives a trigger reminiscent of the lost loved one, which in turn, invokes a physiological response of grief and anxiety via the established neural connections.

Other studies have uncovered related impacts of stress on the brain itself. For example, researchers have observed smaller hippocampal volume in individuals with a history of childhood trauma (Perry & Pollard, 1998; Vythilingam et al., 2002).

Since the hippocampus plays a large role consolidating explicit memory, could this decreased volume translate into poorer memory? Is it also possible that the memory becomes more implicit, which concurs with the somatic marker theory which hinges on unconscious responses? Schwarz and Perry (1994) use the term malignant memories to describe how inaccurate but intense early memories can control our nervous system responses well into adulthood. Although we need more research to discover the specific mechanisms involved, we know that trauma impacts memory in significant ways.

Jenkins and Oatley (1998) introduced the term emotion schemas to describe the tendency toward responding with specific emotions in a particular setting. They suggest that repetitive experiences involving associations between stimuli and reaction create behavioral habits. Within our knowledge of neurobiology, the potential for rigid neural circuits to form as reactions to stimuli makes sense. If grief is triggered regularly, the pathway to this response becomes activated and the concurrent emotions become habitual. These emotions have corresponding behavioral responses, too. What may begin as a new emotional experience—grief—becomes ingrained in the brain and can be generated by any stimuli a person associates with the painful loss.

Stress alters a person's neurobiology to an extent, and this eventuality may be unavoidable in times of trauma. On the other hand, if panic, grief, and fear can program a brain, so can positive emotions. Interactions with caring and empathetic people, which produce good memories, can *reprogram* a brain. The painful feelings of grief may not be erasable, but they can be mitigated. Experiencing stressful events and feelings may be helpful in development. Adults naturally wish to protect children from pain and suffering. Research suggests, though, that stress in childhood can serve to inoculate children as they inevitably face adversity later in life. When parents overprotect kids and shield them from potential problems, the youngsters never learn coping skills. They cannot discern the light at the end of the tunnel because they have never had the opportunity to see for themselves that it exists. In fact, distressed children may be more likely than their shielded counterparts to develop increased levels of empathy (Harris, Brett, Starr, Deary, & McIntosh, 2016). Although a challenging experience will surely affect a child's brain, these changes can be positive. Kids may be quick to hurt, but they will learn to heal when aided by a strong social network. By learning to recognize the triggers and to understand the body's reactions to a stressful past, a child can take the first step to understanding grief and anxiety, and to move on from there (Lawrence, 2015).

Chapter 2

The Role of Memory

Any discussion of our past involves memory. We must keep in mind that our brain is not a black-box recorder that objectively stores the events and information of our lives. On the contrary, our brains perceive stimuli subjectively. The storage of the raw material of memory involves a process of selective attention, addition and subtraction of details, and emotional filtering. Many of us present with an overconfidence bias about one's own memory. When we dredge up a specific recollection into our consciousness, we assume that the details must be correct. We are confident that our memories are right when they are vivid. But consider the number of times in which we find ourselves in a heated debate with a friend or family member when our recollections conflict! Two diametrically opposed reminisces are not both correct. At least one of these memory-holders has the facts wrong, which provides strong evidence that the mind's ability to recall is not infallible.

Our brain forms and stores two primary types of memory: implicit and explicit. Implicit memory includes "automatic" memories, such as repeated procedures and habits. This category includes memories that do not require conscious recall but surface effortlessly. Walking, using a bathroom, and recognizing loved ones in a crowd are examples of implicit memories which, once we consolidate them, are recalled with little overt mental energy. Conversely, explicit memory requires a more conscious effort to bring into awareness. This category holds information such as the names of the United States Presidents and your childhood home address. These are examples of semantic memories, one form of explicit memory. Another other category is episodic memory, which contains personal recollections such as the events of last year's birthday party or Christmas celebration. We can store episodic memory via language or visual formats. One may play episodic memory like a video in the mind's eye, as memories of family vacations and the high school prom flash within the mind. Memories can generate sensory experiences, which we process through the filters of consciousness. Explicit memories can therefore be biased. New experiences develop through the filter of our memories. Our senses detect information we compare to the schemas we already hold, allowing us to store the new memory subjectively. Memories arise through the "film" of emotions which contribute to the way we create, store, and retrieve our memories (Doidge, 2007; Kolb & Whislaw, 2003; Lawrence, 2015; Levine, 2015).

For example, let us consider a memory of a summer vacation. Assume you go to the beach with your family; perhaps to a resort town, Sea City, which is unfamiliar.

The Role of Memory   19

Although this may be your first experience at Sea City, you have been to a different beach community, Ocean Town, years earlier, so you have an idea about what to expect on this trip. Unfortunately, during your time at Ocean Town, you had the nasty experience of being bitten by a jellyfish. On your first day at Sea City, you fear a repeat of the seaside adventure you had in the past. The smell of the ocean triggers memories of the jellyfish sting, generating vague feelings of anxiety. Following your family into the waves, you are vigilant in looking for threatening creatures with any tentacles that might create a danger for you. As a result, you are blatantly aware of any objects floating in the water, from seaweed and other ocean grasses to shells that are tumbling in the surf. Luckily, you find no jellyfish, but later you step on a sharp rock when exiting the surf. The pain in your big toe triggers your heightened anxiety, along with creating a bloody wound. While sitting on your beach blanket applying a Band-Aid to the cut, a seagull swoops over your head and uses your scalp for a toilet. Hastily gathering your beach items to leave the beach, you twist your ankle when stepping into a sandy trench dug by nearby children. You determine this is not your day at all and head back to your hotel for a shower and a much-needed rest (Lawrence, 2015).

How will you encode, store, and retrieve the memories of that day? Do you think you will remember the way events happened, or will your emotions color your recollections—including those generated by your past negative experiences? In most likelihood, you will recount this day at the beach by focusing on emotionally charged, negative circumstances. You may claim that the ocean was filled with "junk" and was too hazardous even when nothing unusual was present. You may remember that the beach was inundated with sharp rocks and shells when the beach was clean. Your surprise and disgust by the actions of the seagull may frame the entire day as a bad experience, resulting in a negative skew in your perceptions of the other day's events. When returning to the beach next summer, the memories of the previous events will affect the new experience, regardless of whether you are visiting Sea City, Ocean Town, or another shore site. Memory is subjective. Our previous experiences, attitudes, cognitive appraisals, and emotional states will influence what we remember and how we recall it (Lawrence, 2015).

In an intriguing example of the fallibility and subjectivity of memory, most individuals cannot recall an explicit memory before the age of 2 years old. There are conflicting theories about why this is true, including the possibility that a young person's hippocampus is still underdeveloped or immature, creating glitches in explicit memory formation. Psychoanalytic theory suggests that many early experiences are traumatic, and we repress them to avoid anxiety. A third possibility suggests that while the brain stores early memories, the encoding processes occur in such a way that a mature brain cannot retrieve them. For example, we may consolidate early memories via visual cues, but our attempts at retrieval involve language cues. In this illustration, the "keys" (retrieval cues) don't fit the "locks" (stored memories). Regardless of the cause, memory in childhood can be difficult to access and check for accuracy (Lawrence, 2015; Levine, 2015).

Several researchers have described how we store traumatic memories within the brain and how our emotions and behavior are impacted. We have previously discussed Damasio's somatic markers, mechanisms by which implicit memories trigger

20   Defining Grief Within a Developmental Context

bodily reactions (Levine, 2010; Rothschild, 2000; Scaer, 2001; van der Kolk, 2014). Sensory experiences, such as smells or sounds, can trigger associations in memory, whether implicit or explicit. Even when the memory of the connection may not be in conscious awareness, the brain may recall the original stressor and then instructs the body to respond accordingly. Bits and pieces of the past may flood consciousness, leading to confused and incomplete recollections. An individual may respond to implicit and explicit memories that may make little sense to the rational mind (Levine, 2015).

In the childhood game "Whisper down the Lane," two people start a story, and then it spreads throughout the group. By the time the information gets to the last person in the series, it bears little resemblance to the original tale. Most of us can appreciate how rumors can begin and become more inaccurate with each retelling. As we have seen, our memories are biased. We selectively attend to the details of the world. We may see and hear what we expect, what shocks us, or what interests us. This is reconstructive memory in action. Our minds reconstruct the memories of events we experience, creating our own personal version of events. This selective encoding and storage processes are largely unintentional. Referring to the previous beach story, next year you may travel to the shore sincerely intending to experience a fun time. However, you may unconsciously attend to specific stimuli. You may scan the ocean for signs of jellyfish or remaining vigilant regarding swooping sea gulls. This selective attention may cause you to ignore other important stimuli. For example, while searching the water for errant stinging sea creatures, you may be unaware of the child nearby surfacing with a mouthful of sea water. Sensory information bombards our brain and generates the internal emotional and cognitive responses in awareness. There is no way we can store all that information, so our brain filters it. We retain relevant details in our memory vaults, while we exclude insignificant information. When we try to recall a detail that received little focus, we may have no true memory. Determined to recall something, we may then add or even fabricate a recollection that fits. For instance, if I ask you about the gasping child who next to you during your jellyfish scan, there may be no explicit memory to recall. Searching the crevices of your mind, you dredge up half-truths and details that seem relevant or which you associate with similar memories. "Why, the child had on a swim suit!" "She was coughing loudly!" These comments are logical given the circumstance, but now these mere assumptions become part of an imagined memory. The motivation to recall details of an experience may be unconscious, and most of us believe what we "remember" because it makes sense. We must remember, however, that a recollection's vivid nature does not assure its accuracy (Lawrence, 2015; Levine, 2015).

Surprising research illustrates the fallible nature of memory, including recollections that are vivid. Researchers asked participants to recall the details surrounding their own whereabouts during the events of September 11, 2001. As expected, most interviewees reported a plethora of details. The respondents rated their memories as highly accurate. Unfortunately, the researchers' attempts to corroborate the recollections were unsuccessful. Almost one-half of the recalled "facts" were unconfirmed or deemed *incorrect*. For instance, some respondents who claimed to be at work were absent that day (Hirst et al., 2009). If we believe that the interviewees were

The Role of Memory 21

truthful, what explains their erroneous reporting? The most reasonable explanation is that the individuals manufactured a highly probable scenario for that day based on normal routine, and then just assumed was true. Their brains "filled-in-the-blanks" when there were gaps in true memory, using information gathered from outside sources (the media) or through logical deductions from personal habits. For instance, respondents knew the first plane crash occurred on a Tuesday morning around 9 o'clock. They also may have understood that on a normal Tuesday, they were riding the train to work or answering emails at the office. Brains make assumptions, which individuals not only accept as true but use as the foundation to build a "memory." What can we take from this study? Memories, even of adults, are frequently erroneous, fabricated, or embellished—even when the memory holder is certain of their accuracy.

Young children, whose minds and mental faculties are still developing and maturing, are more susceptible to building altered memories. If we consider phenomenon such as infantile amnesia, we understand that adequate storage and retrieval of explicit memory is a long developmental process, one that matures along with the hippocampus and related brain structures (Doidge, 2007; Kolb & Whislaw, 2003). Children perceive events through the lens of fantasy and pretend-thinking, skewing the raw material for later memories. These imperfections in information processing may distort childhood memories. Many young people have trouble discerning lies from truth, so it is no wonder that memories are often a hybrid of fact and fiction. Memories formed within a context of intense emotional reactions are vulnerable to biased encoding or storage. Losing a loved one generates high levels of emotionality, potentially influencing the way our brain consolidates recollections.

Memory experts link the amygdala, with its role in primary emotions, to memories of traumatic events. When a stressful event occurs, the body's first reaction is to activate the fight-or-flight response with its concomitant emotion of fear, a primal emotion connected to the amygdala. This is an unconscious connection, but we store the emotional response within the middle part of the brain. The midbrain holds the threat response as an implicit memory, an automatic response to a learned stimulus that created an intense emotional response. Memory consolidation and emotions are linked, just as their related brain anatomies are adjacent in the limbic system. Strong emotions are more likely to trigger any associated memory. Although grief is not always traumatic, it often triggers other powerful emotions. For a child who struggles with rationality, losing a loved one to death may be traumatic. Intense fear and anxiety result. These middle brain's reactions effectively bypass the frontal lobe, so these memories are bereft of logical processing. When a traumatic event occurs, we react on a visceral level first. The resultant memories may be more implicit than explicit. In fact, sufferers from PTSD may have poor explicit recollections of events that trigger their panic. Even when a specific memory exists, it is usually vague or disjointed. Rarely do traumatic memories mirror the clean narratives we can construct surrounding less emotionally charged recollections. When there are gaps in our ability to recall, our brains to fill in the missing pieces (Levine, 2015).

Sometimes, emotional reactions and flimsy memories lay the groundwork for false memories. An individual can "remember" things that never occurred. Other people can unintentionally suggest ideas that become the building blocks of false

22 Defining Grief Within a Developmental Context

memories. When we think back to events from our past, our own recollections intermingle with details from stories told to us by others. If years have passed since the event, perceptions are susceptible to revision, contradiction, and confusion. Severe psychological or physical stress can generate inaccurate remembrances, which can occur when suspects are under police interrogation. Faced with fatigue and anxiety, deprived of water or food, many accused individuals defer to suggestions offered by the interviewers. In a weakened state, many of us will eventually agree to anything, becoming confused between reality and fiction (Levine, 2015).

We could also ask questions about repressed memories, events that an individual unknowingly shoves under consciousness to avoid the pain and anxiety of remembering too much. Sigmund Freud considered repression to be a defense mechanism, undertaken by the psyche to protect itself from negative emotionality (Freud, 1986). As the concentration camp survivor, Primo Levi, suggests in *The Drowned and the Saved* (1988), an individual who is hurt barricades his mind from the memory in order to avoid or blunt the pain. In an excellent description of human memory performance, particularly in times of stress, Levi claims that memory is "marvelous but fallacious" (Levi, 1988). When blocking occurs on an unconscious level, we have repressed the memory into the unconscious. Little can stop these memories from being triggered on an unconscious level, however. This is what occurs in PTSD when an individual reacts physiologically to a triggering stimulus even though an explicit memory is absent. Moreover, repressed memories may emerge into consciousness without warning. Flashbacks can be scary for adults who are unprepared. Kids who are struggling with emotional and behavioral control may not fare well, as they are unequipped to handle the intensity of the uninvited memory.

Although many modern psychologists agree, in theory, that repression occurs, there is dissention regarding how and why this phenomenon happens in specific situations. Controversy also swirls around the methods of uncovering and interpreting repressed memories (Levine, 2015). Some practitioners use techniques such as hypnosis to uncover these secrets. While this technique can allow an individual more control in confronting the painful emotions connected to the memory, there is the risk of overwhelming the memory holder. Typically there is a lack of corroboration when memories emerge in a therapeutic setting. Accuracy may be debatable or unverifiable. Perhaps the objective truth is not always relevant. If the client believes the memory to reflect true events, the emotional impact will also be real. However, it is too tempting to accept the validity of these memories, using them to place blame and responsibility where it might not belong. When dealing with subjective recollections, we must take these with a grain of salt, focusing on the generated emotional reaction and not the accuracy of the memory's details. Levi stresses that are memories are not "carved in stone." He claims that our recollections fade, develop, and transform as we perceive new information (Levi, 1988). When supported a bereaved child through a traumatic event, we should recognize the significant role memory plays in grief.

Should an educator learn the specific details surrounding a student's loss? Many families may be reluctant to share too much information, particularly if the death occurred in a manner that others may judge, such as accidents or substance abuse. Adults may keep kids in the dark at the time of the tragedy, protecting them from

The Role of Memory 23

painful details. The lack of information does not halt an active imagination, however. Kids may find their minds racing as they assume details and fill-in-the-blanks with their own ideas. The risk is that what starts out as assumptions of an active imagination may become the reality to the individual, constructing a "memory" about the loved one's death. The imaginative powers of a young child may create horrific perceptions that are worse than the truth. For example, a child may know his dad died from a car accident, but we adults may shield him from the details of the crash. This youngster may envision a raging inferno with Dad writhing in pain, calling for help (Lawrence, 2015). If the parents or someone could explain the truth, they can keep the young survivor's imagination at bay. The resultant memories have a greater chance of accuracy. Children may not be prepared to hear gory details, and this unabashed honesty is unnecessary. Adults need to know that children will ruminate on what happened, often obsessively, and may jump to inaccurate conclusions if not given enough information. As an educator, you may have a dilemma if you know more details than the child and the student approaches you with questions or incorrect assumptions. In these cases, it is not the educator's place to correct or inform the student, but it would be a good idea to reach out the family and inform them of the child's inquires to encourage them to be more honest. Adults should remember that children can be literal in their interpretations. Their egocentrism, too, may generate misperceptions and misinterpretations. It is natural for young kids to view every detail in ways relevant to them. For example, if someone tells a child that the family dog was "put to sleep" after being sick, fear of bedtime may be the result, as he envisions Fido sleeping into normal slumber and never waking up. This inaccurate mental representation of the pet's death becomes a "memory" of sorts, and if not corrected, the child may continue to believe this distorted view of events. Although knowing facts may be painful, sometimes the truth can aid in creating accurate perceptions and subsequent memories of what actually occurred.

Psychologist Jerome Kagan (1984) writes that both emotion and cognition influence memory, and our childish perceptions become part of the fabric of our recollections. He suggests that our ability to recall our past may dictate the emotional responses we display well into adulthood. Whether we demonstrate apathy, anxiety, failure, pride, fear, or confidence in our adult behaviors, our distant memories may generate these reactions, regardless of their accuracy. Adults who act with honesty help children to develop memories based on fact. Sometimes the imagined "truth" is even worse than the reality.

There are issues and events in our lives we wish we could forget. In his *Untimely Meditations* (1997), philosopher Friedrich Nietzsche describes the blissful lives of cattle, grazing in the field without a care in the world. He states that we humans focus too much on our past, hanging on to our memories to the point that they impede us. He suggests that we "cannot learn to forget" and so our old recollections haunt us throughout our lives (Nietzsche, 1997). The truth of this idea is monumental. As humans, we just cannot flip a switch to enable us to remember and forget at will. Just recall embarrassing or unfortunate episodes in your past that you wish you could block; likewise, we are often chagrined when we forget things we should remember. If we are both blessed and burdened by memory, we

24 Defining Grief Within a Developmental Context

need to understand it. As individuals helping a child struggle with a painful history, we should have a basic knowledge of memory mechanisms to guide a child to a place where remembering strengthens him, as Nietzsche implied (Nietzsche, 1997). Recognizing the power and fallibility of memory is the first step. Memory is an imperfect filter through which we view the past. It would be wise to remember that repressed memories may direct our behavior unconsciously. Kurt Vonnegut's statement in *Slap Stick* (1999) illustrates this point. "The museums in children's minds, I think, automatically empty themselves in times of utmost horror—to protect the children from eternal grief" may ring true for some kids. Perhaps our minds try to protect our psyches from ideas that are too intense, leaving them buried deep in the recesses of our awareness until we are emotionally strong enough to handle them. We may create these repressed memories from bits and pieces of inaccurate tidbits of information. These "false memories" can then influence our behaviors and attitudes for our entire lives (Lawrence, 2015).

Chapter 3

Cognitive Development and Understanding Death

One of the first steps in understanding childhood bereavement is investigating the meaning and implications of death. Comprehending meaning depends on the cognitive abilities of a child which depends on age, experience, and developmental stage (Stuber & Mesrkhani, 2001). Educators understand cognitive maturation but sometimes may overlook how mental abilities influence a child's coping. Kids may reprocess grief and loss many times as their prowess in cognition improves over the years (Black, 1998; James & Friedman, 2001).

In empathizing with how children understand issues surrounding death, we should look at cognition through the lens of Jean Piaget's descriptions of development stages. His theory relies on the schema, his term for general concepts or frameworks in the mind. These concepts are analogous to labels on files, helping us organize our ideas and relate them to associated ideas. Learning involves manipulating these schemas and gaining new information through these frameworks. We compare new sensory input to existing schemas and either incorporate the material into an established concept (assimilation) or alter the old concepts to fit the new data (accommodation). If the input is too novel to work into the current schema, we make a new one. Suppose we have file folders for categories of animals. One file is labeled "Mammals," another is "Reptiles." As we are filing pictures of various creatures, we have no problem finding a correct home for a photograph of a crocodile, an elephant, a killer whale, and a snake. But now we come across a photo of an ostrich. We look at its characteristics, trying to determine if this beast might fit in the files with the others. Eventually, we decide that the two feet and feathers are significantly distinctive, and this animal requires a new folder with a unique label, "Birds." This example is a simplistic way of conceptualizing how we process incoming stimuli. When input relates to what we know, we group this information into existing files—our schemas. When it does not fit, we built a new schema. From that point forward, we have a new concept with which to compare future material. How children use this method changes as their cognitive skills mature, which relates to their neurological development and the quality of experience (Piaget, 1969).

Infants form and manipulate their schemas using their sensory modalities and their motor skills. Give a baby a new toy, and she looks at it, shakes it, or puts it into her mouth. As far as we know, babies do not have mature enough language skills to learn about the world merely from talking and listening—they need to touch, bang, and mouth things in their world. How does a teddy bear differ from a rubber ball? A bear does not roll when kicked! Why is a German shepherd a "dog" like my cocker spaniel, but the zebra at the zoo is not? We learn the differences among these quadrupeds through vision and experience, with the help of language, as we progress through this stage. After direct sensory experience and much practice, a baby learns to distinguish between Mom and Dad, and between a bottle and a breast. A baby bases her knowledge of the world on her senses and motor skills. Early schemas become the foundation for mature thought (Lawrence, 2015).

Piaget considered object permanence to be the milestone of this stage. Children less than a year of age do not realize that objects have an independent existence. If a baby cannot see, hear, taste, smell, or touch something, the item is not there (Piaget, 1969). No wonder older babies go through a period of separation anxiety! Infants of 9 or 10 months of age are cognitively mature enough to know who Mom is—the schema for "mother" is well-established by this time—but cannot comprehend that when Mom leaves the line of sight, she still exists somewhere. No wonder babies are inconsolable; in their mind, Mom has vaporized! After a time, Mom reappears! To the baby, this act is astounding. With practice, this reemergence becomes expected. But what if Mom has died? How long will a baby continue to look for the person who, in their experience, has come back time after time? And how will this infant grasp something that is difficult, sometimes impossible, to see, touch, or hear? When a baby experiences a death in his family, the lack of experience and context makes comprehension too challenging at this point in development. In times of stress, kids may regress to earlier stages of cognitive or emotional development. So, the failure of a deceased individual to reappear may even confuse older children who had mastered object permanence. This is a dilemma because preschoolers are challenged by the concepts of fantasy and reality, as described in Piaget's next stage.

Before we focus on this stage, it might be useful to remember that one of the primary cognitive tasks we undertake as humans is the weakening of egocentrism, or the expanding of awareness of others' perspectives. This idea is a hallmark of advanced consciousness. Our cerebral cortex allows us to master metacognition, which is our ability to think about thinking. We also develop a theory of mind, which refers to our realization that others have perspectives that differ from our own (Santrock, 2017). We come to view ourselves as beings independent of others, with our own thoughts, beliefs, and perspectives. This growth takes time, however. A newborn is egocentric without a solid sense of ego. There is no boundary between him and other; his needs are the only ones that matter. As cognition matures and the cerebral cortex is programmed through neural connections, babies realize that they are separate beings. As development progresses, the line between self and other people becomes more distinct, and children gain the ability to take another's perspective. Object permanence relates to egocentrism (Piaget, 1969). Mom's existence depends solely on my ability to perceive her. As we will see, this innate tendency toward egocentric thinking, and its stubborn persistence throughout the lifespan, can contribute to issues of magical thinking and misplaced guilt when a child is grieving.

Once a child has mastered object permanence, she advances to Piaget's next cognitive stage, the preoperational. During the preschool years, children become aware that others have alternative views, perspectives, and life experiences. Development is gradual, and young kids commonly assume that everyone has identical thoughts and feelings. The lines between fantasy and reality become blurred. Language is now an effective way of learning, although this needs to be made simple. Piaget considered the main achievement in the preoperational stage to be that of understanding symbolic thought. Words, letters, and numbers are symbolic. Pretend play is, too, as dressing up can transform a child into a princess or a superhero. Mental manipulations are beginning, but they are crude and not smoothly transferred from one condition to the next. For example, reversibility can be a confusing principle. We can undo specific actions (picking up an upended bag of crackers) but not others (returning spilled milk into the carton). Egocentrism continues to exert a major influence, and children of this age still find it difficult to put themselves in another's shoes (Piaget, 1969). This is true literally and figuratively. Ask a 3-year-old if a friend across the room can see what's printed in a book held in the viewer's lap, and that child will say "yes" every time. "If *I* know it, *you* know it" becomes the rule of thought.

Now consider an experience with death during this stage of development. The bereaved child may first have issues with understanding the reality of the loss. Dad always returned home before, so certainly he will again! On TV, in movies, and in video games, dead people sometimes pop back into life. Cannot Dad do the same? The incomplete understanding of reversibility, fantasy, and reality set the stage for confusion about death and loss. In a sense, the inability to grasp the finality of death is a form of denial, of not accepting that dying is any different from sleeping (Nagy, 1959). Belief in "magical thinking" also exists at this age. Preschoolers alternate between feelings of impotence and assumptions of power. Lack of rational understanding convinces children that their thoughts and feelings played a role in someone's death. Persistent egocentric views may lead to a child's belief that another's death is a punishment, perhaps for a bad deed the child committed. The lines between cause and effect are blurry as the young child strives to understand the real world of actions and consequences. It is no wonder that a 4-year-old struggles to comprehend a loss in the family. One reason this youngster may act as if everything is normal is because to him, life will revert to an earlier version. Reality is vague to a preschool-aged child.

As the young person moves into the concrete operational stage of thinking during his elementary school years, reality becomes clearer. Concepts such as reversibility are now logical. Perspective-taking and empathy become easier. Concrete experiences are the anchors for this thought (Piaget, 1969). Perceptions exist in the here-and-now. A third grader understands that the term dead means not alive, not breathing, and never returning. She can comprehend what means in terms of her current life. Dad is no longer available for rides to school or bedtime hugs.

Mature cognitive acceptance of death requires recognizing its finality, causality, irreversibility, and universality (Granot, 2005). Other work confirms the ability of children in middle childhood to grasp the concepts of cause and effect (Rosengren, Gutierrez, & Schein, 2014). Believing that every action has a cause leads many elementary-aged kids to view death as bad or evil, serving as a punishment for one's negative behavior. Young children may personify death, conceptualizing it as a figure such as a skeleton, monster, or some other boogeyman (Nagy, 1959).

Death is perceived as frightening, the consequence for horrible thoughts and actions.

Contemplating future implications is difficult. To Piaget's mind, hypothetical and abstract thinking occurs in the formal operational stage, which begins around the age of 12 (Piaget, 1969). Although many experts debate his age limits, eventually a child will shift to thoughts of the future. A young teenager can envision his future, and the ramifications of life without a loved one become painfully obvious.

With intellectual growth, kids will comprehend that death is permanent and definite for every living being. Research by Panagiotaki, Hopkins, Nobes, Ward, and Griffiths (2018) illustrates this stage of thinking. This study found that 10-year-olds not only had a solid knowledge of death in biological terms, but they could consider contradictory ideas, such as various religious viewpoints. This perspective helps kids to understand that death is not evil or always undesirable. The realization that death is inevitable weakens the idea of dying as a punishment, and the deceased are no longer assumed to have behaved badly. It happens to us all, regardless of our personality, lifestyle, or actions (Nagy, 1959).

Formal operational thinking involves a firmer grasp on rationality. Logical, deductive reasoning is not only possible, but should be automatic. The lines between reality and fantasy are well-defined (Piaget, 1969). Remember, that Piaget viewed development through these cognitive stages as a process occurs deliberately. A teen may understand on a rational level that her thoughts did not cause another's death, but established beliefs are not abandoned overnight.

A child's cognitive level extends beyond contemplation and acceptance of a loved one's passing. His sense of self is determined by his abilities, too. Forming an identity and cohesive self-concept is a lengthy task that requires neurological and cognitive maturity. We are born egocentric, with our focus on our own needs, feelings, and desires. As we mature, we gain the ability to think beyond ourselves, and ideally, become more adept at placing ourselves in the shoes of others and understanding the relationship between self and outsiders. According to many psychological theorists, we never fully lose our focus on the self. Freud described how the needs of the id, motivated by a quest for pleasure, stay powerful in our lives (Freud, 1986). We learn to control them. Likewise, Erik Erikson stressed that social relationships decide emotional and psychological development. Our interactions influence the perception of the self (Erikson, 1963). When we experience a death, we must learn how to comprehend the meaning for the deceased but also the implications for the self. A child's immature neurological and cognitive development complicates the issue. No young person fully controls her own life. She requires help from others, and she knows this. She craves nurturance and protection, leading to intense feelings of loneliness, helplessness, and frustration when not provided (Lai, 2013). Adults have similar needs and responses, but children have less power than adults. For all intents and purposes, they are at the mercy of events beyond their control and to the adults who make choices for them. This condition exacerbates the sense of helplessness we experience when we mourn.

We must appreciate a child's cognitive abilities before we can understand their grief. The capacity for understanding is a vital part of grieving, both in the short

Cognitive Development and Understanding Death 29

and long term (Boelen, van den Bout, & van den Hout, 2003; Stuber & Mesrkhani, 2001). The way a young child processes grief will lay the groundwork for adult coping, Poor adjustment in childhood may lead to deficiencies when coping with adult stress (Black, 1998). We must recognize how children reprocess early loss at later developmental stages (Granot, 2005). When reaching out and offering effective coping strategies, we must consider how a student perceives the death. Methods that promote healthy grief in a preteen may be inappropriate for a preschooler. One size does not fit all when considering childhood thought.

When a child's world is upended after a death, something else is lost besides the relationship with the loved one. Also gone is that young person's belief in the world as a safe and orderly place. Children in healthy environments take their security for granted, a construct known as their assumptive world. A significant loss rocks this foundation. Safety, happiness, health, confidence, trust, self-worth—all is jeopardized. The grieving child learns a new way of perceiving his world, and this view may skew toward fear, guilt, and insecurity. This worldview influences not only cognition but emotionality and relationships, too (Goldman, 2002).

Although we think of death as concrete and definitive, abstractions are involved when a loved one dies. For most children, their experience is limited and confined to depictions in movies, books, and TV shows. These encounters are usually based on fictional deaths, often of animals. Consider how many Disney movies a young child sees in which the protagonist mourns a parent's death. (*Bambi* and *The Lion King* at once come to mind.) In these movies, the death is an integral part of the story. In others, such as *Mulan* and *Lilo and Stitch*, a lost relative is on the periphery. These depictions can be inaccurate or misleading. For example, in movies and cartoons, we can conquer death. Characters may narrowly escape death or miraculously return to life. Death follows the same pattern in video games, as players have multiple lives. If the coyote in the Roadrunner cartoon can survive being hit by a train or clocked over the head by an anvil, why can't Dad wake up after his car accident? Moreover, in many action stories, death happens to the bad guy as a direct consequence of his evil actions. Does that mean that my Daddy was bad, too?

Young people are bombarded with constant referrals to actual deaths, too. The media's focus on negative events that include fatalities is intense, and adults will have a difficult time shielding kids from being exposed to news coverage. The spotlight is exceptionally bright when an incident involves children, such as with the coverage of school shootings. The overexposure to horrific acts and loss of life gives us the impression that the world is a dangerous place and threats are ubiquitous (Wass, 2000). A child in a vulnerable emotional state after experiencing a loss is in a heightened state of susceptibility to these news broadcasts, documentaries, and reality TV shows. The worry that he might be the next victim is exacerbated by what he sees on the screen, including social media and online sites.

Grief is transitory and temporary when it is expressed in fictional characters. Within a few scenes, Simba recovers from the trauma of losing his beloved father, Mufasa. Bambi moves on with relative ease after realizing he is an orphan. As adults, we understand that these tales are fictional and meant as entertainment. A story that revolves around trauma and grief will not be a fun movie experience for young viewers! We must remember that immature viewers will assume that what they see on screen reflects reality. Children internalize what they learn from these examples and can assume that real grief will follow this blueprint. No wonder it confuses them when their own grief experiences do not mirror the cases of Simba, Bambi, Jasmine, and Ariel. If Dumbo is doing a great job coping with the loss of his mom, his success is not lost on a child dealing with the same thing. As adults, we know that it takes time, tears, and resilience to adjust to a loss. Reality does not translate well into a fictional story with a neat beginning and end.

Chapter 4

Children's Psychological, Social, and Emotional Development

In modern times, we take for granted the assumption that a psychological aspect of childhood exists. As educators, we learn about the emotional development of children and the effects of issues in childhood on the adult psyche. In past times, society has minimized the role of childhood in adult psychological well-being. When philosopher Jean Jacques Rousseau suggested that children were not just small grownups but had their own unique emotional and mental needs specific to their young age, the idea was radical (Santrock, 2017). At the turn of the 20th century, Freud defined the first specific theory of psychological development (Freud, 1986). His concepts explained emotional growth as progressing in stages, depending on the adequacy of physical pleasure and satisfaction. Development surrounded areas of the body and the related tasks including oral (feeding), anal (toilet training), phallic (gender identity), latency (same-sex friendships and individual growth), and genital (romantic attachments). The concept of the phallic stage garnered the most attention. This time of emotional maturation, which occurs during the preschool years and is highlighted by the Oedipal/Electra Complexes, plays a major role in forming the adult psyche. In this stage, children experience a confluence of unconscious emotions and motives, including the romantic feelings toward the opposite-gender parent, fear, envy, and anger toward the same-sex parent, and the eventual identification with that same adult. In Freud's view, successful ascension through this psychological stage was necessary not only for assuming gender roles but also for the healthy development of a conscience. Psychology students still study Freud's theories today, but many take issue with his focus on sexuality in children and infants (Freud, 1961). As a result, the focus has shifted to other theorists who focus less on physical aspects of maturation.

Arguably, the most prominent of these theorists was, and is, Erik Erikson. In deference to Freud's views, he concurred that childhood circumstances are determinants of psychological maturation in both conscious and unconscious ways, but he disagreed with Freud's emphasis on physical factors as the focal point of emotional maturation. Erikson's ideas involved the description of eight stages of human development, a framework we still accept. Erikson's belief was that social factors in childhood affect kids unconsciously. In his opinion, the quality and nature of a child's relationships are the primary factors that promote a healthy psychological development. He viewed each of the stages as psychological "crises" in which an unconscious tug-of-war begins between two diametrically opposed emotional

32 Defining Grief Within a Developmental Context

constructs. If the interpersonal relationships of the child are strong and healthy ones, the child will gravitate toward the positive end of the psychological dichotomy. Relationships that are lacking will push the child toward negative psychological traits (Erikson, 1963). Erikson's theory has garnered respect in the field of human development, and many experts prefer his ideas to Freud's, not only because of its common-sense nature but also for its flexibility and its emphasis on relationships. For example, the psychoanalytic theorist Alfred Adler (1974) expanded on Erikson's ideas by stressing birth order as a major determinant of personality and emotional growth. Erikson suggests that individuals do not mature psychologically in a linear fashion. On the contrary, the psyche may progress in healthy directions for a time but can become derailed. Psychological back-pedaling may be necessary when an individual must regroup after an emotional hit throughout life. In addition, Erikson theorized that although the first few stages are critically important as the foundation of a healthy sense of self, the development of the psyche continues until the end of life (Erikson, 1963). Freud ostensibly ignored any psychological growth after adolescence. In the modern era, we accept Erikson's belief in the ability to alter ourselves psychologically, socially, and emotionally throughout the lifespan. To his mind, the self is malleable. We have the capacity for learning, growing, and changing throughout the lifespan. The self is a work-in-progress and can by altered by factors in our environment, including loss and grief.

Although most teachers should be familiar with Erikson's ideas, a brief review from the perspective of loss is warranted. Since his theory revolves around relationships, the absence of a significant person in a child's life will alter interpersonal dynamics. Not only will the griever experience the direct loss, but other interpersonal connections will be transformed. If we are to accept Erikson's premise, these alterations will have a significant impact on the child's sense of self and psychological development.

At birth, an infant completely depends on the adults in his world. He is egocentric, perceiving only the world as it appears to him. One-month-old Ian is helpless, and others must meet every one of his needs in his world. He recognizes his own urges, while the needs of others are meaningless to him. When Ian is hungry, wet, sick, or bored, he must attract someone's attention. To do this, he cries. At that point, two outcomes are possible. Either someone attends to Ian's needs, or his cries are unheeded. When caretakers meet a baby's needs, he comes to realize that someone cares in his little world. He learns to trust other people. If they neglect Ian, he comes to perceive that the world is an empty place where help is unavailable. When a baby suffers abuse, his environment is lonely, confusing, and frightening. A baby living in this environment grows up in a state of mistrust. A child who learns mistrust as an infant will struggle with this for the rest of his life (Erikson, 1963). Other researchers reaffirm that early attachment leads to healthy development. Children lacking strong relationships may develop attachment disorders (Bowlby, 1982). Imagine if six-month-old Ian lives with a family coping with death. Although Ian cannot yet empathize with the feelings of his grieving family or even understand the circumstances, he knows when his needs are being ignored. Mourning distracts the family members and they become inattentive to Ian's needs. On the rare occasions in which they interact, grief may alter their

Children's Development   33

demeanor. An upbeat and communicative mother becomes silent, withdrawn, or distraught. Ian does not know why Mom is behaving this way, but he can sense the change in her. Because of egocentrism, he mistakenly assumes the cause is displeasure with him. Babies develop their sense of self from the feedback from others in their environment. When the reaction is muted or negative, an infant can internalize this response. This circumstance is not destined to have a permanent effect on a baby's development. If the relationships with Mom and Dad were good ones before the loss, and if the extreme grief response is temporary, a baby can rebound from a few negative experiences. The potential remains for longstanding issues for Ian when grief creates a roadblock to trust.

Toddler Jill is becoming fiercely independent as she becomes mobile. She wants to do everything on her own, from dressing and feeding herself to using the potty like a big girl. Her favorite words are "no" and "mine," which represent her newfound freedom. Now able to recognize that she is not just an extension of Mom and Dad, she delights in this state of being her own person. This is Erikson's stage of autonomy. This sense of self-reliance will grow if the adults encourage her newfound skills. If parents restrict Jill's desire to do for herself, they may thwart her emerging sense of independence. "Look at that nasty mess" or "You're too slow" can discourage Jill and contribute to feelings of shame and doubt. "Mom doesn't believe that I can do it myself" becomes her manner of thinking after repeatedly hearing these statements. In Erikson's view, adults must set necessary limits, and saying "no" occasionally is appropriate and contributes to a toddler's understanding of limits. However, parents should encourage new skills to develop self-esteem. Without practice and positive feedback, Jill may grow up to act helpless and incompetent. Suppose her family is coping with grief during this developmental stage. Allowing toddlers to practice new skills is time consuming and requires a great deal of patience. A distracted individual may restrain his independence-building behavior by not providing the opportunities for a toddler to try things on their own. A distracted dad finds it easier feed Jill rather than clean the mess from her inexperienced attempts to eat her spaghetti dinner. Sometimes grieving parents overprotect a surviving child. Parents who will not acquiesce to a toddler's attempts at self-sufficiency may send the message they do not trust the child to complete tasks on her own. This little one becomes wary of new experiences and assumes she is incapable of acting on her own. Jill's emotional development may be arrested, and she may develop low self-esteem and learned helplessness (Erikson, 1963). One- and 2-year-olds are not cognitively capable of understanding why Daddy is impatient and why Mom jumps in and completes tasks. The egocentric interpretation reflects the belief that something is flawed with her as a competent individual. This toddler feels ashamed of herself, and she may doubt her own abilities or sense of self-worth. Shame and doubt are shaky foundations on which to build a fortress of self-esteem that can persist into later years.

During the preschool years, between the ages of 3 and 5, children enter the third developmental stage in Erikson's theory. Here the emphasis is on gender roles and conscience development, and Erikson considers this time to be a source of initiative. A more complex version of autonomy, initiative incorporates and expands upon the advanced cognitive abilities of children at this age (Erikson, 1963). For example,

34 Defining Grief Within a Developmental Context

4-year-old Seth is becoming increasingly independent from Mom and Dad. Seth can do many things for himself. He has greater muscle and neurological control, and his understanding of his environment provides enough information for him to decide and act. His play becomes advanced and premeditated, allowing for complex pretend and fantasy play. Seth can empathize with others more because of his growing ability to see others' perspectives. He is more competent in understanding consequences of behavior, but the need to avoid negative ramifications may lead to lying and exaggeration. When 2-year-old Jill spills her milk, she does not yet have the urge to deny it. Seth realizes the trouble he is in and may spin a web of lies to deflect the truth. Seth expresses his cognitive immaturity by telling ridiculous and illogical lies, but his conscious attempt to avoid trouble is notable at this stage. This deepened sense of responsibility and powerfulness over consequences, instead of just superficial doubt or shame, may cause Seth to feel guilty when he does something inappropriate. Guilt arises from our internal censor that lets us know right from wrong. For all intents and purposes, this guilt comprises the conscience, the moral part of our psyches. Our conscience monitors our behavior and provides us with negative feelings when we do something bad, which then becomes the motivation to change our actions or make amends. It is obvious why this stage holds such importance, as a strong conscience provides us with our moral compass throughout life (Erikson, 1963).

How might the death of a loved one influence development at this stage? If Seth's twin sister dies after a brief illness, Seth's nascent conscience may shoulder some responsibility. Immature cognition plays a role, too, as magical thinking contributes to a mistaken sense of guilt. Seth may believe that his own negative thoughts or bad behavior caused his sister's death. "Maybe I am a bad boy, and I deserve punishment." "Maybe she caught her illness from me." "I am a horrible person if I have fun when my sister is dead." Guilt creates these statements. Even if exaggerated, unfounded, or untrue, guilt can become a point of fixation and become an intractable part of the psyche, with profound influence well into adulthood.

Freud stressed the role of guilt in early development. He suggests that this emotion can result from intention alone and not just overt actions. He postulates that when occurring in early childhood, guilt stems from a fear of losing the parent's love. As we discovered through the work of Piaget, children at this age may not differentiate between reality and fantasy, thought and action. For example, a child may hold the mistaken belief that if he thinks negative thoughts about the deceased, he disappoints his parents. The threat of denied love is real to a child without a strong sense of self-esteem or who persists in magical thinking and imagined connections (Freud, 1961).

Freud believed we construct our personality by the age of 6. Events that occur during the critical first years become woven into the tapestry of the psyche will never unravel despite the years of psychoanalysis that Freud often recommended. Erikson did not concur with this extreme view, and he continued in his description of social/emotional stages, which he deemed as important as the earlier ones (Lawrence, 2015). Elementary school becomes the setting for social comparisons as children become cognizant of the views of other people in their lives (Erikson, 1963). When 7-year-old Alex draws a picture for her first-grade teacher,

Ms. Tracey, the reaction will not be as exuberant as that of Mommy or Daddy. At home, they meet Alex's milestones and accomplishments with praise and attention. "Wow, Alex, this drawing is awesome! You should be an artist when you grow up!" Accolades such as these are uttered as Mommy places the picture prominently on the refrigerator. But Ms. Tracey is a busier woman and has seen scores of similar artworks. Without a family connection to Alex, she should be impartial in her reactions. Although she does not want to hurt Alex's feelings, she does not consider the stick figures on the page indicative of an artistic career in Alex's future. Mrs. Tracey will not concede that Alex is the next van Gogh. Her lackluster attitude and corresponding mute reaction may seep into Alex's sense of self. Alex will get the message that her teacher does not agree with Mommy's opinion of her artistic skill.

Similar setting for comparison with peers and social judgments occur during the rest of Alex's day. The class is doing a group reading, and the students in the class know each other's strengths and weaknesses. Luckily for Alex, she reads proficiently, and her natural tendency is to compare herself to the others as each pupil gets a turn to read aloud. On the playground at recess, Alex discovers that her physical abilities do not match the skill of the larger girls. During the afternoon, Alex takes flute lessons with two peers and she realizes that the others are more advanced on the instrument, as the strains of her sour notes fill the room. She is a negative self-critic of her abilities, but the other students and the instructor know she has no musical talent. For Alex, the half-hour music lesson is torturous.

Erikson described this stage of development as establishing competence through industry in social settings. Elementary-aged kids are out in the real world and soon become cognizant of they measure up to society's standards. The opinions of others influence their emerging self-concept and corresponding self-esteem. Erikson does not mean to suggest that a child must consider herself to be the best at everything she attempts. It is necessary to have a realistic and empathetic view of the world, realizing that everyone has strengths and weaknesses. But for a child who believes she never compares favorably to others, this period can create a sense of inferiority. This viewpoint can be pervasive and generalized, leading to a heightened belief of personal incompetence. If this opinion becomes ingrained into the psyche, an individual may find it difficult to override this sense of incompetence later in adulthood (Erikson, 1963).

We can explore how Alex might fare psychologically during this stage after the death of a loved one. If the lost individual is a family member, Alex may be unaware of other children in the same circumstance. She may believe that no one understands, and she may be lonely and isolate herself. A growing sense of alienation can result. Observing the grief of others, especially parents, may be unsettling. Alex may strive to be the perfect child so she does not create stress for her family. She may try to compensate for the loss by taking on more tasks, perhaps more than she can handle. As a result, her self-standards may be rigid and elevated, resulting in a bar that too high. Her unrealistic expectations lead to failure, creating a deepened sense of inferiority. The family may idealize the deceased. If this individual was a sibling or peer who attended the same school, Alex may aspire to live up to real or imagined comparisons. Competing with the elevated persona of the dead individual is a set-up for failure and can shatter the illusion of relative perfection.

36 Defining Grief Within a Developmental Context

In Erikson's theory, middle childhood lasts until around the age of 12, which starts adolescence. This period serves as a second "terrible twos," as teens struggle to separate from their parents and establish an independent version of themselves. Peers play a major role in their lives. One of the biggest paradoxes of this phase is that just as a teen struggles to be his own person, he experiences the simultaneous attraction and conformity to cliques. Erikson claims that the goal of this stage is identity formation. The need to discover identity leads to experimentation with different roles and ideas, creating an identity crisis. Identity encompasses every aspect of the person, including personal appearance, values, opinions, attitudes, career and educational plans, relationships, and sexuality. If teens emerge from this time of personal discovery with an intact and positive sense of self, it sets the foundation for a framework for future growth as an independent adult. Conversely, if an adolescent ends his teenage years confused about one's sense of self, we call this role diffusion. Not only may this teen have little sense of direction, he may have little motivation to continue a positive quest for identity, leading to inaction or self-destructive consequences (Erikson, 1963).

How might 14-year-old Randy, whose 16-year-old sister has died from a lifelong medical condition, react when in the stage of identity formation? While Randy attempts to distance himself from his family, he might experience pressure to remain close to his emotionally needy parents and other siblings. If his sister's identity becomes larger than life, this can become a great sense of stress for Randy. Mixed and ambivalent emotions, compounded by the hormonal and social influences of normal adolescence, create emotional confusion and conflict within Randy's teenage psyche. In an attempt at self-preservation, Randy may isolate himself from the others, if no one else identifies with his experiences. His teenager status leads Randy to risk-taking opportunities. Randy may jeopardize his own health or safety through these dangerous behaviors, using them either as a way of distancing himself from the family or escaping his own pain. Bereavement in the teenage years may force Randy to grow closer to his family or go to great pains to distance himself. In either event, this will affect identity. The role of griever can become a part of the identity itself.

Writing on adolescent egocentrism, Elkind (1967) describes distinct peculiarities of teenage thought. The "imaginary audience" refers to the exaggerated belief that one is in the spotlight, that others perceive every flaw and imperfection. The "personal and invincibility fables" refer to the misguided beliefs that one is extra-special and unique, which serves a protective purpose. Because he has a special status, a person is exempt from experiencing negative consequences that might befall others. These are cognitive distortions which can lead to risk-taking behaviors and succumbing to the undue influence of peer pressure (Elkind, 1967). If an adolescent is grieving, these common cognitive exaggerations can magnify.

Although psychosocial development continues throughout the lifespan, educators will find the first five stages most relevant to their work. Understanding normal development and superimposing grief unto these phases build the framework for grief education. It is helpful to remember that although the maturation of the self and psyche is ideally linear, back-tracking often occurs during times of stress. A child who is grieving may find his established sense of trust, autonomy, or identity

Children's Development   37

shaken. Kids may need to emotionally regroup before continuing in their psychological development.

A child's social influences can be positive or negative throughout this development. Most times, circumstances can have variable effects. The death of a loved one is a powerful event that will become a major influence in the life of a child. But just because the event is stressful doesn't mean that subsequent effects must be troublesome. The experience can help a child grow closer to his family, develop a greater sense of empathy and compassion, develop a larger purpose and well-defined direction in life, and strengthen the impact of relationships (Lawrence, 2015). By defining Erikson's stages, we suggest a framework for adults to appreciate a child's growth and maturation. The psychosocial perspective can serve as a guide in helping a child navigate his world when a child is struggling with grief.

The essence of Erikson's theory boils down to relationships, and healthy, solid attachments build the foundations. Today's neurological research has shown that strong bonds become wired into the brain. This synaptic network is a crucial component in grieving. There are two major ways in which this connection directs a child's reaction to the loss of someone close.

First, it disrupts the neurological "program" the relationship with the deceased had created. The stronger the attachment we have to our loved one, the greater the effect. Our minds and bodies function via learned neurological connections. When a relationship changes because of the physical loss of one partner, normal neural connections derail. The circuit ceases normal function, and new patterns of connection will form. Time to adapt is necessary whenever a familiar pattern of behavior changes in any way (new job, beginning of a school year, moving to a new town, etc.). Loss of a cherished individual is a similar change but has greater intensity. We often lose faith and hope after a death, leaving despair in their place. The griever learns he cannot go back and reconnect the threads of the relationship. The neural circuitry is altered, and our brains need to develop new patterns of thought, feeling, and behavior.

Second, loss can influence the entire nature of attachment. Children are inexperienced with broken attachments, and they do not yet understand how life will continue without the object of their love. As we grow and mature, we become familiar with loss in our lives, and we learn that we will survive. We gain coping skills, and we learn to become resilient, sometimes for no other reason than we have no choice but to forge ahead. These reactions form new neural programs that run any time circumstances dictate. The connections may create positive or negative coping styles. They become the go-to plans for coping when loss creeps up on us again later in life.

The key to mitigating the negative effects of these disrupted neuronal connections is to strengthen alternative attachments, just as Erikson suggested when he focused on interpersonal relationships in healthy psychological adjustment. When a significant person in a child's life dies, that child needs new emotional connections to help repair the neuropsychological damage. She may build these bonds with people that enter her life after the loss. Other attachments can entail reinforcing and reconfiguring older ones, such as deepening bonds with siblings that are sharing the same horrible experience. These relationships help the brain build new connections

38 Defining Grief Within a Developmental Context

that allow for healthy coping. New neural programs do not necessarily replace the old ones but may serve as alternate routes for traveling the path of life. When one road gets washed away from a flash flood, other routes become available to keep us on our journey. We need those detours, or else we will get stuck on the old road waiting for the waters to recede. Sometimes, the road may be closed permanently, and we must find new routes. But our memories of the old ways linger.

As adults who play a major role in children's lives, educators have a unique opportunity to bond with students and create healthy attachments. Teachers are already familiar with how the nature of interpersonal relationships with the pupils in class allow for more effective teaching and learning. We can say the same for helping a grieving child. The key to maximizing this opportunity is by demonstrating true concern. Children have an uncanny ability to recognize when adults fret over them. They sense honest respect and empathy. By being present and expressing sincerity regarding the child's welfare, teachers become lifesavers in the floodwaters of grief.

Chapter 5

Attachment and Relationships

Our feelings of attachment to a loved one are at the core of the grief response. When someone dies, those left behind are struggling with the loss of the relationship. The closer we feel to the individual, the more intense grief reaction we should experience. We mourn the loss of the deceased's presence, and our minds turn to the regrets we have about the past and the lost future (James & Friedman, 2009). Since the intimacy of the bond is paramount in grief, we should investigate the nature of attachment to better understand mourning.

John Bowlby is one of psychology's leading theorists on this topic. In a series of books published in the 1970s and 1980s, Bowlby described the way human beings form these early relationships (Bowlby, 1969, 1982). In 1970, Mary Ainsworth extended his work by testing infants' attachment to their mothers. She used an experimental set-up known as the "strange situation." In these research trials, Ainsworth tested older infants in several scenarios that involved their mothers leaving them in a strange room. Sometimes the babies were left with a stranger. In other trials, the infants were left alone. The researchers observed the reactions of the children when the mothers returned. By systematically recording and describing these responses, Ainsworth defined several attachment styles. The major styles included secure attachment, in which an upset baby was easily soothed by the presence of the bonded adult, i.e., the mother. Fortunately, most of the infants fell into this designation. A second category, ambivalent-insecure attachment, included babies who became upset when the mother left, then was clingy but inconsolable upon her return. A third classification identified by Ainsworth was the avoidant-insecure attachment, which described the behavior of another group of babies. These children were detached and disinterested when Mom came back into the room. They often ignored her and did not return for comfort or a warm greeting. More stoic than the ambivalent babies, they appear to adopt an "I-don't-care" emotional facade. Because attachment theory is largely a psychoanalytic perspective, the theory presupposes that the nature of these early bonds has huge implications for future relationships (Ainsworth & Bell, 1970). Not surprisingly, research has illustrated this effect (Higgins, 2003; Jones et al., 2018; Schimmenti & Bifulco, 2015; Sroufe, 2005). Years later, securely attached individuals reported the most satisfying and intimate bonds with others. Having that first positive tie with Mom set the stage for similar patterns in the future. Although psychologists predominantly assumed that these patterns were behaviorally conditioned, current neurological

40 Defining Grief Within a Developmental Context

research suggests a neurological route for this phenomenon. I will cover this topic in the next chapter, but for now, understanding the importance and persistence of this original emotional bond to a significant other will suffice for grasping this concept.

Babies who exhibited an ambivalent attachment grew up to have similar problems with other adults. They may be very insecure about their loved one's feelings for them, and this lack of faith in the bond can lead to excessive anxiety regarding the relationship, clinginess, and neediness (Dilworth & Hildreth, 1997; Sroufe, 2005). For these individuals, no amount of reassurance calms their fears that their loved one will leave, just as the infants in Ainsworth's study were not sure if mother was coming or going, returning or leaving for good. When a relationship ends, ambivalently attached people hold on for dear life, perceiving the break-up as a devastating blow. The bonds are tight, but no safety net appears.

Like their infant counterparts, avoidant adults lack the ability to bond comfortably. For these people, the lack of a secure base resulted in the tendency to protect themselves from the pain of loss. These adults tend to be emotionally guarded and withdrawn, and they do not enter close relationships easily. They behave as if they prefer to back away rather than risk abandonment. They are standoffish and may act as though they do not need, or even desire, a close connection with another. The pain of not having a stable relationship early in life results in the tendency to avoid this potential later (Sroufe, 2005). "If I don't bond, there can't be any pain of disappointment or loss" seems to be their credo.

Years after Ainsworth's study, Main and Solomon (1986) described a fourth attachment style: disorganized-insecure. Behaviors that demonstrated a sense of confusion regarding the relationship with the caregiver defined this category. These babies acted inconsistently upon the parent's return in a strange situation. They may approach, then appear fearful, or they might be confused. Adults display similar patterns of behavior. These individuals handled their relationships with a sense of inconsistency, acting as if they wished to develop close bonds but then shy away. This approach-avoidance behavior is frustrating for the significant other, resulting in relationships that lack intimacy and security. The researchers suggest that this attachment style may result when parents alternate between loving and intimidating behaviors, creating a child who is uncertain what to expect from the parent. As adults, these kids may seek similar relationships, creating associations that send them on emotional roller coasters.

The importance of understanding attachment when considering reactions to loss of a loved one cannot be overstated. Remember, underlying grief is the loss of a connection to someone or something. When a bond is with a person, this tie becomes a relationship. The subsequent nature of that relationship and the intensity of attachment contribute to the characteristics of grief when the connection is threatened or lost. Grief is often more pathological when "unfinished business" remains within the relationship (James & Friedman, 2009). Since these attachment styles develop during the early years, they are relevant when focusing on childhood bereavement.

Most attachment researchers focus on the early years when these styles are being developed. The actions and attention of loving adults set the stage for a child's ability to bond with others later. This research largely looks at the normal course of infancy and the usual issues in childhood (Jacobs, 1999; Sroufe, 2005). However, other research has suggested that these styles influence our way of coping with grief. In times of intense stress, we revert to the behavior patterns of infancy to help us find support and security (Bowlby, 1980). If those ways were not effective when we were babies, they are likely not to help us through grief either.

Children and adults who show secure attachment styles will reach out when they need help in coping. One purpose of attachment is to allow babies to regulate emotions and grieving children look to trusted adults for the same thing (Sroufe, 2005). Connecting to a secure base helps to ground the griever, at least to an extent. What happens, though, when the lost loved one is the usual, go-to person the child turns to in times of stress? This is an anxiety-producing event. Even when the secure person is physically available, he or she may not be emotionally accessible if grief is overwhelming them. Researchers acknowledge that when a powerful emotion such as grief is triggered, the bond with a secure person may not be enough to lessen the anxiety. If a child discovers no one is available, or if the support is insufficient to match grief's intensity, the child may oscillate between two different coping strategies. On one hand, there may be hyper-activation, or an increase in the degree of neediness shown by the child. Children may be clingy and anxious, as if they are frantically searching for someone to lessen their rising sense of discomfort (Bowlby, 1976). Conversely, they may withdraw and put on a brave face, as if denying their need for support. This is not true resilience but an act designed for their own benefit, to convince themselves they are fine on their own. It is not uncommon to find young kids waffling between these extremes in behavior (Fraley & Bonanno, 2004). They need help, and they know it, but the usual techniques for getting security are ineffectual.

If we see these behaviors in people who have secure attachments, it makes sense that the situation is even direr in individuals with ambivalent or avoidant attachment styles (Shear et al., 2007). They, too, will revert to their default method of coping, either by becoming needy or refusing offers of help. Although these actions remind us of those exhibited by Ainsworth's securely attached babies, grief triggers the reactions. There are no interjections of positive, secure interactions with others. With no secure base, the mourner does not know where to turn. There is no one to help regulate the intensity of these intense human emotions. If this is the first time experiencing the painful emotions that a loss triggers, the panic of dysregulated emotions can be overwhelming. We revert to old attachment patterns, desperately latching on to anyone (as seen with ambivalent/insecurely attached individuals) or recusing ourselves from any or all attempts of comfort and support (which occurs with avoidant-insecurely attached people). With a disorganized/insecurely attached, person behaviors can vacillate erratically. Alternately, support is accepted and rejected, leaving the griever emotionally vulnerable.

Some research has focused on the connection between attachment and neurological development during the early years (Cozolino, 2006; Jacobs, 1999; Siegel, 2001). Although there are individual differences regarding the specialization of the brain's cerebral cortex hemispheres, or lateralization, there may be inherent differences between the right and left hemispheres. For most of us, language capability resides in the left side, while nonverbal activities originate in the right. Studies

42 Defining Grief Within a Developmental Context

suggest that the right brain is more intricately connected to the emotional centers of the limbic system. Therefore, a baby who has been traumatized and forms a poor attachment to others may be deficient in right brain neurological connections. The results in an emotional short-circuit, leading to poor self-regulation (Schore, 2001). This child never learns healthy emotional reactions to stress and may have a difficult time regulating his or her emotions and related behaviors.

Research has described specific patterns of attachment problems that arise after a child has experienced the death of someone in their lives, especially a caregiver. Some of these kids manifest an avoidant attachment personality. This style is characterized by a lack of trust in other people along with an inflated view of the self. The idea is that only oneself can be trusted, creating a lack of intimacy with others. These individuals become highly self-reliant and independent, refusing to accept help. This leads to competitiveness and a lack of emotional expression, which people may interpret as coldness. Another group of children demonstrate a preoccupied anxious/ambivalent pattern of personality traits. In this scenario, kids become excessively clingy and dependent. Separation anxiety and phobias are common. Interestingly, although helplessness is the rule in this individual, receiving the sought-after care and reassurance does little to placate him. A third fraction of people act in a way that indicates disorganized/chaotic personality characteristics. Related behaviors include extreme caution, paranoia, self-consciousness, and occasionally, psychosis. In this manifestation, the person is distrustful of everyone, himself included (DiCiacco, 2008). While not all grievers will exhibit these traits, many will behave in related ways as they work their way through grief.

When the death involves traumatic circumstances, disruptions with attachment are more likely. This tendency also occurs when the loved one is a close relative to a child, like a parent (Jacobs, 1999). We must remember, however, that a child's perception of trauma may vary from ours as adults. A young person is dependent on others to care for them and keep them safe, and as a result, he may interpret any scary or threatening situation as traumatic.

When grieving, we need a positive and healthy attachment to a significant other. When a child does not have a secure attachment style in the first place, forming new bonds is challenging. Even in the best of circumstances, a young person may not trust new attachments in the wake of losing one. Forming strong bonds with others is the best way of dealing with grief and maintaining a new version of attachment to the deceased is part of the process of mourning (Kosminsky & Jordan, 2016; Neimeyer et al., 2002). Strong attachments can even create new neural connections in the brain (Siegel, 2001). Educators have a large role to play in offering support, especially those who have daily contact with a child in emotional need. Later in this book, I will suggest ways to reach a grieving child; but for now, it is enough to keep this aim in the forefront of our minds in our interactions with the bereaved.

Chapter 6

Loss as Potential Trauma

Centuries ago, parents and educators paid little attention to the psychological development of children, especially regarding the effects of negative experiences. Society considered young people to be resilient because their immature perceptions sheltered them from worry and grief. When Sigmund Freud described his psychosexual stages of development around the turn of the 20th century, he spearheaded a movement that recognized the psychological life of children. Decades later, Erik Erikson developed his psychosocial stages of development, and society no longer minimized children's emotional. Children may be resilient, but they are still susceptible to lasting effects from traumatic situations encountered during the early years.

While theorists such as Freud and Erikson understood the potential for psychological harm in youth, most of the threats to well-being they described were commonplace circumstances. Erikson described feelings of shame that can develop when parents interfere or scold too much (Erikson, 1963). Kids who do not keep up with their peers may feel inferior. But what happens when a child encounters a traumatic situation? What effects can these events have on the immature psyche?

In 1998, researchers completed a multiyear study that investigated the effects of serious stressors on young people. This study is known as the Adverse Childhood Experiences Study, or ACEs. The results are familiar to those who work with children and school personnel included. The researchers defined ten situations that could be traumatic to a child. These conditions included physical, sexual, and emotional abuse; physical and emotional neglect; exposure to violence in the home, toward the mother; experience with substance abuse, incarceration, and mental illness in family members; and divorce. All these life events adversely impacted children. Effects ranged from at-risk behaviors such as substance abuse, promiscuity, and unprotected sex during later adulthood. Moreover, negative behaviors persisted, often resulting in health problems such as chronic illnesses and early death (Felitti et al., 1998). Further research showed that these effects were consistent across racial and SES groups (Cronholm et al., 2015). Other studies stressed individual differences in response to trauma, including the nature of the complex relationships in a child's life (Finkelhor, Shattuck, Turner, & Hamby, 2013). Despite the multitude of influential variables that may dictate the specific results of early trauma, focus shifted to the potential for significant, long-term influence of such factors. The tide of awareness was rising. With these findings, society overlooked children's suffering no more. We learned how major, negative life happenstances can have long-term, permanent effects on a child.

44 Defining Grief Within a Developmental Context

After reading these studies, however, one must consider the operational definition of "trauma." A common definition refers to an experience that is "emotionally painful or distressful," resulting in long-term effects, either physical or psychological (National Institute of Mental Health, n.d.). The ACEs study neglected to focus on a death in the family as traumatic. If we hold to a strict definition of trauma as being a direct effect to the perceiver, then a death of another may not be a trauma in the usual sense. However, a definite blow to emotional well-being occurs. After a loved one dies, the remaining family members sustain damage to their psychological health. Little children do not have a clear view of reality and fantasy. Their egocentrism causes them to see things in relation to themselves. It is not a huge leap for a child to think another's death might be contagious or otherwise threatening. If true, this is trauma on two counts: the emotional shock of the loss and the perceived personal threat. Grief and bereavement are not identical to chronic child abuse, but we could assume that trauma creates similar consequences. When a loss is traumatic, can the effects persist into adulthood, as the ACEs study revealed for other types of childhood crises?

To investigate this question, it is important to support the idea that a loss is, in fact, traumatic at the time of the event. McClatchey, Vonk, and Palardy (2009) looked at 158 children between the ages of 7 and 16 who had suffered the loss of a parent. They found that the majority experienced symptoms of "traumatic grief," including self-reported feelings of anxiety, social withdrawal, and low self-esteem. These effects existed regardless of whether the parent's death was expected (such as in a long-term illness) or sudden. These findings support the idea that loss is a trauma even when anticipated or indirectly threatening to the griever. When children lose a mother or father, it can jeopardize mental health.

Cerniglia et al. (2014) focused on adolescents. Investigating 151 preteens, these researchers found that the children who had lost a parent displayed more psychological symptoms than did the nongrievers. Effects included obsessiveness, depression, and anxiety, continuing years after the death. The subjects whose loss had occurred prior to the age of three presented with symptoms with more severity, leading the authors to conclude that preteens may struggle with a grief experience even if the death had occurred years before and there were few explicit memories. Brent et al. (2009) studied 176 young people between the ages of 7 and 25, half of whom had lost a parent without warning. Surveying them at 9 months after the loss and again at 21 months, the grievers reported significantly more mental health issues than did the controls. These symptoms included feelings of depression, low self-esteem, guilt, and anger. Interestingly, the anxiety and PTSD symptoms in the grieving subjects decreased significantly by the 21-month point, while the signs of depression held constant. Studies such as these lend support to the hypothesis that loss during childhood, particularly of a parent, can create effects that suggest that grievers are, in fact, traumatized by this event. This is true irrespective of race, gender, SES, or manner of death.

Layne (2014) took this research one step further, questioning 3785 subjects who had sought help from the National Traumatic Stress Network. Although Layne was looking at several varieties of trauma in this study, he specifically asked them to recount their experience with death and loss. He found that trauma, regardless of its

Loss as Potential Trauma   45

nature, had a cumulative effect. Those with multiple occasions of trauma suffered the most ill effects. These subjects reported higher rates of negative behaviors such as truancy, substance use, suicidality, and criminal actions. One of the major problems reported by the respondents dealt with attachment. Subjects reported struggling to bond with others after multiple experiences with trauma, including loss. One of the leading theorists on attachment, John Bowlby, wrote prolifically on the potential for grief and loss to affect attachment (Bowlby, 1960). It is not surprising that researchers such as Layne (2014) found results that suggested fewer attachment behaviors in bereaved subjects.

Other studies declared that the effects of a loss during childhood are not just psychological or emotional. Virk, Ritz, Li, Obel, and Olsen (2016) conducted a large-scale study of over 94,000 Danish citizens who had lost a parent or sibling when they were between 5 and 17 years of age. Over 6000 of these individuals had developed Type 1 diabetes during childhood, a statistically significant number. The authors concluded that loss in a family creates stress, which can increase the chances for illness and other health conditions to occur. Since we accept that emotional stress can impact the body, this possibility of a traumatic loss to create or at least contribute to the emergence makes intuitive sense. Is it reasonable to infer that young people would be more susceptible to health issues because of continuing growth and maturation? Possibly.

If we assume losses to be traumatic, often wreaking psychological and physical havoc on a child, can these effects persist into adulthood? Several studies suggest that this is the case.

Hurd (1999) conducted a qualitative study in which he interviewed 43 adults who had experienced the loss of a parent when they were between the ages of 3 and 10 years old. Although the experiences were different, Hurd found definite similarities in the reactions lasting into adulthood. A group of respondents discussed feelings of appreciation and respect for the deceased, while others felt frustration toward the surviving parent. Others described their feelings with the survivor as "enmeshment"; the relationship went through tough times early but grew closer over time. These subjects reported negative effects as adults, including strong feelings of guilt, anxiety, worry, fear, and low self-esteem, which they attributed to their loss experience. Another group of subjects claimed that they were not sure if the loss still influenced them. Hurd considered this group to be "ambivalent." They reported high levels of anxiety and fear yet were unable to connect these feelings to the early loss. Many of the subjects reported diagnoses of depression as adults. Hurd's findings suggest that although there are individual differences in terms of specific effects, a loss during one's childhood has the potential for long-ranging influence. His findings implied that the level of communication in the family was the key to directing these influences in a positive way.

Kaplow et al. (2010) compared three groups of young adults between the ages of 11 and 21. One group had lost a parent; one had lost another family member; and the third had suffered no loss. The researchers surveyed the subjects over several years, discovering that both bereaved groups reported lower levels of global functioning and higher rates of substance use and separation anxiety when compared to the control. These effects lasted over the period of the study. Interestingly, the

46   Defining Grief Within a Developmental Context

group designated as "other bereaved" reported higher levels of depression than did either of the other groups. The authors suggested that this may result from less social support given to children who lose someone other than a parent. This idea relates to Hurd's (1999) work; well-meaning adults may talk more with children who have lost a parent because they view the loss as significant. On the other hand, when the deceased is not a mother or father, the intensity of the bereavement may be underestimated. Children in these circumstances may experience indirect, or disenfranchised, grief. This term, defined as unacknowledged grief, is less familiar to laypeople (Doka, 1989). As a result, this child may grieve without sufficient support, potentially creating negative long-term consequences.

McLeod (1991) looked at 1755 married individuals between the ages of 18 and 64. She compared those who had lost a parent during their childhood to those who had experienced a parental divorce. Although both groups suffered after the events, children of divorce showed higher rates of substance abuse and marital problems than did the grievers, females reported higher levels of persistent depression. The author surmises that communication and relationship with the surviving parent may have minimized negative effects. Divorce implies family dysfunction, while a death does not. She suggests that in both cases, males may be more likely to suppress their emotions and report no unhealthy consequences, possibly a result of male stereotypes regarding emotional expression.

Maier and Lachman (2000) looked at 4242 adults between the ages of 30 and 60. They identified two groups: 182 had experienced the loss of a parent prior to age 17, while another 380 had experienced a parental divorce. As in previous studies, these researchers discovered a gender difference in responses. Females who had lost a parent through death reported higher rates of depression than did the nongrievers, while males reported higher rates of autonomy. These findings agree with those of McLeod (1991) and may support her conclusion that children who lose a parent are not only better supported that those who have dealt with a divorce, and girls and boys differ in their reactions. This study admits that long-range findings would be useful, admitting that these studies focus only parental death. Other research has suggested that the death of siblings or other close family members may affect survivors in drastically different ways.

A study by Mash et al. (2013) focused on these types of losses. They studied 107 individuals between the ages of 17 and 29, some of whom had lost a sibling or close friend within the last three years. Sibling survivors reported significantly higher levels of depression and complicated grief than those who had lost a friend. Both grieving groups were more depressed than the controls. The sibling survivors reported a greater number of health and somatic symptoms and a more pessimistic world view overall. The level of complicated grief was positively correlated with the reported level of intimacy and depth of relationship with the sibling. Complicated grief persists over a long period and is characterized by lack of acceptance and inability to resume a normal life (Schupp, 2004). If we assume that sibling loss is disenfranchised grief, and if these siblings are ignored or unsupported, we would expect these findings. The authors' conclusions were statistically significant even for grievers three years removed from the death. This provides more evidence that loss has enduring effects and creates unique reactions from different people.

Another study that focused sibling relationships was that of Fanos and Nickerson (1991). These researchers surveyed 75 adults who had lost a sibling to cystic fibrosis before the age of 17. Cystic fibrosis is a chronic, progressive, and often fatal genetic disorder in which sufferers produce abnormal mucous, causing digestive and respiratory problems. Respondents in this study reported the greatest level of negative effects if the death had occurred when the survivor was between the ages of 13 and 17. These individuals reported higher rates of anxiety, more sense of vulnerability, more concern about physical health, greater feelings of depression, and higher levels of guilt than the other subjects. The authors suggest that the pre-teens exhibit ambivalent, volatile, and complicated feelings. Although surviving siblings often report persistent psychological symptoms, those who were preteens at the time of the loss had greater difficulty coping.

Prigerson et al. (1999) focused on the effects on survivors of the death of a friend by suicide. Surveying 146 friends of suicide victims, the authors found that level of grief positively correlates with suicidal ideation. This significant effect was true regardless of elapsed time since the death, reaffirming the tenacity of grief.

Other research indicated that bereavement may trigger stubborn physical consequences, too. Baker, Norris, Jones, and Murphy (2009) studied 1308 Mexican respondents who reported childhood trauma, including bereavement. They discovered that the subjects reported high rates not only of depression and PTSD but also physical symptoms such as gastrointestinal, muscular-skeletal, cardiovascular, and respiratory problems. The authors controlled for other links such as SES, education, and home environment, and they were persisting years beyond the actual trauma. Goodwin and Stein (2004) looked at Americans in a similar study. By performing regression analyses on data from the National Comorbidity Survey, the researchers discovered a link between early trauma and physical illness. Those subjects who reported childhood maltreatment also were more likely to report respiratory problems, peptic ulcers, and arthritis; sexual abuse was linked with cardiovascular illnesses. Respondents reporting neglect displayed higher rates of diabetes and other autoimmune disorders. Although this study was correlational and focused on abuse, when considered with other findings, the data imply link a link between traumatic grief and poor health in later years.

A study by Zall (1994) suggests that there is a potential for these long-term effects to have important implications not only for the individual in question but also for his or her families. Zall studied women who had lost a mother when they were children or adolescents, comparing them to a control group whose moms were alive. The grievers reported significantly higher rates of depression and suicidality when they were younger which continued into well into adulthood. As new moms themselves, they showed higher levels of overprotectiveness and worry about health and safety than did their control group counterparts. They also admitted being demanding and controlling toward their children. Zall found that despite these results, the grieving group's overall level of parental functioning was not significantly different. One interpretation is that while early loss may create uncomfortable symptoms in the griever (e.g., worry about health); these may translate to positive actions toward others (protection of their own children).

48   Defining Grief Within a Developmental Context

Are long-range effects always negative? Some research suggests that positive reactions are possible. Standing and Ringo (2016) examined links between early loss of a mother or father and achievement level in adulthood. Earlier research had described such an effect, called the "Phaeton effect." Many prominent historical figures, including American Presidents, British Prime Ministers, and literary writers, have experienced the loss of a parent when they were children. These researchers discovered that a multitude of famous individuals lost fathers before they were 4 years old. Experiencing a loss that occurred between the ages of 5 and 10 had more negative than positive effects, however. Standing and Ringo suggest that because younger children (less than 4 years old) had fewer explicit memories, their experiences were not as intense. Older kids would possess more recollections of Dad. The authors hypothesize that early loss creates a desire for achievement and success as compensation for feelings of loss, deprivation, and emptiness. Although the emotions might cause distress, the eventual results and expression could be positive.

Other research provides more pieces to this puzzle. Some of these investigate whether manner of death is a variable that influences grief. For example, Pfeffer, Karus, Siegel, and Jiang (2000) compared children whose parents had died from a suicide to those who lost a parent to cancer. The former group of children had significantly more symptoms of depression and reported more problems with their relationships. Wilcox et al. (2010) also compared children whose parents had died from suicide, accidents, or illnesses. Kids whose mother or father had ended their own lives were more likely to be suicidal themselves; they were also more likely to be hospitalized for psychiatric disorders. All the grievers, however, were more prone to criminal activities when compared to the control group. In a similar light, Breier et al. (1988) studied adult psychiatric problems in subjects who had lost a parent during childhood. They found that the quality of the home life after the loss was a huge factor in lessening the chances of psychiatric disturbance in adulthood. Not only that, they suggest that the actual mechanism for future psychological dysfunction lies in the altered mechanism of the hypothalamic-pituitary-adrenal (HPA) axis. The authors hypothesize that early traumatic loss has the potential for permanent effects to this neurological function, and a healthy social environment has the potential to mitigate this. Other studies have further investigated the neurobiological consequences of trauma. Vythilingam et al. (2002) studied 32 depressed women, 21 of whom had suffered childhood abuse. The findings revealed smaller hippocampal volume in those who were abused than in those who had not; the implication was that abuse caused the smaller volume, not the depression itself. Although these authors do not explicitly make the connection between memory loss after trauma and smaller hippocampal volume, that could be a rational explanation for their findings. Carrion and Wong (2012) also found similar effects of trauma on the brain structure and physiology. Through functional imaging, they found reduced activity in the hippocampus and prefrontal cortex of many youths who had experienced traumatic stress when compared to normal controls. They suggest that the findings imply there is an effect on the brain of altered levels of cortisol. This hormone is secreted in large amounts during stress and is associated with poor hippocampal physiology. The implication, according to these researchers, is that trauma creates chemical responses in the brain which lead to poor memory processing (hippocampus) and executive functioning (prefrontal cortex). The end result is impairments in learning and cognition.

While these studies provide interesting ideas for thought, there are limitations. A handful focuses solely on loss of a parent, neglecting other forms of grief. Others have small or homogeneous samples. Many assume that the effects of grief will manifest as mental health symptoms or transform into physical problems. Current research focuses on how grief and trauma alters brain anatomy, physiology, or chemistry. A select few suggest how grievers can channel their pain into positive outlets, and most do not enter the realm of therapies or support. Grief is not a rare experience, and it would be prudent to continue research on this topic to validate grief as a trauma and illustrate how the effects can be "writ large" on the adult. The potential for long-ranging consequences is real.

Erikson maintained that strong relationships were the key to healthy psychosocial development (Whitbourne & Whitbourne, 2014). When a close bond is severed following a death, not only is the connection between the two individuals lost, but other relationships may suffer, too. We should recognize that coping with a death in the family will have a significant impact on a child's development across the lifespan.

We have stated that death and grief are facts of life, even in childhood. As adults, we may understand the reality of situations and control our behaviors and emotions, but that is easier said than done. The effects of grief, even in adulthood, can be intense and permanent. It seems reasonable to assume that loss can also have a major influence on children. Because of their neurological, cognitive, emotional, and social stages of development, children may interpret and handle a grief situation differently than an adult. In a vulnerable child, the influence of this situation can be potentially strong. The unpredictability because of so many variables makes it difficult to determine exactly how a child will react, but children *will* react eventually. We may be unable to prevent this life event from occurring, but we can become more informed and better able to support suffering young people. The goal is to lessen the negative effects and accentuate any positive ones. Research is necessary to provide the roadmap and rationale for this trip in aiding bereaved children.

Chapter 7

Definitions of Grief

As is true with most topics in psychology, the concepts of grief and mourning are abstract and difficult to define. The processes themselves do not always follow a predictable path. I prefer not to use the word "normal" when I speak of humans' behaviors and reactions. This word may be appropriate if we think of the term "normal" in its most basic sense, meaning what most people say, do, or feel. Given the wide variety of human characteristics and extraneous variables that influence us, it should not surprise us that social scientists have difficulty finding definitive patterns. So, when we say a reaction is normal, we merely imply that it falls somewhere on the bell curve of typical. In terms of mental health, psychologists use the term to describe behaviors that are maladaptive, not just rare. The problem when applying these concepts to bereavement is that the tendency for a behavior pattern to be maladaptive may vary from person to person. For example, an introvert's social withdrawal may work well for him (quiet time to recharge) but be detrimental for an extrovert (disconnection from beneficial social connections). There is no one right way to grieve, nor is there one clear pattern of reactions. There are behaviors that are unhealthy because they are not conducive to productive living or they result in negative consequences. Social scientists lean on descriptions that represent most people, but an individual may engage in unique behaviors that are personally effective even if we classify them as outliers. In this book, I am considering the term abnormal to mean counterproductive or ineffective. I will rely on the social scientist's method of summarizing patterns of behavior and descriptions of common reactions. It is important to keep in mind that no book can cover every variation of normal. Grief is unique even as it is universal.

To complicate the issue, experts take great pains to distinguish among the terms, grief, mourning, and bereavement. We think of grief as the internal emotional reactions to a loss, while we often define mourning as the behavioral manifestations of that loss. Bereavement refers to the long-term process of feeling the loved one's absence; we are bereft of his or her presence. Although we can make distinctions among these terms, the connections are obvious (Bow, 2018). To determine where the emotional and psychological reactions stop and the behavioral manifestations begin, for example, is a difficult task. Likewise, we may find it hard to distinguish the pain created from the absence of a loved one from the negative reaction to the facts of the death itself. For the purposes of this book, the distinctions are minor. To experience the loss of a loved one creates a grief response, which results in

Definitions of Grief 51

mourning behavior. We consider this person bereaved. For ease of our conversation, we will think of these as three aspects of the same phenomenon, reacting to the loss of a significant person in our lives. We can apply the same thought when referencing children.

In 1942, a devastating fire occurred at the Cocoanut Grove nightclub in Boston, Massachusetts, killing almost 500 people. Erich Lindermann was a psychiatry professor at Harvard Medical School who was asked to help with the survivors, and he became one of the first individuals to study grief in a clinical setting. He defined terms such as acute grief, which included not only emotional responses but physical symptoms such as tightness in the throat, muscle aches, choking sensations, and frequent sighing. Lindemann also described morbid grief reactions, which he defined as distortions of the normal process. One sign of morbid grief is a delayed response, which can occur weeks or months after the event. He described cases in which the survivor displayed symptoms of the deceased's illnesses along with other dramatic somatic complaints. Occasionally, the mourner may acquire personality traits and behavioral mannerisms of the person who died. Kids may exhibit an exaggerated sense of hostility, a severe lack of social interaction, or "agitated depression." This last condition includes feelings of sadness and hopelessness combined with tension, irritability, guilt, and lack of sleep. Suicidality is a real possibility in these cases (Lindemann, 1944). Lindemann's work was valuable not only for the importance he placed on describing normal and abnormal grief responses but also for his acknowledgement that grief can result from many circumstances, including witnessing the death of strangers.

Attig (2010) describes the difference between grief reactions and grief responses. To his way of thinking, grief reactions are the feelings, thoughts, and physiological changes that occur soon after a death. These are largely involuntary and can be difficult to control. Emotions are raw, and they basically happen *to* us. Later, grief responses occur. This term refers to the choices we make to express and cope with our grief. We can control our behaviors along with our internal responses. We can consciously decide to act in specific ways, such as purposely choosing to participate in positive activities. We can actively strive to "relearn" our world, forming new relationships, environments, and behavior patterns (Attig, 2010). Rasmussen (2019) suggests that we can even choose happiness, reclaiming our natural state of being. We are meant to be joyful, playful, and calm. A death within our social circle destroys this condition, but after a time, we can voluntarily work to make ourselves feel better. Of course, we may struggle mightily to achieve this.

In its purest form, grief is the price we pay for loving someone (Parkes, 2011). Anytime we sense a connection to another, the unfortunate possibility exists that one day we might lose that person. When we grieve, we are not just lamenting the loss of another soul but losing the *relationship* we have with that other. This cold, hard fact means that grief and attachment go together. We cannot discuss one without the other. This is our starting point in understanding how and why we grieve. Since we are referring to loss of a relationship, this implies that any loss will cause a level of grief. Life events such as divorce and romantic breakups, moving, and changes in schools can cause grief. These sources of loss and death differ significantly in their level of finality and irreversibility. In these occurrences, we can

52 Defining Grief Within a Developmental Context

reestablish prior connections or states of being. In many of these instances, relationships continue, albeit in an altered form. When loved ones die, the hope of physically reconnecting dies along with them. While alternative bonds with the deceased are possible, we cannot escape the fact that the loved one is gone, forever, from one's physical interactions. Because this creates a different approach to both grief and adjustment, this book focuses on losses from death, both confirmed, assumed, or expected.

Losses are not all created equal, however. When we think about how we feel after someone dies, we realize that the intensity of our response depends on many factors. Children, too, will have variable reactions depending on the deceased's identity and the role that individual played in their lives, as well as their perception of the events. However, kids are unpredictable, and adults may not necessarily be correct in their assumptions about the effects in a specific case. Not all kids will be inconsolable after a grandparent dies, for example, but some will. Presupposing specific reactions from a grieving child is difficult and becomes even more challenging when the circumstances and details of the loss are less clear.

Let us consider the case of ambiguous loss, for example. Pauline Boss (1999) used this term to describe two distinct states. In the first, a loved one is absent psychologically but present physically. This may occur in cases of dementia or brain injury. The loved one's body is alive, but not the familiar spirit and personality. These conditions result in a death of the personality, and physical death is often imminent. The second case occurs when an individual is presumed to be deceased, but the death is not fully acknowledged or verified. This happens if a person is missing or when a body is never recovered. Closure is difficult in these instances. When a mourner holds out too much hope for a reversal of a circumstance, acceptance of reality is impossible.

We label other losses as disenfranchised. This occurs when society minimizes or invalidates the level of pain experienced by the bereaved. This lack of acceptance leads to heightened perceptions of alienation and guilt. A few examples of cases that can create disenfranchised grief include miscarriages, loss of pets, or the death of someone who was not close, such as a celebrity or schoolmate. Disenfranchised grief may magnify children's suffering as adults minimize the intensity of a child's reactions. This situation can result in incomplete mourning, since the survivor may not feel permitted to express their emotions (Volkan & Zintl, 1993). Frequently, we are sensitive to societal expectations that death should not impact us as deeply as it does (Doka, 1989). After the death of my brother, for example, a teacher told my 14-year-old daughter that "she shouldn't be that upset because it was only her uncle who passed away." This attitude adds pressure and contributes to guilt, as the mourner fears he is not grieving properly in the eyes of society. When support from other people is crucial to helping navigate grief, when family and friends ignore or belittle feelings, the griever becomes more isolated.

Other times grief and loss are anticipatory. This occurs when the loved one's death is expected or imminent, as in the case with a terminal illness patient. Although the death has not yet occurred, its specter hangs over everyone involved. Certain individuals mourn prematurely in preparation of what is coming, attempting to make a preemptive strike to combat the pain of the inevitable loss (Rando, 1988).

Definitions of Grief 53

Anticipatory grief, however, does little to prepare anyone, and it often prevents those involved from fully appreciating the remaining time. Pointing out this fact to those experiencing this grief often adds fuel to the fire of guilt that is already burning. Although no loss has yet occurred, the accompanying grief is no less real.

Grief can also be complicated, or prolonged. These terms refer to grief that does not follow a normal path and becomes intertwined with excess emotional baggage as to weigh down the mourner (Dyregrov & Dyregrov, 2013). This reaction may include dysfunctional behaviors or irrational thoughts, such as magical thinking and insistence that the loved one will come back to life (Rando, 2012). The bereaved may be in a state of denial for an extended time. In other cases, the mourner becomes obsessed with the dead loved one, allowing thoughts and behaviors of the person to invade every aspect of the day, long after the actual death (Volkan & Zintl, 1993). Some young people may pathologically identify with the deceased, blurring the lines between self and other (Garber, 2008). Complicated grief correlates with higher rates of PTSD and suicidality (Szanto et al., 2006). Despite the high rates of this condition, there has been little research or outreach to improve the ability of professionals to recognize the signs (Dickens, 2014). In the early stages of acute grief, denial and irrationality may be normal and even expected. After more time has passed, though, this thinking and behavior are detrimental. Eventually, diagnosable conditions may present themselves, necessitating referral to a mental health professional. Grief that requires this level of help is labeled as pathological. Although this term sounds ominous, it merely refers to longstanding reactions that continue to affect the mourner negatively.

Traumatic grief is another classification. This term refers to a grief response that occurs after a loss that is devastating to the bereaved. While this may apply to a death that is violent or sudden, we may also use this classification when there was a close personal connection to the deceased (Jacobs, 1999; Schupp, 2004). Traumatic grief may occur when the griever himself was in jeopardy, such as in a car accident. In general, we label a death as traumatic when it involves elements such as suddenness, violence, and randomness. Incidents in which more than one person has died can also fall into the category of traumatic (Range, 2013). While these criteria are helpful to keep in mind, they are merely guidelines. From a young person's viewpoint, these descriptions are vague. For example, 7-year-old Claude was not told about his grandmother's imminent death from breast cancer. While he knew she was sick, he had no idea that she would soon die. When she passed away in her sleep one night, her death was sudden and random to Claude.

Symptoms of traumatic grief are similar to those of PTSD, including obsessive thoughts, flashbacks, and sleep disturbances. For a child who may receive misinformation or perceives an experience egocentrically, any death of a close individual has the potential to be traumatic. If our criterion is that the loss is personally "devastating," the bar to clear this hurdle is much lower for a child than for an adult.

Regardless of the label we assign to grief, no one can deny the pain it creates. The intensity of our feelings results not only from the obvious reasons but also from the "unfinished business" we may have with the deceased. Things left said or unsaid, missed opportunities, and regretted interactions all feed our emotional reactions to the death of someone in our lives (James & Friedman, 2009). We are plagued with

54 Defining Grief Within a Developmental Context

nagging thoughts of "if only" (Noel & Blair, 2008). When we are not fully free to express ourselves or tie up the loose ends that were untied with the death, we suffer doubly (Volkan & Zintl, 1993). Accepting the loss and processing our grief becomes a daunting task. The multitude of variables inherent in our complicated relationships and responses to their losses make for convoluted paths of grief. Supporters of the bereaved should respond to their reactions, not technical labels.

Despite the need to pay attention to grief, we should remember that while painful, bereavement and mourning are natural processes. At the same time, grief creates a state of imbalance in our physical and emotional states. Some experts have suggested that grief could be considered a disease. While it is natural in that we expect it to occur after the loss of a love, it can create havoc within us all the same. Grief can be equated with a burn or an illness such as a cold or flu. These are certainly natural, but they are still chaotic and difficult to endure (Engel, 1994). Diseases are debilitating and correlated with pain, distress, and physical suffering. So is grief. Diseases have consistent causes and corresponding reactions; so does grief. People suffer *from* a disease; they do not usually actively *create* it. The same is true for grief (Averill & Nunley, 1993). Thinking of grief and bereavement as disease processes may create the idea of something needing a cure (which is impossible), this perspective does allow us to recognize the challenges that grief presents and the real effects it has on our well-being (Engel, 1994). Although many of us, including children, are resilient and will rebound into a sense of normalcy after a loss, this reaction does not minimize the experience nor diminish the lasting effects of bereavement (Wortman & Silver, 1989). People in a state of sadness, fear, and guilt following the loss of a loved one require special considerations. Even normal and common negative events can create major emotional and social upheaval to a child. Healing is a relative term.

Section 2

Reactions to Grief and Loss During Early and Middle Childhood

Chapter 8

General Principles of Childhood Grief

We can place children's reactions to death within the context of the theories of Erikson, Piaget, Bowlby, and other developmental psychologists. Factors such as nature of relationship to the deceased, family structure, and availability of support systems will influence kids' reactions. When we identify these variables, we improve our chances of understanding our grieving students. We know that children grieve differently than adults, and this point provides the foundation for support. Being insensitive to this truth leads to a misinterpretation of a child's grieving process. It might be useful to discuss specific patterns unique to childhood bereavement.

1. Kids grieve in spurts. Once an adult accepts the reality of a loss, feelings of grief are difficult to ignore. Distraction is challenging, and although sadness may ebb and flow between waves of acute anguish and suppressed pain, there is a prevailing depressed affect. This may be untrue with young people. It is not unusual for a little girl or boy to cry one minute, and then run off laughing the next. We can attribute this behavior to short attention spans (Bowlby, 1960; Brohl, 2007; Lawrence, 2015; Worden, 1996). Just as 3-year-old Jimmy cannot sit and read a book for more than a few minutes, neither can he concentrate on mourning for long stretches of time. His immature understanding contributes to his Jekyll and Hyde reactions. ("What do you mean when you say that Daddy died?") We can see why children do not spend inordinate amounts of time in despair. This denial is a defense mechanism designed to protect us from a painful emotion. A similar reaction is dissociation, a way of "zoning out" and avoiding what we do not want to face. We also dissociate when we are distracted (Epstein, 2013). For instance, many of us can recall a time when we find ourselves at a destination without a specific memory of arriving there; this phenomenon frequently occurs when we are in a heightened emotional state while driving. For a brief period, it is as if we are experiencing two states of consciousness. A young person may withdraw when observing the intense or uncomfortable reactions of others. When the support person suffers, it brings a child's insecurity to the surface. A young child may find it easier to repress what is happening and retreat to life as usual. "If I act as if things are normal, maybe they are."

2. Children's reactions can appear inappropriate to adults. We should remember that these behaviors may arise from a lack of understanding, a need to deny reality, or inexperience with social customs. A young one's grief is multiplied by fears for safety, misplaced guilt, and unexpressed anger. This maelstrom of intense thoughts

and feelings can erupt in a barrage of temper tantrums, clinginess, regressive behaviors, or phobias. Children may act younger than their age. They can experience nightmares and bed-wetting. School-aged students may become disorganized and indecisive. A few might lose academic skills they had previously acquired. Some react with hyperactivity, including excessive talking. They may become defiant and fly into a rage any time someone approaches. Older kids may resort to lying, stealing, and other rule-breaking behaviors (Bowlby, 1960; Brohl, 2007; Lawrence, 2015; Weymont & Rae, 2006; Worden, 1996). Extraverted kids refuse to talk to family and other well-wishers, while shy youngsters attach themselves to strangers. After the death of my brother, I gravitated to a young pastor from our church. My parents often described their surprise upon finding me snuggled up next to my new friend! Apparently, they had warned him I was painfully introverted, so he was just as confused by my response. Like many stressed kids, I had severe nightmares for years. Adults need patience, recognizing that odd behaviors may be part of that child's attempt to deal with grief.

3. Effects may present as somatic symptoms. The emotions of grief are powerful, contradictory, and often ambivalent, and they may be too much to bear for a young person with limited coping skills. Therefore, in addition to behavioral expression, heightened feelings may be manifested through psychosomatic illnesses and physiological signs. For instance, heart and breathing rates may be increased for some time, even when triggered by unrelated emotional stimuli (LeBlanc, Unger, & McNally, 2016). Sleep patterns may be disrupted, creating problems associated with sleep deprivation such as lack of concentration and irritability. Nightmares often contribute to sleep loss, too (Pynoos et al., 1987). Children in preschool and the early elementary grades frequently transform fear into creature-like personas, imagining beasts and monsters that typically emerge when it is dark (Nagy, 1959). Kids may complain frequently of muscle pains and headaches. Digestive problems such as nausea, vomiting, and diarrhea are common. Some kids show allergic-type symptoms such as breathing difficulties and skin rashes. Appetite changes may occur (Granot, 2005). Because it is a major stressor, grief has been shown to lower immunity by interfering with lymphocyte responses. As a result, a child may suffer from frequent colds or other minor illnesses following the death (Schleifer, Keller, & Stein, 1985). Some studies have shown correlations between severe grief reactions and increased visits to doctors and hospitals (Hensley & Clayton, 2008). Whether vague symptoms are the product of suggestibility, hypochondria, avoidance techniques, or true physical illness, the discomfort is real. Emotional injury frequency translates to physical pain.

4. Grief reactions may be delayed, sometimes for years. Children may respond in age-appropriate ways at the time of the loss, but they will need to reprocess the experience at subsequent stages (Bowlby, 1960; Brohl, 2007; Lawrence, 2015; Worden, 1996). A baby, for example, may have a muted response to the death of a family member at the time it occurs. Because an infant is egocentric and cognitively immature, she will not comprehend the meaning of the death, but she will sense how the event has affected their family life. She can sense the atmosphere of sadness and/or anxiety around her. When family members interact with her, they are distracted and inadvertently neglect her needs. An infant has no choice but to adjust

General Principles of Childhood Grief 59

to these changes, but she will not truly understand the reasons for the change in the home environment. If the situation is extreme or extended, she may internalize this sensory input egocentrically, thinking that she must be to blame for her family's disinterest. Even when a baby has a reliable support system, such as a caregiver who is emotionally removed enough to continue with positive connections, that child will still go through periods of "regrieving" as he reaches new stages (Oltjenbruns, 2013).

For example, when baby Judith reaches late toddlerhood or early childhood, she will gain a new experience with the loss. Suppose that Judith's dad died when she was a baby. Three years later, reminders of him decorate the home. Mommy tells Judith that she has Daddy's eyes and impish laugh. Her older brother Curt, who was 8 years old when Dad passed away, has definitive memories and tells stories about him. Daddy's mother, Judith's Nana, plays a significant role in her life. Although the death occurred years earlier, the loss has current relevance for Judith. Her maturing abilities in reasoning, memory, and comprehension allow her the ability to understand that she once had a father, but now he is gone. She will need to do lots of mental gymnastics to cope with the idea of a "ghost dad." She must reprocess this loss again at the concrete operational stage and later at the formal operational level. Her interpretations and social support will determine how she accepts her father's death and the way her identity develops. What affects the brain affects the heart, and vice versa.

Older children continue to react years after the death, too. One study found that a significant number of school-aged kids who lost a parent demonstrated problems in adjustment over two years after the event. In many cases, these difficulties were more severe than effects occurring in the immediate period following the death, especially when the event was perceived as traumatic by the surviving individuals (Corr, 2010; Lima & Gittleman, 2004). Physiological changes and negative behavior patterns persist for years, perhaps decades (Saavedra et al., 2017; Walter & McCoyd, 2015). For a young person, there is no statute of limitations on grief and bereavement.

5. Children respond in unexpected ways to deaths of specific family members. If grief is the response to the loss of a relationship with a loved one, then the intensity of the reaction correlates with the strength and importance of the lost relationship, not to the label affixed by others. Ten-year-old Scotty's bond with his friend Coby might be stronger than the ties he has with a cousin, so he is more distraught after the death of the best pal. Nine-year-old Amelia is close to her Aunt Molly whom she visited daily, while 7-year-old Nina only met her aunt once and barely recognizes her. We cannot expect that a person's level of grief after losing a friend or relative correlates exactly with that individual's role in the family. As a result, allowing specific numbers of bereavement days for school students based solely on the relationship rarely makes sense.

We may also be deeply affected by the death of someone we have not met or do not know well. For example, a big brother or sister-to-be might be devastated by Mom's miscarriage or the delivery of a preterm sibling (Jonas-Simpson, Steele, Granek, Davies, & O'Leary, 2015). Although a mutual relationship had no time to develop, a child responds to the loss of the potential bond and corresponding hopes

60 Grief During Early and Middle Childhood

and dreams. He senses his parents' distress, too, which emphasizes the reality of the tragedy in the family. Adults and children can develop strong attachments to public figures, such as TV or movie personalities. Although these relationships are one-sided, we connect to celebrities as our exposure to them gives us the impression of familiarity. We need only remember the public outpouring of intense grief demonstrated after the death of Princess Diana, for example. Young people who are still blurring the lines between reality and fantasy are prone to building strong bonds with individuals known only through the screen or the pages of a book.

Moreover, the circumstances of the passing may play a role in reactions. For instance, we adults depend on the natural order of life. Older people die before the young, and when this pattern is broken, we struggle with unfairness. We may also react to death's circumstances. For example, most adults might accept a death following a long, painful health condition; the end of pain may be a blessing. Youngsters may not comprehend these nuances. To a child, a death is a death, and the fact that the deceased was a 90-year-old grandfather suffering from cancer is no consolation. Immaturity and egocentrism create reactions unique to early developmental stages. "Granddad was always playing games with me, and I miss that about being with him." That thought saddens 6-year-old Lily, whether or not it was grandfather's "time."

Reactions can be disproportional if multiple losses or stressors have occurred within a compressed time period. Grief can be cumulative, and a current loss may trigger the expression of pain from past hurts (Cox, 2013). For example, everyone in the family was impressed with how stoically 12-year-old Mia handled the loss of her older brother. She stepped up and helped her mother and younger siblings when a few months after the death, her father abandoned the family. But when the family dog died from cancer a few weeks later, Mia cracked. While barely shedding a tear at her brother's funeral or her Dad's rejection, she becomes distraught and inconsolable over her puppy's demise. While she surely loved her pet, this intense reaction was the result of the progression of stressful incidents after which Mia bottled up her feelings. If someone were unaware of the previous losses, it might be hard to understand the intensity of Mia's response to her dog's death.

6. Children have difficulty identifying and managing negative emotions. Adults can understand the ambiguity, ambivalence, and contradictory nature of grief. Not only do they understand the primary emotions of sadness and anger that might rear their ugly heads during a time of bereavement, but grownups are familiar with complex, social emotions such as guilt, jealousy, regret, and resentment. These feelings require higher-level brain processing, which occurs concomitantly with attainments in cognitive development. As far as we can ascertain, a baby does not yet grasp what it means to experience remorse or pity. But as he matures, these nascent feelings can emerge. Two-year-old Jackson may be sad that Mom is gone, but he may not envy his playmates in the sandbox whose mothers are nearby. It makes sense to believe, however, that the seeds are there to grow these secondary emotions, and as the older child reprocesses their loss, these feelings may develop and surface. Since these feelings are new, a child may not perceive them accurately and could be scared by them. Jealousy and guilt are powerful and frequently negated by society. Many of us consider these emotions to be unhealthy and go to great lengths to deny

and obliterate them. This is easier said than done, and as many psychologists would suggest, may be impossible and ill-advised. Modern counseling protocols encourage the expression and labeling of negative emotions, all to regulate and control them. In order to self-regulate, one must realize what is being regulated. Caregivers can assist a child to accept any socially undesirable feelings by guiding her to name them and discover positive ways to express and channel them. All of this will help achieve self-control in expressing painful and intense emotions.

We cannot overstate how variable grief reactions are in children. Factors such as the manner of death, developmental age of the child, availability of positive support systems and services, attachment to the deceased, elapsed time since the death, and coping skills of role models are just some variables to consider when assessing how well a child is handling a loss. Whether we can label grief as complicated, pathological, or traumatic depends on these risk factors, too (Dickens, 2014; Horowitz et al., 2003). Grief may trigger or correlate with other psychological problems, such as PTSD, phobias, depression, and bipolar disorder (Boelen & Spuij, 2013; Fenichel, 1943). Children copy what they see; therefore, they are apt to imitate the coping behaviors of those around them (Bandura, 1986). Adults must inform themselves of the diverse expressions and consequences of grief in children, without falling into the trap of attributing every problematic response to bereavement. This is a challenging tightrope to walk, and the only way to navigate well is to pay attention and prepare ourselves. Kids are relying on knowledgeable and empathetic grownups to hold their hands through their losses.

Chapter 9

Patterns of Grief Reactions

Dr. Elisabeth Kubler-Ross (1969) was the first individual to describe patterns of grieving. Her groundbreaking work with dying patients set the groundwork for the research to come in subsequent decades. She suggested that grievers move through five stages just as the dying person himself goes through the stages when coming to terms with his own fate. These stages include:

- Denial: The inability to reconcile with the reality of the loss. We can see this reaction when a person refuses to admit that a loved one dies.
- Anger: Rage directed at the situation or the deceased. We can also turn this anger on God, fate, or even oneself.
- Bargaining: In accepting reality, the griever may attempt to change what has happened by making a deal with God or Mother Nature. Such thoughts can take the form of "If I do this, I can change that," or "If I am a better person, can my loved one return?" This is an obvious connection to denial. Although the griever is slowly coming to terms that the death occurred, there is still magical thinking about the potential for changing the events.
- Depression: Once reality is established, sadness can plant its roots. Along with this emotion is the realization that the event is real and cannot be undone. Prolonged and intense sadness can even lead to clinical depression.
- Acceptance: This stage consists not only of admission to the reality of the situation but also includes continuing life with the "new normal." Also included are attempts to develop a life without the loved one's physical presence and to incorporate the memory of the lost relationship into the griever's future.

These stages imply that there is a common, linear bereavement process. As is clear from the previous discussion regarding individual differences in reactions, grief does not take such a course in every case. Eventually, Kubler-Ross herself admitted that these are guidelines and common reactions, but they are not absolutes. There really is no "average griever." First, a bereaved individual may not go through every stage, and the stages can vary in duration and rate of progress. Second, coping with the loss of a loved one is not a linear progression. For example, there may be times in which anger and depression rear their ugly heads even as acceptance has taken hold. Because of the debate regarding the appropriateness of Kubler-Ross's ideas, other researchers have attempted to define their stage theories. Worden (1996) described four stages:

- Accepting the reality of the loss. In a nod to Kubler-Ross, Worden acknowledges the original feelings of denial and time needed for the truth to sink in. We must accept that death is not arguable, just like we cannot debate questions about other natural phenomena such as weather forecasts (Greene, 2019). To quote a colloquial phrase, "It is what it is." If we do not realize the truth, we will have difficulty moving forward.
- Working through the pain. Using the word "pain," Worden (1996) incorporates all the negative emotions connecting with losing a loved one. Feelings such as anger, guilt, sadness, depression, confusion, frustration, and longing would fit into this stage. This stage might not even have a clear endpoint, as painful emotions can reemerge long after loss is "worked through."
- Adjusting to a new environment and life circumstance in which the loved one is no longer a physical part. This process is logistical. For example, the mourner will need to establish new routines and procedures. Who will walk the dog now that the usual dog-walker passed away? How will we pay bills without the loved one's paycheck? What should we do with the deceased's possessions? This process includes psychological and emotional aspects. The griever must continue their lives with the knowledge of the loss and accommodate a new self-image that incorporates the role of a bereaved individual. Finally, this process is also social. Not only is life continuing without the deceased, but other relationships may suffer (Worden, 1996). It is no wonder that this stage may vary in duration, as we must perform many tasks in the grip of weakened emotional defenses.
- Developing a new, long-lasting connection with the lost individual. As the griever readies himself to move on, he cannot jettison the deceased from his life. Maintaining a new connection to the deceased is an important part of the adjustment process (Kosminsky & Jordan, 2016). Memorializing the individual and cherishing positive feelings are part of redefining the role this person continues to have in one's life. Part of this stage may also involve finding meaning and purpose in the loss and the relationship, and this may be the impetus some grievers need to make concrete tributes, such as planning charity events or offering scholarships in the deceased's name.

Although Worden's stages are broader than Kubler-Ross's, we could levy many of the same criticisms. Although he defines his stages broadly enough to allow for a wide range of reactions, but there are still many individual cases that do not fit into these steps or progress smoothly through them. The myriad of variables in the circumstances again create no clear blueprint for grief.

Granot (2005) describes stages that are more emotion-centered, and her ideas are grounded in children's responses. This author states that after learning of a loved one's death, a child reacts with shock, a basic reaction on a visceral level. Kids may "forget" that the person has died (denial), but at other times may imagine the individual's presence via auditory or visual hallucinations (hearing footsteps, for

64 Grief During Early and Middle Childhood

example). Physical symptoms such as eating disturbances, nightmares and insomnia, or respiratory issues can accompany this early stage. As the child moves into the second stage of internalizing the loss, she undertakes the intense work of mourning. We characterize this phase through complex emotions such as guilt, sadness, and depression. The child now understands the reality of the person's absence, and emotions are easily triggered. Once he accepts the finality of the situation, he enters the third stage of integration and acceptance. He has achieved the new normal, although there may be a remaining sense of reluctance to resume everyday activities. The child will reluctantly adjust to the changed lifestyle and circumstances. For example, 6-year-old Erin may prepare the dinner table with one fewer place-setting, or perhaps assume a new seat when traveling in the family car, after the death of her little brother. New behaviors that accommodate the loss become routine. The previous progression of grief stages may take extended time for young children as they reprocess their sense of loss over time and through their maturing cognitive development. Many young people may have blips along the way, resulting in periods of relative dysfunction. Sometimes the tasks take an intense emotional toll, culminating in aggressive or regressive behaviors. Granot states that to facilitate a smooth progression through the stages, adults should provide honest information and remember to include the children in the family grief. If the child is permitted to isolate himself and withdraw from others, this will only hinder adjustment.

Theresa Rando (2012) took a similar approach in her "6 Rs" theory. In her view, grief processes through a half-dozen steps, all beginning with the letter R; she also groups these stages into three different phases:

- Recognize the loss—avoidance stage. In this first step, the mourner realizes that the death occurred and is irreversible. Inherent in this stage is the recognition of what the concept of death means.
- React to the separation—confrontation stage. Once we accept reality, emotions will follow. We must find an outlet to express these feelings; Rando suggests that we acknowledge secondary losses in this stage. Secondary losses include other situations (or people) that disappear along with the deceased. For example, death of a bread-winner may mean moving to a new home, neighborhood, and school. The death of a close friend may cause the loss of other relationships attached to that person, such as their families.

  Loss begets other losses and rarely is one absent attachment not accompanied by others. We must mourn all of these.
- Recollect and re-experience—confrontation phase. With feelings acknowledged and expressed, the mourner can plan new connections with the deceased which incorporate memories. This is the stage in which the relationship changes from one involving two living beings to one in which the object of attachment exists primarily in memory and feeling instead of in the flesh.
- Relinquish old attachments—confrontation phase. Inherent in forming a new attachment is loosening the old ties. The nature of the old relationship changes and makes way for new attachments in the present reality.
- Readjust—accommodation phase. Besides altering relationships, the griever must also adjust his own sense of identity. Part of this new persona includes

the role of "bereaved." For example, the individual who lost a parent must now see himself as the grieving son without a living mother rather than the child of a dynamic, flesh-and-blood relationship. Moreover, the individual must acknowledge that others view him as a mourner, and this altered perception will become part of the self-concept. Life will continue with new roles to play, and these changes will affect identity.

- Reinvest—accommodation phase. The griever now shifts his focus to new relationships, goals, and directions—all of which proceed with the loved one as a memory. Although we do not forget the deceased, we redirect our focus outwardly toward our new life. We spend emotional energy making new connections rather than the maintaining old one.

(Rando, 2013)

Although there are pointed differences among these theories, there are also some clear similarities. These stage theories involve the same certain steps: acknowledging and accepting reality; experiencing the feelings that accompany the loss of a loved one; and adjusting to a new life without the object of attachment. This last step allows for maintaining the previous bond in some form while shifting focus to new relationships and routines. The similarity in the theories means they suffer from the same pitfalls. A multitude of factors influences these processes and as a result, grief is chaotic. It is as if grief did not read these well-researched theories and instead, decided to just wing it. Grief discovers its own way, not only from person to person but from relationship to relationship.

So, what do we gain from learning about these theories? Although not perfect and obviously not definitive, they can give us a guideline for how grief may progress. It may be like a road map or Google directions: these give us the general idea of how to get to our destination of coping with grief, but it is prudent to be aware that there may be roadblocks or detours along the way. It's good to have a plan, but it's even better to understand that sometimes adjustments are necessary.

One of the main reasons a specific course of bereavement is so difficult to define is because of the numerous extraneous variables involved. What are some of these factors? Many of these are obvious, but others might be less apparent. Although not an exhaustive list, included are some major determinants of an individual's unique experience with grief. As you might guess, several aspects are interrelated.

- Nature and intensity of the relationship with the deceased. Although there are no universal truths here, grief takes on different tasks depending on the connection. For example, losing a parent might differ in significant ways from losing a sibling or a partner. Implicit in this bond is the level of intensity and closeness. This means that sometimes the death of a close friend might impact an individual more intensely than losing an estranged parent. Although some aspects of bereavement may be limited to certain relationships, (such as guilt about not protecting a deceased child may not be a factor in coping with the loss of a mother or father), grief often correlates with the intimacy of a specific relationship. Gender, too, may play a role, especially when we consider the

66 Grief During Early and Middle Childhood

griever. For instance, society teaches males to hide strong emotions and inhibit crying, while we instruct girls to repress anger. (Granot, 2005).

- History and backstory of the relationship. Together with the first factor, the details of the experiences with the deceased create the feelings of attachment, but they can also add weight to a load of grief. Past hurts, regrets, things said and not said, can all wreak havoc on one's ability to acknowledge a loss. Likewise, positive experiences and shared feelings can sometimes ease the pain of considering what might have been. These factors will also be important in constructing new attachment patterns with the deceased (Kosminsky & Jordan, 2016).
- Manner and circumstances of the death. Knowledge that a loved one was not in pain, for example, can mitigate some suffering that results from grief. Was the deceased, and the loved ones, aware of an impending death? Or was the demise sudden, therefore giving friends and relatives no time to brace themselves? Was someone at fault? Who? Could the death have been prevented? How? Are there clear facts surrounding the loss, or are the circumstances somewhat ambiguous, leaving unanswered questions for survivors to contemplate? Although no loss is easy to cope with, believing that events took a natural and pain-free course is certainly more reassuring than a situation in which extenuating and preventable circumstances were at play. Traumatic deaths are particularly challenging to handle and bring along their own set of baggage that needs unpacking. Likewise, studies have shown that deaths from overdoses, violence, or suicide carry a great amount of extra baggage that is hoisted onto the shoulders of the griever (Granot, 2005).
- Ages of griever and deceased. The age of the person who is coping with a loss is a crucial factor that dictates the grief experience. The age of the loved one is likewise significant. Did the death occur before its time, out of the natural order of things? (Son before father, for example.) This point not only contributes to feelings of regret but also to how one views death.
- Prior experiences with stress. There is an interesting paradox when considering this factor. On one hand, the effects of stressors, especially losses, can be cumulative (Granot, 2005). A person who has had to deal with multiple challenges, especially several losses, may be on a shakier emotional ground than someone starting off their course of grief without their psychological resources depleted. On the other hand, navigating previous tough situations can foster resilience. The individual adds tools to their bag of coping skills, and they know from experience they can rise to meet heavy demands on hearts and minds. We learn from our past encounters with stress and trauma, whether it is in a good or bad way. Frequently, it is both.
- Level of intensity regarding concurrent stressors. Many of these issues are practical ones that relate to how rituals and routines will continue in the future. For example, after a mother's death, children may worry about who will do their laundry or prepare their meals. Sometimes the loss of a family member may mean financial problems or changes in housing situations. These are considered secondary losses, and it is natural for a bereaved person to consider these things, if only fleetingly (Hone, 2017). It is also normal for guilt to result

from entertaining such mundane problems. However trivial, these questions and concerns can add to one's burden of grief.

- Strength and availability of social support systems. If death is the cost of losing an attachment, one of the most powerful ways of coping is to depend on other relationships in our lives. Not that these replace the lost love; we know that can never happen. But feeling loved and cared about, having a shoulder to cry on and an ear to listen, along with realizing you are not alone, all contribute to greater feelings of hope and the belief that life can go on (Rando, 2012). People who isolate themselves in their grief may suffer much more than those who mourn collectively.
- Reactions of others. While we need accessible supports, this is insufficient for healthy grief. We must also consider the nature of the helper's reactions. If a grieving person relies on a friend or relative for support and that individual is struggling, he may not be the best influence. Although sometimes there is a benefit to stumbling together, it helps if there is a support person who is dealing in positive ways. Watching a family member fall apart emotionally, perhaps turning to self-medicating or other less constructive methods by which to cope with the intensity of grief, may negatively influence others that need positive support (Rando, 2012).

There are many other variables, but these provide us with a foundation for comprehending the enormity of grief and bereavement. Since each person is unique, every relationship is too. As each attachment differs from others, so does reactions to its loss. Keeping a basic framework in mind while we transverse grief can be useful despite the individual differences we encounter, just as a roadmap helps to orient us on our physical journeys.

Chapter 10

Emotions of Grief—Sadness

When most of us contemplate grief, sadness is the emotion that first comes to mind. After a loved one dies, it is logical and understandable to mourn the loss from our lives and feel sympathy for the person whose life is now over. In fact, this emotion may be most obvious to an observer immediately after the death for adults and children alike. A child may cry, often at random times. He may find no pleasure or excitement in anything, a condition known as anhedonia. For instance, the ardent Philadelphia Eagles fan displays little enthusiasm when presented with tickets to the big game, and the drummer who typically awakened hours early to prepare for a band concert struggles to get out of bed in time for the performance. Because of the cyclical nature of grief, episodes of melancholy or despair can appear periodically while a child mourns (Edelman, 2014). A handful of kids will be consistently teary and go to great lengths to hide this from others. Lack of any signs of happiness, such as smiling, is common. Forlorn children may refuse to take part in class activities, including those that typically piqued their interest. A few may withdraw from other kids, while others may become clingy to peers or to the teacher. Misery can create disinterest in appearance, health, or eating. Acute sadness may be difficult to hide, but many children learn to ignore the constant sense of chronic unhappiness. There are signs, however, if a teacher looks hard enough. A child who just seems different from his usual self is a cause for concern. Apathy and low energy can plague a woeful kid, too.

Feeling heartbroken after a death is not restricted to merely missing the loved one. Keep in mind that children often experience secondary losses, too (Hone, 2017). For instance, when Dad died, Amelia, 9, had to leave her home and school since Mom could not afford their mortgage. When her twin sister succumbed after a long battle with cancer, 6-year-old Kathleen lost her roommate and some mutual friends. Coby, 11, has no one to make his lunch or wash his clothes after Mom passed away suddenly. While feeling upset about these ancillary losses is normal, a child may feel guilty about worrying about relatively mundane issues. But when a person dies, the sense of loss extends way beyond their physical absence. Tears are shed for the deceased, the missed opportunities, the break with routine, and for ourselves.

Occasionally, with children who are prone to repression, sadness can rear its head in more indirect ways. An unhappy child may focus on distressing topics or become fascinated by melancholy stories and books. A morbid sense of humor or interest

Emotions of Grief—Sadness 69

in the macabre can also be a manifestation of blue feelings. Adults can empathize, realizing that sadness is painful, often excruciatingly so. To protect themselves, many people, kids included, will hide their feelings behind a wall of bravado or comedic tendencies. A young girl or boy may not be self-aware enough to recognize the sorrow behind the curtain, while older people may act purposefully. Keep in mind that adults may be oblivious to the real reasons and motives behind their actions. The same is true of students in your schools.

Intense feelings of sadness can lead to concomitant emotions such as worthlessness, hopelessness, and helplessness. A person in the depths of despair may see no way out from the gloomy feelings. Just as in depression, sadness's cousin who digs in and refuses to leave, symptoms of low self-esteem may manifest. Unhappiness colors everything, and finding a way out from under this cloud is challenging As a result, the consequences are pervasive. Eight-year-old Millie, who despairs over the loss of her mother, is in no mood to find any joy in an extra few minutes of recess. Hopelessness concerning an event that is uncontrollable and irreversible—like Mom's death—can spill over into a similar sense of learned helplessness regarding grades. Powerlessness equates to a lack of control, so kids may wonder why they should bother with something as mundane as schoolwork. Life seems arbitrary, so school success may be, too. Sadness coupled with futility result in a lack of initiative. A despairing student may decide it is easier to just give up. Millie, formerly a straight-A student, now exerts little effort and is unconcerned by her report card of Cs and Ds.

Here is a list of common statements an educator may hear from a student that signifies overwhelming sadness after a loss:

- I miss _____
- I am so lonely.
- No one understands how I feel.
- Everything I see or hear reminds me of _____
- I am afraid I will forget _____
- I am having problems remembering how my _____ looked and talked.
- I don't want to have fun anymore.
- I am not hungry.
- Food makes me queasy or tastes like cardboard.
- I want to cry all the time, but sometimes I can't.
- I don't know why I am crying so much.
- I wish I could sleep forever.
- I am always tired.
- I have nightmares every night.
- I dream about _____ all the time.
- I can't stop thinking about _____
- People keep bothering me.
- I have no energy.
- Even boring TV shows upset me.
- I just want to sit here.
- I want to be alone.

70 Grief During Early and Middle Childhood

Since it is a short leap from sadness into bona fide depression, it is critical for adults to be cognizant of the potential for suicidality in children of any age. When a person experiences emotional pain, thoughts of stopping the suffering emerge. If the pain is unpreventable, (there is no way to bring back to life the lost love, for example), escape may be the next thought. Suicidal ideation is common in any depression, and it can manifest in grief reactions. After a loved one dies, many of us will feel the pull to join them in death. The intensity of the sorrow can be overwhelming, and the peace of dying is a welcome option. Writers on grief frequently and eloquently recount losing their will to live, whether to escape pain or to reunite with the deceased in an afterlife (Greene, 2019). Often, these ideas will pass. Ideation does not necessarily imply action. Considering the allure of death is not the same as actively planning one's own demise. The distinction between thought and action, however, can be hard to discern. We must err on the side of caution. If a student suggests suicide or any other form of self-harm, we must take his comments seriously. Grievers are in a fragile state, and emotionality may overtake rationality.

Interacting with someone who might be suicidal can intimidate us and make us uncomfortable. The alternative to not intervening is too serious to ignore. Many people hesitate to start this conversation with a depressed person. They may worry that by broaching the subject, ideas are being planted into the heads of the depressed. This is categorically not true. Suicidal ideation is so common that most depressed individuals have one form or another, even if they are not intending to follow through. The ideas are there. A well-intentioned inquiry does not cause a person to hurt himself. The fact that someone cares enough to inquire is often a life-affirming realization.

Young children may express their heavy hearts inconsistently or not at all. A child's reasons for sadness may be unlike those of older students with a solid comprehension of death. Some respondents in our study reported that to their way of thinking, the loved one was just gone, away on a trip, perhaps. If unaccustomed to death and bereavement, they often misunderstood the finality of the circumstance, and these children did not respond with the same degree of unhappiness as did their older, more experienced, counterparts. Young people may find it difficult to show their emotions publicly and may go to great lengths to hide their feelings or act tough. Putting on the persona of a strong, perhaps overconfident, an individual who is coping well can be a mere act. Keep in mind that any extreme reaction, or behavior foreign to the child's normal manner and personality, may be smokescreens to a child's true internal reactions. Acting brave is not the same thing as feeling brave.

Case Example

Twelve-year-old Jailyn lost her older brother in a motorcycle accident a month ago. Her seventh-grade teachers report that since the loss, they have not seen Jailyn smile even once. She returned to school after a week's bereavement, and for the first few days, she would request to leave the classroom several times a day. When she reentered the class, both teachers and classmates noticed the red eyes that signified her crying while in the bathroom. Jailyn had a friendly personality and was well-liked by most of her peers, and many of her classmates offered their condolences when she first came back to class. Jailyn brushed off the kind words and drew into herself, turning down offers to sit with her friends or otherwise interact. After weeks of rejections, the other kids stopped talking to Jailyn. Well-groomed and fastidious about her fashion choices, Jailyn now comes to school in sweatpants and tee shirts, her hair uncombed. She has stopped cheerleading, a former favorite activity. When asked a question, even in class, Jailyn either shrugs her shoulders or replies in one-word responses.

Chapter 11

Emotions of Grief—Anger

Anger is a common emotional response following the death of a loved one. Elisabeth Kubler-Ross (1969) recognized this condition and even specified anger as one of the major reactions, evidence of the level of importance she assigned to it. For children unable to understand the tidal wave of thoughts and feelings created in the wake of loss, anger may dominate their reaction.

To whom is this fury directed? In most cases, there are moving targets. Mourners may direct their rage at the deceased for leaving this world. Children may blame adults for not preventing death or protecting them from heartache. Remember that, to a small child, parents are ultra-powerful; the loss in the family shatters this perception of omnipotence. Anger is directed to the event itself, or to God or fate or other religious figures. Life is irrevocably changed. This reality is enough to create an emotional response of fury. Sometimes, the bitterness is self-directed. Children may be annoyed at themselves for their own helplessness, frustrated with their inability to prevent the loss. Kids can chastise themselves for poor coping skills and for misperceived weaknesses of character. Anger and aggression are natural responses to uncontrollable, painful events, and the intensity can be overwhelming.

Animal studies have demonstrated that expressing aggression after a traumatic event can be cathartic. For instance, rats that attacked others after receiving an electric shock showed fewer physiological signs of distress than did a control group that tried to escape (Williams & Eichelman, 1971; Conner, Vernikos-Danellis, & Levine, 1971). Those of us who have hit pillows or smacked a punching bag know how satisfying those actions can be when our emotions are out of control. Children are no different, but they frequently lack the self-control to curb these tendencies and direct them to appropriate targets. Unfortunately, they may lash out in physical ways to other living creatures, including themselves. For many mourners, there is a tendency to self-harm, whether from anger, guilt, or pure anguish. Even when rage is physically suppressed, repressed bitterness can eat at us psychologically (Archer, 1999). Bottling up our feelings creates a powder keg that is ready to explode when the fuse is lit.

Anger worsens when a responsible party actually *does* exist, such as in cases of murder or suicide. If someone is to blame, we naturally wish to direct anger toward this target. As sensitive human beings, we may find fault with our own thoughts and actions even when others do not. After the death of a loved one, we obsess over the would-haves, could-haves, and should-haves. This emotional self-flagellation

Emotions of Grief—Anger 73

is counterproductive and unwarranted, but grieving individuals often struggle to recognize the irrationality of their thoughts. Children are particularly vulnerable to this thinking because of their immature cognitive development. Their misguided sense of power, inherent in the belief that mere bad thoughts can create reality, strengthens nascent feelings of guilt and responsibility. The result is anger toward the self.

Societal stress can exacerbate anger when we believe that being mad is "not nice." Parents teach us to minimize feelings of wrath and aggression as if they are undesirable emotions. The trouble is, anger does not recede at will and may intensify under the psychic surface. When rage turns inward, self-directed fury can create low self-esteem, learned helplessness, and guilt.

Repressed, muted, or blatant anger is reflected through statements such as these:

- I am mad at _____ for messing up my life.
- My parents should have protected me (or the loved one).
- My mom and dad should have been there for me.
- God should have prevented this.
- The doctors and nurses weren't good enough to fix _____.
- My friends don't understand me. They have let me down.
- My life is ruined; I will never be happy again.
- I can't do the things I wanted to do since _____ died.
- My family ignores me.
- They left me out from planning the funeral.
- Adults didn't tell me the truth.
- I have a right to know the truth.
- Life stinks if horrible things can happen.
- Everyone else's life is perfect. Why is mine so awful?
- Why is everybody else having such a good time?
- I do not have the right to be happy.
- It's my parent's fault for not doing their job to make a good life for me.
- It's the doctor's fault for being stupid.
- It's God's fault; He could have done something to stop this.
- God hates me.
- I hate God.
- I hate my parents.
- I hate _____.

Although many of these statements may not sound like anger on the surface, they are masking deep rooted outrage at the core. Notice that wrath can take the form of name-calling and blaming. We express anger directly or subtly, but it is there, all the same.

We must recognize that most people confronted with a loss will experience a level of annoyance or resentment, even though they may spend enormous amounts of psychological energy to repress and deny it. However, any emotion is normal and healthy and should be acknowledged without guilt. Children require guidance in managing acrimonious emotions, since misdirected anger leads to behavior

74 Grief During Early and Middle Childhood

problems and aggression. But encouraging desirable behaviors does not mean ignoring the feelings themselves. Sometimes a child just needs to "blow off steam," and the availability of a safe, nonjudgmental place is crucial for healing. At the risk of sounding Freudian, we might remember that sometimes anger is just a projection—an outward expression of the guilt and pain a person is experiencing internally. The best way to cope is to express emotions openly, without pressure or shame. Children need to accept that feelings themselves are not wrong or abnormal. We are human, after all.

Of the various emotions that can result after loss, anger may be the one that is most commonly repressed. Just as children may try to suppress the memory of the event itself to block the pain and guilt, kids can push their rage under the surface where it can simmer. If we remember Vonnegut's statement about the "museums in children's minds" that was mentioned in Chapter 2, we can appreciate how these "museums" protect kids from feelings of infuriation as well as well as sadness, shock, and fear (Vonnegut, 1999). Society teaches young people that irritation and resentment are impolite and unacceptable, and embitterment toward a sad situation or the victim would make one a "bad girl" or a "mean boy." Animosity and indignation are normal and expected, and the child craves reassurance that he is still a good person. He may require help to discover a constructive outlet for his powerful thoughts and feelings.

Case Study

Four-year-old Jesse has recently begun Pre-K. Although he had spent most of his life attending day care, this is the first time he has been enrolled in an academic program. Jesse's father died in a motorcycle crash when Jesse was only a baby, so he has few, if any, explicit memories of him. To Jesse, "normal" means living in a home without a dad. It also means living in the shadow of this deceased parent. Mom and Dad, although married, had a rocky relationship. On the night of the accident, they had been arguing before Dad stormed off to clear his head on a ride through the country—a ride from which he never returned. Mom has spent the last few years struggling with her feelings of guilt and regret about words said and unsaid on the night of his death. Financial problems loom large in the household since Dad had no life insurance. Mom was obligated to find a full-time job soon after the funeral, creating more strain in the household as they shunted the children off to daycare. Jesse has an older sister, Sara, who was 5 at the time of Dad's accident and who has vivid memories of her deceased parent. Sara constantly speaks of Dad, often in glowing terms. As is common after a loved one dies, survivors often elevate the status of the deceased. Sara was close to her father in life, but now in death, everyone idolizes him. Jesse cannot relate, and he regrets having no relationship with his dad. Although he is unable to articulate his feelings, anger fuels Jesse over the unfairness of his life. Old enough to understand that the other kids in his PreK class have father figures, Jesse struggles with a distracted mother. He is angry at Mom for her physical and emotional distance. Jesse cannot comprehend the choices she makes, and he recognizes her unavailability to him. He resents Sara because she had more time with Dad, enough to have memories of a strong bond.

Jesse has nothing except the second-hand perception of others' stories. Even at the young age of 4, the sense of loss and injustice is simmering under the surface. Jesse does not appreciate where the source of his anger arises, but the emotions bubble to the surface and dictate much of his behavior. He has become defiant, especially around his mother. His resentment of his sister and other children is expressed through aggression and bullying. Recently he was suspended from school when he tried to stab a classmate with a sharpened pencil. This event occurred after weeks of more minor transgressions, from pushing, shoving, and smacking other kids with toys. When asked why he hurts his friends, Jesse has no response other than "I don't know." In truth, Jesse really is clueless about his motives. He is acting on the urge to lash out after his anger reaches a boiling point. On an unconscious level, he wants to hurt others to avenge the pain festering inside him. If the adults took the time to study the circumstances in more detail, they might discover that most of Jesse's outbursts occur soon after someone mentions their own fathers. Clearly, these comments trigger Jesse's feelings of deprivation caused by the absence of his now larger-than-life father.

Chapter 12

Emotions of Grief—Fear

In his memoir *A Grief Observed*, C.S. Lewis (2001) writes that while he was deeply saddened by his wife's death, he was surprised to find himself afraid, too. Fear is a common reaction, and it often overwhelms a grieving individual, particularly a child (Martin & Ferris, 2013; Smith, 2018). When someone dies, we naturally extend the horror of the death into our own lives, creating worry and anxiety. We may focus on relationships and circumstances that remind us of what was lost. For example, a child whose mother has died may fear for her father's well-being. As an adult, she may be excessively nervous about becoming a mother herself, her mind racing to the possibility of leaving her children motherless, like she was (Edelman, 2014). For some grievers, anxiety over personal well-being takes center stage. Others fear the unknown aspects of the future and the upcoming changes in their lives (Smith, 2018). Frequently, a child may not articulate fear directly, but an astute teacher or other concerned adult can detect this emotion in statements such as these:

- I don't want to go to school/home.
- What happens if the lights go out?
- Can someone come with me to the bathroom?
- I don't like the movie we are seeing in class. Please turn it off!
- I am worried about my Mom/Dad who is going away on a trip.
- Please let me eat lunch with you!
- Do I have to read this story?
- Can I come with you?
- Can I bring in my teddy bear from home?
- You can't make me go on the field trip.
- I am worried a monster is hiding under the bed, so I am not sleeping.
- I don't like nighttime.
- There is a monster in my closet!
- Something is trying to get me!
- What if something happens to you/me?

Our autonomic nervous system, along with the hormones secreted by the adrenal glands, ensures that our body is prepared to counter a threat. In this fight-or-flight response, the dominant emotion is fear. In *Why Zebras Don't Get Ulcers*, author Robert Sapolsky (2004) makes a compelling point when he explains how and why

Emotions of Grief—Fear   77

people are more susceptible to long-term stress than are animals. He suggests the illustration of a zebra on the savannah that encounters a lion. The zebra's fight-or-flight response kicks in as expected. There are only two possible outcomes at this point: either the zebra runs and gets away, or the lion catches him. In either event, the zebra's fear is short-lived. The case is different in humans, however. For most of the time, because of the evolutionary stance we now assume as humans, the threats we encounter daily are less life-threatening. Not only that, but our highly developed cerebral cortex allows us to consider *possible* threats, not only those that are immediately at hand. Zebras do not lie in bed at night worrying about taxes, job security, tomorrow's test, or boyfriend problems. We do, and our worry triggers the fight-or-flight response as if there were a real emergency at hand. Our biological response to threats programmed for the long term. We are designed to confront the problem immediately, one way or another. But mental worries are a whole different story, and the fear and apprehension that result can last indefinitely. This chronic anxiety can take a physical toll on the body, in the form of gastrointestinal problems, cardiovascular consequences, lowered immunity, fatigue, and a variety of aches and pains. Another possible ramification is emotional problems such as an anxiety disorder, posttraumatic stress, and depression. These conditions can persist even in the absence of actual stress. Combine these reactions with the egocentrism of young children, and you have a child terrified of illness and injury (Lawrence, 2015; Sapolsky, 2004).

Phobias and other trepidations can become learned, or conditioned, and grow stronger with time. When fear is encountered in youth, it can become ingrained in the brain pathways and remain entrenched for years. Imagine that 10-year-old Carlton's family received a late-night phone call informing them of a grandparent's death. He now associates the phone with painful news, and the ringtone will elicit anxiety and panic every time he hears it. Eight-year-old Michaela stopped at a Dunkin' Donuts before visiting her brother in the hospital for the last time; now she associates the pastry establishment with painful memories and anxiety. Fear can be rewarding, especially if the child receives attention or other reinforcement for the negative emotion. It may be self-rewarding as when 6-year-old Lee avoids his twin's bedroom to lessen the associated anxiety. In ways such as these, children's terror may never be challenged and may become self-fulfilling.

Very young kids may personify their fears, creating monsters and other imaginary creatures as projections of apprehension surrounding death. Children may develop these characterizations after any exposure to death, whether on TV, in the movies, or in a story. Most of us remember irrational fears from our childhoods. Why were we scared of beings in our closets or under our beds? These fictional forms represented the unknown, and the worries surrounding the uncertainty of dying are easily projected onto dark figures and eerie shadows (Nagy, 1959). When a child has experienced a loss, these projections move front and center. If death is perceived as a punishment for misdeeds, the image of these horrific beings becomes larger than life when a child gets in trouble. It is easy to see how these fears can get the better of young children due to their immature grasp on the reality of death.

Fear can manifest in the form of hypochondria, when a child's uneasiness revolves around her physical health. Every minor illness becomes a cause for panic as illness

78 Grief During Early and Middle Childhood

anxiety becomes powerful. She perceives any ache or pain in exaggerated ways. A child's inner thoughts create a whirlwind of worst-case scenarios. Younger kids may have the mistaken idea that death itself is contagious, and they may worry they are next in line to "catch" the likelihood of dying (Stuber & Mesrkhani, 2001). Twelve-year-old Laynie worries every time her neck glands swell in response to a respiratory infection. She is sure this is the first sign of cancer! Everyday events require a heightened risk assessment. Fourteen-year-old Vinnie has a panic attack each time he steps on the school bus after his friend died in a rare bus accident. In these hypothetical cases, the connections are obvious even if misguided. Sometimes, however, a child becomes fearful by seemingly random stimuli. An adult may need to orchestrate a little detective work to uncover the connection that a child has made between the loss and the source of panic. Occasionally, the correlation is nearly impossible to determine. The logic of a child does not compare to that of an adult, so associations may appear irrational to you as a grownup. Try to see the circumstances from the child's point of view. Whether the connection is logical is irrelevant; what matters is that the child's reaction comes from fear. Even when the exact nature of the link between stimulus and anxiety is not clear, we can mitigate the issue by talking, expressing, explaining, and relearning. Calm reassurance, and even the passage of time, will naturally change a few of the negative associations (consider how positive phone calls can replace the memory of the bad one, for example).

Another clue that a grieving child is struggling with feelings of fear can be seen in his or her interpersonal relationships. It is not unusual for a child who has lost a loved one to be reluctant to form emotional ties with anyone. The pain of losing the connection may be stronger than the anticipation of being alone, so the bereaved may put up an emotional wall between himself and others. While this is a protective mechanism that works to shield pain to an extent, it has the added effect preventing any real closeness or intimacy. This restricts the intensity of present and future relationships. Moreover, this disconnect prevents others from supporting the child and helping with the coping process. If we assume that love and friendships are the main sources of happiness in life, we can understand how this issue is an obstacle to future contentment, satisfaction, and meaning as we live our lives.

In other cases, a child may react to excessive fear by becoming inordinately attached to family members or friends. Her intense fear of losing a specific loved one may result in a compulsion to stay physically close, refusing to let this person out of her sight. She may balk at being left alone, preferring the company of others. Terror is frequently worse at nighttime, when the dark can get the better of us. We are usually most scared of what we cannot see or understand, and darkness represents the unknown. Fatigue serves to exacerbate the problem. As a result, kids may insist on rooming with parents or sleeping with open doors and burning lights. Other times, the ties are primarily emotional, and a child may become fiercely loyal to significant people in her life (Edelman, 2014). The bonding can be obsessive, at times to the exclusion of nurturing new relationships.

When a bereaved child is consumed by fear, the availability of a trusted adult offers a sense of security she desperately needs. As we have seen in our amusement park example, having a companion along for a scary ride provides us with a dose of bravery. Our sidekick can distract us, and conversations are excellent ways to avoid our fearful, obsessive thoughts. Moreover, we are calmed merely by keeping tabs on our loved ones. "If I can see Mom, I know she is alive and well." After a significant person dies, we naturally fear that others can be snatched away from us, too. For children who physically *need* the security and protection of an adult, the concern that others might die, leaving them alone, builds to panicky levels. Calm reassurance and the comfort of your physical presence will go a long way in comforting a scared child.

Research and anecdotal evidence have suggested that many siblings become excessively fearful of their own death after a brother or sister has passed away. For instance, when a child dies of a specific disease, the sibling may have an obsessional fear of the same illness (White, 2008). If the death occurred accidentally, the sibling commonly becomes terrified of similar events. This apprehension and anxiety can be overcome in time and can eventually empower the child. Imagine the trepidation Senator Ted Kennedy must have had upon entering the Presidential race in 1980 after losing both his brother John and his brother Robert to assassins. In a TV interview on *20/20* in 2009, Ted's son Ted, Jr. speaks to his own concern for his dad, remarking on the bullet-proof vests that adorned the family closet (Dwinell, 2009). Yet, Ted, Sr. was not only able to overcome any qualms or anxieties for one election cycle, but he spent decades in the political spectrum and public eye. Sometimes meeting the fears head-on is the best antidote, and as time goes by and nasty things don't always happen, the panic begins to fade to a degree. Facing one's fears is part of life. We can probably remember a time at a favorite amusement park when the roller coaster or Ferris wheel was an intimidating behemoth that made our skin sweat, our lungs hyperventilate, and our hearts race. If we can stifle our anxiety enough to climb aboard the ride and survive the experience, no doubt our fears will be fewer the next time. Our bravery is enhanced with the support of others; riding the Cyclone with a group of confident friends goes a long way in bolstering our own positivity. The same thing is true with grief. Sharing the experience with a brave associate can help us to act courageously and tackle whatever is horrifying or panic-inducing.

In his essay entitled "Mourning and Melancholia" (1957), Sigmund Freud writes that people who are in deep grief may, in his words, suffer the "loss of the capacity to love." Although we could argue that he is exaggerating about losing this "capacity" permanently, we can understand how the social withdrawal of mourners serves as a protective armor against further pain. Loving and losing a cherished person is immensely painful, and fear of this potential trauma can prohibit interaction with others. So, fear can manifest itself indirectly, not only as anxiety regarding death itself but as a reluctance to form intimate attachments as a defense from pain of loss. In other words, fear may be a projection of feelings of loss. It can stop us from forming new bonds that can be broken and therefore shield us from further grief.

Children may have enormous difficulty dealing with their fears. Their heightened sense of powerlessness, implicit in their weaker social status, combined with their lack of real-life experience, may create a panic that appears insurmountable. Scary stories and movies exacerbate the situation. A young child's imagination easily spirals out of control. Moreover, confusion reigns as they look back at the lost past while realizing the future is uncertain (Corr, 2010). Grief creates fertile ground for phobias to take root and grow unchecked.

80 Grief During Early and Middle Childhood

Consider the story of Corinne, a 12-year-old girl whose mother suddenly passed away from a heart attack. Corrine was present when her mother collapsed, and she witnessed the arrival of the paramedics and their unsuccessful attempts to revive her. This incident happened in the evening, and Corrine remembers the dark house that enveloped her as the ambulance raced off with her dying mom. Corrinne's body has experienced the fight-or-flight response, with its rush of adrenaline and the other physiological responses. The resolution of this state, however, is not the same as that of the zebra who narrowly escaped from the hungry lion. The immediate emergency is past, but grief remains and impedes a tidy resolution of the sympathetic response. Corrinne's anxiety level may not resolve completely, and she has no opportunity to express her fear through catharsis. Anxieties multiply, including uncertainty about what happens next in her young life. The fight-or-flight response, as we have seen, generates the emotion of fear. Corrine may associate these physiological and emotional sensations with any stimuli that occurred during the event, from the sound of the sirens to the emptiness of the dark house. It is not surprising that she trembles with anxiety when the lights go out or exhibits a full-blown panic attack at the sound of sirens during the next few weeks or years.

Certain manifestations of fear are notable. A handful of kids may develop school phobia after a loss. Children may be reluctant to leave their parents, worried that one of them may die and only being reassured through continual contact. Kids may assume responsibility for helping the other family members, who are being left to their own grief while the child is away at school. If the death occurred while the child was not at home, an association can be made between leaving the household and loved one's dying; staying home becomes the only way to alleviate the anxiety that is created when the young person ventures outside. In these cases, home becomes the secure base. If the death occurred in the home, however, the association can be flipped, and the source of fear reversed. A child in these circumstances may avoid returning home at the end of the school day and may search for activities and commitments to keep him at school after hours. A few children form a closer attachment to the teacher, preferring to stay in the classroom rather than run home to the family. Even when the death did not occur at home, the house can be a reminder of the loss as it becomes the setting for grief. In this case, phobias occur more at home than at school.

Another common fear expressed in a school setting is germ phobia. This possibility is likely when the loved one died from illness. Children do not yet grasp ideas of germ theory and virology, and they may be misinformed about contagion. Therefore, any sickness that results in death can be a potential threat to a young child. Egocentric thinking may create a cognitive environment in which fears of fatal illnesses find fertile ground. A child's heightened awareness of illness may mean that he perceives any cough or sneeze as a potentially fatal "bullet" to the target of one's good health. This fear of getting sick may cause a child to wash hands obsessively or avoid touching infected surfaces. Youngers may refuse to eat in the cafeteria out of concern that the food might make them ill. Fear of catching something from other people creates a scenario in which a child withdraws from social interactions— exactly the opposite of helpful behaviors for mitigating grief.

Regardless of the specific form that fear takes in a child, the common responses are discomfort and distraction. No one likes to be afraid. We may achieve catharsis by fearing a villain in a movie, but on a conscious level we understand that this apprehension is being generated by something fictional. Real life is different. It is hard to rationalize a threat that is right in front of you! Children's tendency toward fear is heightened by their vulnerability, and the lines between reality and fantasy are blurry. As a result, grieving children are likely to become frightened and panic-stricken when confronting any potential danger.

Case Example

Six-year-old Jesse's dad died after a long bout with cancer. During the two years of his father's illness, Jesse was dragged along to the hospital, doctor appointments, and other medical facilities. In his preoperational mind, the sights, sounds, and smells of the medical field became easily associated with his father's deadly illness. As a matter of fact, Jesse may have mistakenly assumed a causal connection between the hospital visits and his dad's death, which occurred during an overnight stay. Additionally, the day before his death, Jesse's father was rushed by ambulance after his mom called 911. After the funeral, Jesse became increasingly anxious any time he perceived reminders of the medical field. The sight of the school nurse or the sound of a siren outside the classroom window causes Jesse to become panicky and run to the teacher. Since his school is near a fire station, alarms and sirens are heard daily. The triggers are so common, in fact, that Jesse is now constantly on edge in class. The teacher notices how he frequently looks out the window or toward the classroom door for any signs of a passing ambulance or the school nurse walking by in the hallway. Jesse has become reluctant to come to school, as his mother reports increasing difficulty in getting him up and out the door every morning. At home, Jesse has insisted that his mother hide all medical equipment (even thermometers). His mother is dreading his next check-up, as Jesse has yet to see his own physician since the death of his dad.

Chapter 13

Emotions of Grief—Guilt

Many children who have lost a loved one shoulder the burden of responsibility, whether real or imagined. Guilt is the result. This is a complex emotion that hides in the psyche and rears its ugly head in sly, ambiguous ways. Because guilt is generated by misinterpretations and manifests in a myriad of ways, we should explore this feeling in more detail.

We must first define the term itself. Along with its twin emotion shame, guilt is a self-conscious emotion. To experience guilt, we must know ourselves as an individual person, separate from others and responsible for our own actions. The implication is that guilt is complicated and requires a degree of cognitive development. We assume that babies and toddlers do not yet have the mental capacity to experience guilt (Lewis, 1971). According to developmental theorists such as Freud and Erikson, children have the capacity for guilt between the ages of 3 and 5 years, when the skill of perspective taking becomes more refined (Erikson, 1963; Freud, 1986). The issue is muddied by the subtle distinction between guilt and shame, a difference that laypeople miss or ignore. Shame is global and self-directed; it is the individual self that is faulty and unworthy. Guilt is more specific and directed toward a singular event or behavior (Lewis. 1971). Over the last couple of decades researchers have studied this distinction (Ferguson & Stegge, 1998; Ferguson, Stegge, & Damhuis, 1991; Lindsay-Hartz, 1984; Tangney, 1995; Tangney, 1998; Tangney & Dearing, 2002; Tangney, Miller, Flicker, & Barlow, 1996). We consider guilt less painful than shame because of its focus on a well-defined action rather than on the self as a whole. Guilt can be useful, motivating us to make amends and repair any damage we have caused (Tangney, 1998). Shame is a value judgment regarding one's own self-worth that is difficult to fix in any simple way. As Erikson (1963) theorized, shame develops earlier in psychological development before the schema of the self is established. In fact, shame can become woven into the fabric of one's self-image. Guilt, on the other hand, needs a distinct, recognizable self to develop. Clearly, the two emotions are connected. A child who views himself as shameful may easily create pangs of guilt later, as he believes his actions are unacceptable. We can feel constructive guilt about a negative behavior without internalizing it into our sense of self. Differentiating between these emotions takes advanced mental manipulations, so we can understand how young children struggle with distinguishing between the self as a person and the self as an actor in an environment. Guilt and shame are often defined similarly because of the potential for interdependence (Tangney & Dearing, 2002). In reality, subtle differences matter a great deal.

Another way of looking at the cognitive somersaults that define these terms is to see them in the light of attribution theory. Attributions are the causes we assign to different emotions and behaviors. If I fail a test, I can blame that problem on myself (internal) or the teacher (external). If I decide to take responsibility, I might express this culpability by believing I am dumb and incapable of doing well (stable and global/dispositional), or by rationalizing, saying I did not study effectively and will improve my performance the next time (unstable and situation-specific). Guilt is limited to a particular action, place, and time, and therefore we can atone for and correct this by changing course. Shame is more wide-ranging and inclusive (Tangney, 1998). We may find it easy to apologize for spilling the milk and then make amends by cleaning it. A more difficult task is transforming from a flawed person into a perfect human being.

The self-conscious emotions are harder to comprehend than primary emotions (such as fear, happiness, and sadness) for reasons beyond their need for sophisticated mental capabilities. A child can present an emotionless face, interpreting emotions through body language and paralanguage. The stimuli that elicit these emotions are not universal, and they can differ from one individual to the next (Lewis, 1971). Although both emotions have their roots in childhood, they can persist well into adult life. Triggers of these emotions can have the power to influence us years, perhaps decades, later.

Young people may internalize their feelings of discomfort after a loss into a global sense of shame (Lewis, 1971). Not yet able to connect the dots between act and feeling, or between self and outside world, these children may continue to build their self-concept with shame as part of the foundation. The vague sense of "I did something wrong" generates negative regard for the self. With immature language capabilities, this child may never realize how and why this painful self-image emerged. Shame is often the result of relational trauma that occurs early in life. For example, a child whose caregiver is abusive or neglectful may unconsciously assume that he somehow invited the poor treatment and that he is unworthy of being loved (DeYoung, 2015). The same dynamic can occur when a loved one leaves. Although older kids and adults understand that most deceased individuals did not willingly abandon their child to a cognitively immature child, however, no distinctions are made. "If Daddy is gone, he must have had a good reason. I am bad, and he wants nothing to do with me. I drove him away, and he no longer loves me." This internal monologue may be unspoken and unacknowledged by the child, but its unconscious toxicity will poison the little one's emerging sense of self.

When shame is the cornerstone of cognitive and emotional development, the consequences are enduring. The guilt springing from a deep-rooted sense of shame is called debilitating guilt. This emotion is more intense than the normal feelings we have after we do something wrong. In normal cases, we can make amends or apologize after a bad deed, and we can separate the act from our persona. People with an identity interwoven with shame cannot let go of guilty feelings. No amount of compensation can erase the negative self-concept. Shame is persistent, and it pervades every other aspect of the personality (Wicker, Payne, &

84 Grief During Early and Middle Childhood

Morgan, 1983). Moreover, this individual may begin to feel guilty about the shame itself. The mindset of shame and its accompanying guilt can linger, becoming part of a person's adult identity. Long-term effects on mental health are common, too, as many shame-ridden people eventually develop symptoms of depression or anxiety (Middleton-Moz, 1990). While healthy guilt keeps us on the straight and narrow, debilitating guilt and shame wreak havoc with our self-esteem.

Most of us understand how grief can incorporate feelings of guilt. There are many sources of this emotion, from regrets of things undone and unsaid to remorse for actions that caused pain to another. Guilt can result from responsibility inherent in the relationship itself. For example, parents are by nature protective, and they may believe they have failed when an offspring dies, even if this fear is unfounded. Survivor guilt is common, particularly when the death is out of the natural order of things, e.g., a younger person dies before the older parent, spouse, or sibling. In these instances, no logical reason for guilt exists, but the emotion can occur, nonetheless. Since guilt's purpose is to nudge us with enough of a sense of discomfort so we act to correct our mistakes, it is misplaced in these circumstances. We cannot atone for the "sin" of outliving our sibling, for example. The inability to make amends may be the reason guilt is so persistent after a death. The obsession to fix things is a strong motivator when one suffers from guilt. Without recourse for this drive, we keep guilt close at hand.

There are other sources of guilt beyond the obvious. Many of these affect children, arising from their immature cognitive development. If a child's perception of death is in error, the misunderstanding may create assumptions of neglect or even malicious responsibility. Magical thinking may heighten thoughts of "if only" that even adults entertain (Noel & Blair, 2008). It is difficult to stop our internal obsessions, suggesting that if we had done something differently, the loved one would still be alive. If we truly accept the truth of these ruminations, guilt is the inevitable result.

For example, a preschooler may have an exaggerated sense of his own power. Because of egocentrism, combined with the convoluted senses of reality and fantasy, young children may mistakenly believe they could have prevented a death. They worry that mean thoughts and angry feelings contributed to the death. Kids are frequently convinced that their negative thoughts had the power to kill their loved one. Adults understand the lack of cause-and-effect nature of this magical thinking, but kids do not yet have the emotional and cognitive maturity to appreciate that fact.

The circumstances of the death play a role, too. If the grieving child was somehow involved or witnessed the death itself, the stage is set for the emergence of guilt. Even when the child is not responsible, he may believe that he is. Consider the guilt of the surviving child after a car accident that killed his parent or sibling. What if he had been sitting in their place? Would he have died instead? Not only are those thoughts guilt-producing, but the child may recoil at the concomitant sense of relief he experiences. A young person's lack of understanding of the circumstances may contribute to intense guilt. For example, as a 5-year-old, I was convinced I had given my brother the mumps, after which he received his leukemia diagnosis, was my fault. Maybe this illness triggered his cancer, but is this necessarily true? And if it is, am I responsible? Maybe I should blame my school friends whose original contagion affected me? My adult self can see the folly in this line of thought, but as a kindergartner, I could not. To an extent, my brain retains those neurological connections involved in that reasoning, even if other thoughts have made new pathways. Undoubtedly, traces of guilt remain when a loss affects a brain so young.

There are unfortunate cases in which a child may be directly or indirectly responsible, or if they are blamed for the death. For example, Ray Charles's younger brother drowned in a bucket of water after he fell in head-first, right in front of young Ray's eyes. Frozen by fear, Ray was traumatized and too weak to save his brother. Although the stories are conflicting, Ray reported longstanding feelings of guilt regarding his inaction (Charles & Ritz, 2004). When we remember that Ray was only 5 years old, it is hard to point the finger at him regardless of whether there was theoretically anything he could have done to save him. As adults, we understand that kids are just kids, and they are unable to act or think maturely. That is no comfort to Ray, who bore the burden of that guilt for a lifetime.

Guilt may arise when observing others as *they* suffer. Watching parents and other adults struggling with grief is scary for a child. Angela, age 6, knows that crying or talking about her late grandmother will trigger strong reactions in Mom, so she keeps silent. The fear of upsetting others may motivate children to deny, repress, and ignore their own grief. Numerous respondents in our college interview studies explained that witness their parents' pain was an extremely difficult aspect of their own grief process. Many actively repressed their feelings in front of Mom and Dad, going to great lengths to avoid saddening them.

The period immediately after the death is a vulnerable time for feeling bad about oneself. Many of us experience pangs of guilt when we laugh or have fun after a loss. Worrying about trivial things makes us feel ashamed for not focusing on the important aspects of life. As time progresses after a loss, a child may believe he is not mourning sufficiently or appropriately. Many bereaved individuals lament that they can no longer recall vivid memories of the loved ones, including the details of their face and sound of their voices (Lewis, 2001). The bereaved might struggle to make their loved one proud, pressuring ourselves to find meaning or do something purposeful with our lives. But when grief is new, it creates fatigue and inertia, leading to more guilt. A vicious cycle presents itself.

The act of displaying sadness can also generate guilty feelings. For example, several of our student respondents reported that both children and adults accused them of not being "sad enough." Others were blamed for the opposite issue, being too upset and emotional because the deceased was "just your uncle." For a young person struggling with her first experience with loss, emotions can be confusing and paradoxical, and no blueprint or map is available for "doing it right." When another person implies that you are "doing it wrong," he administers another dose of guilt-inducing medicine.

The expression of guilt, or even shame, can take many forms that may be evident in a classroom setting. These reactions are like those displayed by children who *truly* are guilty for an action. The difference, of course, is that these manifestations of guilt result from a loss for which the child is not actually responsible. But in looking with a keen eye, an educator can spot guilt rearing its head.

86 Grief During Early and Middle Childhood

Actions stemming from guilt include:

- Avoidance of certain settings or people. Shamed individuals may literally run away, while others might take more indirect means to distance themselves from anything that triggers their guilt (Bybee, Merisca, & Velasco, 1998).
- Attempts to rectify the situation (Bybee et al., 1998). Obviously, in the case of the loss of a loved one, this is impossible. A guilt-ridden child, however, often frantically attempts to undo what she believes she did wrong. This unachievable task may cause the child to ask for forgiveness repeatedly, even for vague transgressions. Attempts at perfectionism and emotional meltdowns are related behaviors.
- Confessions regarding actual and perceived misdeeds. These may be connected to the death or be seemingly nonsensical (Bybee et al., 1998). Regrets about forgetting to say "I love you" or not spending time with the person are common. A few children may express regrets about missing the death itself, such as when other family members have gathered around the bedside of a hospice patient while excluding the kids. They may express remorse for past actions that had created conflict. (Worden, 1996). Along with confessing, youngsters may apologize profusely for the perceived transgression for which one is at fault. (Bybee et al., 1998).
- Becoming overly altruistic. To compensate for the misdeed, a few children will become obsessively empathic, cooperative, and law-abiding. Since the true damage in their life is irreparable, they may go to extremes to be prosocial and charitable in other settings (Bybee et al., 1998). Kids may also strive to be the perfect child, not only to ease the burden on distraught parents but to compensate for their perceived imperfections of the past. Behaviors may include overprotection and nurturance of others, to the point of ignoring their own needs and wants (Corr, 2010).
- Aggression and other forms of acting out. This expression can be verbal or behavioral, and directed at either the deceased or others (Worden, 1996). Suppressed anger is liable to explode at inappropriate times. Triggers can be random or obvious. When anger stems from guilt, the anger is self-directed; however, the outburst may be displaced to an external target. Acting-out behaviors are often expressions of inward anger turned outward. The true, but unacknowledged, target is one's self.
- Phobias, panic attacks, and nightmares. In a child whose guilt is out of control, the emotion can be projected onto external targets that become metaphorical bogeymen. This reaction is rooted in fear of punishment. When we feel responsible, we anticipate negative consequences for our horrible actions. When none are forthcoming, we may project our dread of punishment onto a person or monster that will "get" us. This worry turns to fear, which creates panicky behaviors and outright terror.
- Self-harm and self-punishments. To force retributions from themselves, a portion of kids will intentionally do penance. This can be blatant harm to self, such as attempts at suicide or cutting. Self-punishments can be subtle, such as depriving oneself of anything pleasurable. A child may become obsessed

with punishments, either of themselves or others (Bybee et al., 1998). As the individual grows into adolescence and adulthood, addictions can result from feelings of chronic shame and guilt (DeYoung, 2015).

- More serious pathologies such as obsessive-compulsive disorder (OCD). A meta-analysis by Shapiro and Stewart (2011) found that guilt is a correlated emotion with OCD behaviors. If we consider that the rituals, or compulsions, in OCD exist to confront negative obsessions and prevent them from becoming a reality, this correlation makes sense. Instead of undoing or stopping mere bad thoughts, a child displaying OCD-like ritualistic behaviors may be unconsciously trying to undo the horrible event that triggered the guilt. When we remember that magical thinking may play a role not only in OCD but in the young child's immature cognitive processes, the connection is obvious. A guilt-ridden child who believes her thoughts caused someone's death may go to extreme lengths to perform a compulsion they think will prevent other terrible things from happening. For example, author and mortician Caitlin Doughty resorted to a series of rituals to prevent further deaths after she witnessed a child die in a fatal fall. She was 8 years old at the time, and this incident was her first experience with death and trauma. Her constant tapping, checking, and counting behaviors were her attempts to regain control (Doughty, 2014). No matter how reassuring these actions are in the short term, there is a vicious cycle involved in these scenarios. The more one tries to stop thinking a thought, the more it stays in the mind. There is no surprise that a child may turn to a ritual to break the pattern.

Here is a list of comments a guilt-ridden child may utter. Although expressed indirectly, guilt is the emotion fueling these statements.

- I am the older brother, so I should have been able to protect him.
- If I am older, why didn't I die first?
- I was sick, too, so why didn't I die?
- I shouldn't have thought those nasty things about _____
- I should have been nicer.
- I'm sorry I fought so much with _____
- The last time I saw _____ I said really mean things.
- _____ is a better person than I am.
- I was a horrible sister/brother/son/daughter/friend.
- I am a bad person, and this experience is God's way of punishing me.
- I know I can never be as successful as _____ would have been.
- My parents want me to take the place of my sibling, but I am failing.
- Mom and dad favored my sibling, so why I am left?
- Perhaps the cold he caught from me caused his death?
- I smacked him last week; maybe that's why he died?
- I never had a chance to say goodbye.
- I never told her I loved her.
- I am a disappointment.
- I am not crying enough.

88   Grief During Early and Middle Childhood

- I am crying too much.
- Maybe I didn't love _____very much if I don't feel as sad as I should.
- I am not as sad as I'm supposed to be.
- I cannot even grieve correctly.
- Why don't I feel as bad as everyone else does?
- I know I am failing in my attempt to live for two people.
- _____ would be ashamed of me.
- Sometimes I think it should have been me.
- _____ was a much better person than I am.
- I should have done something to stop what happened.
- It was probably my fault, but I don't really know what I did wrong.
- I don't believe I am entitled to have fun anymore because _____ can't.
- I shouldn't be able to have new experiences because _____ cannot.
- God hates me.
- I hate myself.

Case Example

Lindsey is a 10-year-old girl whose little brother, Leo, died at the age of 5 from complications due to chicken pox. Lindsey had contracted the illness too, but she had a milder case. Her brother had been sickly since his premature birth, and his immune system was too weak to fight the virus. Lindsey grieved in typical ways in the period immediately after the death. She had occasional crying spells and periods of sadness but seemed to rebound quickly. For the next few years, Lindsey rarely discussed Leo, busying herself with schoolwork, socializing with friends, and learning to play the saxophone. One day during her fifth-grade year, Lindsey watched a movie about some individuals who were falsely accused and then executed. Lindsey became fearful and withdrawn. She had horrible nightmares in which people were coming to kill her. She became obsessed with the possibility of getting into trouble at school for something she did not do, and she worried about receiving unfair punishment. After a week or two, Lindsey became so distraught that she had trouble sleeping at night and paying attention during the day. Her frequent crying spells alienated her friends, and she withdrew from extracurricular events. She exhibited compulsive behaviors, such as flipping light switches repeatedly and washing her hands until they bled. When asked why she was doing these odd behaviors, she replied that completing these actions was the only way to stop the fears twirling around in her head.

A visit to a child therapist led to the discovery that Lindsey had been fermenting feelings of guilt about Leo's death for years. She had never directly expressed her fear that she was the cause of Leo's fatal illness. Immature cognitive processing prevented her from a rational understanding, and she unconsciously assumed responsibility for infecting, and eventually killing, Leo. Lindsey refrained from sharing her concerns with her parents, since upsetting them would increase her guilt. Years later, the repressed feelings found sunlight when they were triggered by the story of an innocent person receiving the ultimate punishment. Lindsay related to this victim who was wrongly accused and punished. She feared that the same fate awaited her, since horrific things were imminent as retribution for "killing" her brother. Although her 10-year-old mind realized that she was not responsible for Leo's death, her early misperception and its resultant guilt became programmed in her plastic brain. Feelings of remorse and regret were automatic responses. By helping Lindsey understand the connections and confront her unresolved guilt in therapy, Lindsey's OCD behaviors, panic attacks, and nightmares diminished.

Chapter 14

Learned Helplessness After a Loss

Behavioral psychologist B. F. Skinner (1958) described the power of reinforcement in encouraging behaviors. His work followed in the footsteps of that by Thorndike (1933), who used animals such as mice and rats to illustrate the law of effect in social science. His theory assumed that living beings operate via behaviors and their consequences. To continue an activity, most people require validation for their efforts. We must expect a positive consequence of our actions or we stop performing them. Suppose you have a job you hate; not only are the hours long and difficult, but you suspect your job is pointless. You despise your boss and your coworkers, and to top it off, the boss refuses to pay you. Instead of a salary, you receive a blow to the head when you walk in the door. Do you continue with this employment? Of course not. You need to be getting *something* out of your job, whether that is a paycheck, friendships, or an internal sense of achievement. If not, you will surely stop what you are doing (Lawrence, 2015).

But what if you find yourself in circumstances where you are not being rewarded? What if you commit to a job because of family obligations but do not receive a paycheck? Some individuals may resort to rationalization to explain their actions. For example, a son may convince himself that he loves his work, or at least enjoys helping his father in the family business. Or the person may just quit, removing themselves from an unrewarding position. But what occurs when we cannot avoid the negative conditions? When we have no control over our fate, we predictably just give up.

Lost in a hopeless scenario, even the most resilient of us will feel powerlessness. This phenomenon was first described by Martin Seligman and his colleague from the University of Pennsylvania, Steven Maier, who worked with dogs as subjects. After placing the animals into pens, the researchers exposed them to randomized electric shocks that were unpredictable, unpreventable, and inescapable. Seligman and Maier discovered that the animals gradually stopped trying to avoid the shocks. In future trials, this group of dogs entered a new pen from which escape was obvious. Still, the dogs sat stoically, accepting the shocks. The researchers' interpretation of this behavior was that once the dogs realized there would be no positive outcome, they gave up and accepted their fate. Further research showed that this state of learned helplessness can continue even when the environment changes. Because the dogs learned that they were powerless in one setting, they were ineffective in others, too. Seligman and Maier suggested that if dogs displayed this behavior,

Learned Helplessness After a Loss   91

humans might do the same. Seligman and Maier demonstrated that powerlessness can bleed into subsequent occasions, resulting in an overwhelming sense of helplessness that pervades one's life. These psychologists surmised that the dogs in their study appeared to be "depressed," acting in ways reminiscent of adults with that mental health disorder. If this generalization is true, the potential exists for a person to become sad and withdrawn in similar uncontrollable, negative circumstances. In fact, inherent in the diagnosis of depression are the symptoms of feelings of hopelessness, signifying the loss of control over one's life (Seligman & Maier, 1967).

Researcher Kurt Richter (1957) found a similar phenomenon in rats, with dire consequences. He discovered that many of these animals, when confronted with a series of major stressors from which there was no escape, died. This was especially true for wild rats, who were easily threatened by restraining them and cutting their whiskers. When placed in narrow tubes of water, a large number quickly stopped swimming, dying quickly. Domesticated rats, who were not fazed by the earlier handling, persisted in their swimming efforts, some for over 60 hours. Those who had been rescued in an earlier trial continued to paddle the longest. Richter's interpretation was that these animals had *hope*. They did not perceive the immersion in the tube as a permanent threat, so they tried desperately to help themselves. Although Richter could be accused of anthropomorphizing at bit, his point is relevant. Bombard a living creature with too many unexpected stressors, then remove ways to lessen the burden or expel the pent-up energy, and you have defeated him. When there is no way out of a dilemma, resignation is the best option. Although humans are not rats, we can empathize with the need to believe that our efforts matter and that the situation will improve. Hope is crucial.

After a loved one dies, most people experience an intense feeling of impotence and weakness. This loss is real; we can do nothing to bring back the deceased. Children, by necessity, may naturally accept the loss of control. Adults in their family, school, and society already direct much of their lives. In normal circumstances, a child gains a modicum of control as he or she matures and gains responsibility. A loss reinforces a perception of powerlessness because the trauma is irreversible and uncontrollable. Paradoxically, a youngster may respond to negative events by insisting he is ultra-powerful, which further fuels his suspicion that angry words or thoughts caused the death. Or, he may revert to a state of total helplessness in an unconscious attempt to absolve himself of any responsibility. The discrepancy between omnipotence and powerlessness creates conflicting feelings in the child, but in both cases, the child perceives exaggerated and misunderstood levels of responsibility and involvement. Children in these circumstances may grow up with a distorted sense of reality that can contribute to adult depression, along with residual guilt, hopelessness, and helplessness. With no way of escaping his ineffectiveness, the child may behave like the unfortunate dogs in the learned helplessness experiments or the doomed rats in the tubes.

The natural progression is from situational learned helplessness to a global pessimistic attitude. Once a person assumes that he has no control over negative events, he might expect more undesirable circumstances to occur. This belief is a defense mechanism. While the circumstance itself may be uncontrollable, by being vigilant and anticipating every possible negative outcome, an individual retains a sense of

92 Grief During Early and Middle Childhood

control, at least over his own reactions. Preparing for the worst-case scenario builds protective armor against the incoming stresses. Poet Robert Lowell once wrote about how the metaphorical light at the end of the tunnel is likely to be a train thundering in our direction (Jamison, 1995; Lowell, 1977). The pessimist can talk herself into a false sense of preparedness by assuming the worst. This may prove to be an ineffective strategy for coping. Rarely is grief lessened because we expect it. When we only see the glass as half empty, we struggle with life.

The most important takeaway from his information is that empathetic adults, including educators, would be wise to help children establish a realistic sense of power in their lives. We should allow young children to talk over their feelings and learn how to express these emotions appropriately. If they display attitudes of guilt, as caring adults, we can reassure youngsters that thoughts and words do not make them responsible. Death is not typically within our control. Although helping children learn this fact of life can be a depressing and challenging task, we can focus on what is within our power. For example, Mae, 9, worries about car accidents after a friend dies in a crash. Although we cannot make guarantees, we might show Mae how to minimize potential danger, such as using seatbelts and eliminating distractions. We offer perspective, reminding Mae that severe accidents are uncommon. We can teach her how to react in an emergency and whom to call for help. In these ways, we allow her to own her fear and realize she is not powerless. Grown-ups can include the child in decision making, enhancing self-efficacy. Mae can be taught to confront her emotions and develop coping mechanisms for dealing with the grief. Although we cannot always prevent horrific events, we can find comfort in knowing we influence and direct our reactions. Adults empower children by fostering confidence in their own resilience. Although we may perceive this as a challenging task in stressful times, adults should model feelings of optimism and resist the inevitable pessimistic feelings. Educators can play a vital role by reminding bereaved students that although there are times in life when the light ahead signals the next scheduled train, occasionally the light signals the way out of the darkness (Lawrence, 2015).

Chapter 15

Effects in the Classroom

The effects of grief can present themselves in many individualized ways that are as unique as the students. Sometimes, behaviors will correspond to a stereotypical grief scenario and will be obvious to any teacher. In other cases, the connection to the loss may be vague or ambiguous. Perhaps the behavior appears unrelated to sadness, or there may be a delay before the development of symptoms, making it difficult to connect the dots to a loss. Obviously, we cannot blame grief as the source for every problematical behavior, but we must consider the possibility that they could be linked. Trauma-sensitive educators are trained to ask not what is "wrong" with a child who exhibits challenging behaviors, but "what happened" to that child that caused maladaptive reactions (Briere & Scott, 2014; Courtois, 2014). We should be mindful of these associations when dealing with grief in the classroom.

The specific behaviors displayed by a young person can be tied to several factors, including his age, his developmental stage, and the nature of the relationship with the deceased. Family coping styles will also play a role. The behavioral manifestations will follow a path that correlates with the emotions of the griever. Since these feelings are variable and often explosive, the behavioral components may follow suit. Despite the wide variety of grief-related behaviors in a classroom, we can consider some common scenarios. Teachers can adapt these general ideas to fit the specific issues.

For students who have a firm grasp of their feelings, behaviors usually reflect the expected reactions. For example, tears may show sadness, while they may channel anger into aggression. In these cases, teachers will have no trouble appreciating the child's struggles to adjust. However, grief can be expressed indirectly through behavioral changes that may be much more subtle. In these situations, a teacher will find it harder to make the connection to the loss.

For instance, a student who returns to school after a death can manifest her emotions by losing concentration. Many students in our interview study indicated that they often "spaced out" during lessons. Several had trouble focusing on the academic tasks at hand as their minds wandered to home or other reminders of their loss. This distraction is typical in most cases of trauma. As Maslow's hierarchy of needs suggests, when we lack feelings of safety or security, we lose motivation to attain higher-level goals, such as learning and achieving (Maslow, 1943). Since a death in the family signifies change and disruption of a child's normal environment, there is often a concomitant feeling of insecurity and perhaps loss of perceived

94   Grief During Early and Middle Childhood

personal safety. A child experiencing major interruptions in his personal life may "zone out" in school during lessons and activities considered irrelevant or uninteresting. He may cease listening to instructions or shift focus frantically from stimuli to stimuli. Homework might be neglected (Goldman, 2002). Additionally, quite a few individuals disassociate by daydreaming and engaging in fantastical thinking to avoid reality. In these cases, too, a grieving child may appear distracted.

Another outward sign of sadness and depression includes lack of proper hygiene and disregard for personal appearance. A student may withdraw from friends or activities and may cease participating in class discussions. This self-imposed isolation may be especially apparent during recess and other periods of socialization. After-school activities may be neglected. Alexithymia, the inability to express one's emotions is another common reaction (Cozolino, 2006). Children may tell their stories with no outward expression of feelings, as if they are detached and uncaring. While this behavior is slightly disconcerting to the listener, it does not indicate a lack of empathy but rather an attempt to repress pain and sorrow (Brohl, 2007). Symptoms of physical illness, such as headaches and digestive issues, may surface. Others may become obsessively anxious over their health, focusing and worrying when any small sign of illness arises. Karen, age 7, exhibited this sign by asking to visit the nurse on a daily basis for minor symptoms. Caregivers at home might report incidents of bedwetting and sleep disturbances (Brohl, 2007; Goldman, 2002). Karen may not be sleeping well, contributing to vague signs of illness such as fatigue and headaches, increasing her level of worry and requests to run to the nurse's office. Moreover, stress may weaken her immune system, making her more susceptible to viruses and infections (Brohl, 2007; Cozolino, 2006).

When anger is the prevailing emotion, the resultant behavior typically involves aggression. A child in your classroom may lash out at others without provocation, either verbally or physically. Rage can be turned inward, and a young person may resort to actions of self-harm. A handful of people will project their anger outwardly, finding a host of reasons to bully others. Children in this emotional state are likely to have a short fuse, and they may be easily triggered into violent acts. This circumstance requires a great deal of understanding on the teacher's part, since the behaviors will need correction, and other students need protection. Realizing the source and reason for the hurtful actions can help adults respond sensitively, acknowledging the real issue without minimizing the negative behaviors that are being addressed.

Sometimes grief increases a child's activity level. Students may become hyperactive, restless, and disorganized. A few will engage in risky behaviors through impulsivity. They may speak out of turn or become uncharacteristically talkative, monopolizing class discussions. Others may take on the role as the class clown, using humor as a way of seeking attention or blowing off steam (Goldman, 2002). Children who act in these disruptive ways may generate negative reactions from staff. It is no wonder that some schools may come to see bereaved kids as discipline issues (James & Friedman, 2001). In order to properly and effectively address troublesome behavior, teachers and principals must identify the source of the issue—the underlying grief. While bad behavior need not be tolerated, harsh punishment may only make the problem worse.

Acquiring phobias of objects or situations associated with the classroom environment occurs frequently, especially with elementary-aged children. They may express fear as separation anxiety or a school phobia. While a few students may find themselves strongly attached to a parent or other individual at home, thereby refusing to go to school, others may focus their desire for connection to the teacher or someone else in the school setting. This latter scenario is likely if a student had a close bond with the individual prior to the loss. Clinginess stems from the fear of losing that person and the desire to feel safe. Since the death of his father, Tyler, 5, refuses to leave his mother's side when she drops him at kindergarten every morning. She represents safety and security to Tyler, and he worries that she may disappear, too. Children who are naturally fearful may be more prone to abnormal attachment behaviors. They may cry or remain hypervigilant throughout the day. As we have seen, anxiety is a common component of grief, as the child's nervous system becomes primed to react to the scary changes it has encountered. Some experience bona fide panic attacks (Smith, 2018). It is common for phobic behaviors to extend into the home environment. Tyler, for example, insists on sleeping in Mom's bed every night. An anxious child is easily distracted from his or her schoolwork and may have enormous difficulty paying attention in class while their antennae are directed elsewhere.

Moreover, bereaved kids can idealize the deceased. They may exaggerate this person's accomplishments and minimize details surrounding the death. Many children will imitate their loved one, assuming behaviors and speech patterns. This idolatry may be accompanied by heightened spirituality or religiosity (Hayes, 2016). These coping attempts may be off-putting to others, further ostracizing kids from social support systems. Attempts to dispute the child's perception may meet with anger, defiance, or frustration.

Because grief is such an intense emotional response, it makes sense that its effects will spill over into classroom performance. In the New York Life study, teachers reported several other common behaviors from their bereaved students. These included poorer academic performance, lateness with work and in attendance, withdrawing from social activities, and failing to complete assignments (Supporting the Grieving Student, n.d.). These behaviors may result from emotional distraction and lack of interest due to heightened emotions, or they could emerge from practical considerations such as excessive absences or new home responsibilities that conflict with homework and study time. The effects of grief can be direct or indirect on academic performance.

Social factors can and will also play roles in a child's functioning in school. Unfortunately, some bereaved children have reported episodes of taunting or bullying by classmates. In a 2015 study that investigated this topic, 20% of the interviewed children reported some amount of negative and derisive talk from their peers. Comments such as "I have a mom/dad and you don't" were recounted. Several remarks placed blame on the bereaved or their families, such as "your dad died because your mom is ugly" (Cain & Lafreniere, 2015). Unbelievably, students in support groups described similar instances. In one hurtful accusation, a 12-year-old girl recalled how another child told her that "if her mother weren't already dead, she would be because she'd kill herself for having you for a daughter." Taunting is more common when the loved one passed from "controversial" causes such as drug overdoses or suicide. Other times, the teasing refers to the bereavement behaviors themselves. Children were ridiculed for crying or holding on to items of the deceased, such as Sarah, 8, who was teased for wearing her father's army jacket, and Jake, 4, who carries one of his sister's teddy bears. Harassment can continue via online forums, such as comments made on memorial pages, and these remarks have the possibility of remaining in perpetuity (Mitchell, Stephenson, Cadell, & MacDonald, 2012). Even when teasing and bullying is not overt, subtle forms may seep into peer interactions. A few students, for example, report being left out of peer activities, often outright rejected by other students (Cain & LaFreniere, 2015). Whether this avoidance is because of discomfort, fear, and uncertainty, or if it results from blatant cruelty, is hard to say. Becoming a social pariah, however, will hurt in any case. For a grieving child who feels different, having this sense of ostracism validated through the behavior of peers deepens the sense of low self-worth and alienation (Dyregrov, bie Wikander, & Vigerust, 1999). Educators should recognize this issue in order to nip in the bud. By addressing issues of grief with the class, in ways that are suggested later in this book, awkwardness and misunderstanding might be lessened. Confusion and ignorance feeds bullying, in whatever form it ultimately takes.

Even when a bereaved child is not blatantly mistreated, she still may find herself ostracized. Adults in similar circumstances report how others frequently avoid them after the loss. The reasons are varied. Friends and relatives may be clueless about what to say, others may wish to avoid feeling uncomfortable or sad. One writer stated that his friends and family seemed "spooked" by him, as if loss is contagious (Greene, 2019). Despite our rational selves, we may worry that associating with a grieving person will somehow affect us, too. When we consider children's immature rationality, this avoidance behavior is more likely to occur. No one wants to be sad or expose themselves to loss. Ignoring the griever is a more comfortable option. When bereaved individuals report feelings of loneliness, they are not always unwarranted. Teachers in the classroom setting should be observant and monitor interactions among the students. Watch for attempts to exclude the grieving pupil and encourage actions that are inclusive.

In your classroom, a child may present in ways varied and individual. Look for changes in normal functioning—for that particular student. A normally passive pupil turned aggressive, or a talkative one who becomes laconic, for example, are two examples of personality and behavioral alterations symbolic of emotional disruption. As an observant educator, be on the lookout for these kinds of behavioral changes as signs that a child may be exhibiting signs of their grief.

Chapter 16

Diagnosable Issues

At least once in our lives, we will lose a loved one and experience grief. Most of us will navigate this road to an endpoint of relative acceptance, moving on with our lives in a new state of normalcy. For others, grief is a roadblock that creates a major detour from the usual route. We should always consider the potential for a grief reaction to be the trigger that leads to a clinical diagnosis. Anyone is vulnerable to the pathological consequences of grief.

The dilemma inherent in any mental health diagnosis revolves around distinguishing what is "normal" and what is "abnormal" in terms of behaviors, thoughts, and feelings. We use this latter term in many college courses to label people who have a mental illness. This nomenclature creates problems. In the strictest definition of the word, "abnormal" means out of the norm. When a symptom occurs in a minority of people, it is potentially abnormal. This is a strict statistical designation. But if we use this definition to assess people's behaviors, everyone engages in "abnormal" actions sometimes. People who dye their hair, for example, are "abnormal" if we mean that most human beings at any one time are not engaging in this activity. Likewise, operating a hover board or surfing in the ocean is "abnormal," too. But no one would consider these acts symptoms of mental illness. When using this label in psychological circles, the meaning goes well beyond the "in the minority" definition. Typically, we use this term as a necessary qualifier but not an absolute sign of pathology. If the majority members of a societal group are exhibiting a behavior, we will not use this action as symptomatic of a problem (Wood, Wood, & Boyd, 2013). For example, if most people in a community love hot dogs and enjoy dining on them, a person who orders this product for his evening meal does not act abnormally. Only when the behavior deviates from what is customary in a specific group can this be labeled as problematical. This designation as "abnormal," however, is necessary but not sufficient to signify a diagnosable condition. For that eventuality, the behavior must also be dysfunctional. Often, the level of dysfunction is clear. If Jim likes to eat paint instead of chicken, he is jeopardizing his health. Other times, however, there is a value judgment involved. If Jim prefers to eat guinea pigs, is this a sign of mental illness? In certain cultures, people view this rodent as a meal rather than as a pet, so dining on the furry animals is not abnormal. In the United States, this predilection is atypical—but is it dysfunctional? Eating guinea pigs is not a health problem, since they are as consumable as other animals like chickens and pigs, which most Americans have no problem ingesting. If Jim does not make a

98 Grief During Early and Middle Childhood

habit of raiding pet stores and slaughtering the potential pets, is his behavior harmful? We could argue it is not.

This discussion leads to one obvious fact: there is a level of subjectivity involved in diagnosing mental health problems. All of us do things that could be considered "abnormal." All of us have issues and problems. All of us struggle with negative thoughts, emotions, and behaviors from time to time. All of us perform actions that could be dysfunctional or maladaptive. But do we all have a diagnosable mental illness?

Suppressing the desire to answer that question in the affirmative, let us assume that most people in a society are "normal." Then we can develop criteria to determine which behaviors or symptoms displayed by an individual are *not* normal and also pathological. To do this, we consider two other criteria.

First, the counselor will assess the level of distress. Atypical behaviors irritate others in a society, regardless of whether they bother the perpetrator (Wood, Wood, & Boyd, 2013). A person suffering from frotteurism enjoys rubbing his private areas up against strangers in public, not unlike an unneutered male canine who finds human legs sexually stimulating. The perpetrator of such activity will not be upset, but the object of his "affection" will be. This behavior not only infringes on the rights of others, it is downright unnerving. Keep in mind the level of distress involved in these criteria. We cringe at a fellow diner's loud phone conversation, but this rude behavior does not meet the criteria for mental illness.

With most behavioral health issues, the affected person is the one who is suffering. Anxiety and depression have external manifestations, but the brunt of these feelings falls squarely on the shoulders of the person who is experiencing them. Negative thoughts, known as obsessions, create panic and guilt, which are intrinsic feelings of distress. Although many people may become adept at hiding these negative thoughts and feelings, the internal turmoil can be crippling.

The most significant criterion of a mental health diagnosis is that of being maladaptive (Wood, Wood, & Boyd, 2013). How does the current issue affect or disrupt a person's life? Can the individual act in the way she wishes? Is his life influenced in such a way by the symptoms that the person cannot perform basic functions or take part in desired activities? If so, there may be grounds for reaching a diagnosis.

Suppose repetitive thoughts plague Mary each morning after she leaves her house. As she starts her car, she suspects she forgot to unplug her coffee maker. Pushing the thought to the back of her mind, she puts her car in gear and backs out of the driveway. It is no use. The fear that the appliance remains plugged into the outlet, overheating as the remaining liquid evaporates and starting a raging fire in the newly renovated kitchen, overwhelms Mary. The fear gives way to panic as visions of her home fully engulfed in flames because of her irresponsibility becomes too much to bear. Mary stops the car for a moment and runs back into the house to confirm what she already knew—the coffee brewer is safe and sound, with the plug lying next to the cooled carafe. Glad that no one witnessed this reassuring behavior, Mary returns to her car and starts off to work. Is Mary's behavior diagnosable as a mental health disorder?

The key criterion is whether her behavior is maladaptive. Is it?

We could argue that if Mary returns to her home *once* to double check her plugs, it is not a dysfunctional act. The fear is distressing to Mary, true, but she squelches it by taking 30 seconds to reassure herself that all is well. If Mary can continue with her day free from further anxiety over her home appliances, this action will not be enough to earn her a mental health diagnosis.

On the other hand, if Mary's repetitive thoughts continue to plague her and create greater anxiety, and if she succumbs to this fear by *repeatedly* returning home to check on her electrical cords, there may be a bigger problem. If her compulsive behavior delays her punctuality by forcing her to return many times throughout the day to recheck, this behavior has become maladaptive. Not only is Mary's day interrupted, but she will soon be unemployed! Here, a diagnosis of a mental health disorder like obsessive compulsive disorder, abbreviated as OCD, might be appropriate.

Professionals in the mental health field refer to the Diagnostic and Statistical Manual (2013), published by the American Psychiatric Association, as the go-to source on symptoms and information on current diagnostic criteria. This volume, in its 5th revision, has the most up-to-date listing of disorders with symptomology, etiology, and treatment plans. Over the six decades since its first publication, it has undergone frequent changes and revisions as knowledge of mental illness has increased. Likewise, the book reflects societal norms and values, meaning that the criteria changes with time. Despite attempts to describe symptoms and disorders in painstaking detail, the criteria can be subjective. The most experienced and well-educated practitioners frequently disagree on diagnoses. It is this subjective nature of psychological disorders that often creates confusion surrounding labels and differences in treatment approaches.

To make matters worse, society holds a social stigma regarding mental illness. Most of us have few qualms about seeing a physician for strep throat or bronchitis; no one is ashamed of suffering from such ailments. But many people are reluctant to admit they are depressed or anxious, let alone struggle with substance abuse or violent mood swings. That a large portion of society continues to see mental health problems as signs of personal weakness rather than a medical condition is a holdover from centuries of misunderstandings and falsehoods. In the 21st century, we may no longer consider a person who holds conversations with their personal visions to be a witch, but many still blame these victims for their "crazy" behaviors and lack of functioning. Mental health labels stick, too. A diagnosis such as bipolar disorder has a long shelf-life, most likely because no curative treatment currently exists. However, the subjectivity involved in the diagnostic process suggests that on over one occasion, diagnoses are incorrect. When a child receives this label early in development, growth may alter behaviors, which then require reevaluation. Unfortunately, reassessments do not always occur, and diagnostic labels may be permanent.

Can grief become a disorder? If we consider the criteria of deviating from the norm, distressing, and preventing normal functioning, then intense grief can fit. On the other hand, this reaction is expected when the loss is new. Various factors may contribute to the enormity of the grief response, such as the manner of death, the preparedness of the mourners, the age of the individuals involved, and the coping skills of the mourners. Although people do not "get over" grief, after a reasonable time, those who are coping with a loss come to accept their "new normal" and learn how to function despite their grief. A few psychologists consider this person to have "recovered" (Bonanno, 2009; James & Friedman, 2009). In other cases, this resolution takes time, although time itself is usually not enough for effective healing (Martin & Ferris, 2013). When unresolved feelings and issues dominant a reaction, the grief itself can become pathological and warrant a diagnosis (Lichtenthal, Cruess, & Prigerson, 2004). Professionals consider developmental level when making this diagnosis, as patterns of grief are unique in young patients (Kaplow, Layne, Pynoos, Cohen, & Lieberman, 2012). In other cases, particularly involving those individuals who are genetically predisposed, grief can trigger mental health conditions.

When loss is the key triggering event and there is no prior history of underlying disorders in an individual, grief that meets specific criteria could potential diagnosed as Persistent Complex Bereavement Disorder. This diagnosis is appropriate for both adults and children, but the time frame of symptomology is different. To receive this diagnosis, an individual must have experienced the death of a person with whom they had a close relationship. The second criterion involves the experiencing of at least one of these symptoms, on most days, for 6 months for a child (12 months for an adult):

- Persistent yearning for the lost loved one, as evidenced through thoughts, behaviors, or play. This longing can involve fantasies of being reunited with the loved one.
- Intense levels of emotional distress.
- Preoccupation with the deceased individual which can manifest in compulsive behaviors and repetitive thoughts and conversations surrounding the lost person.
- Preoccupation with the death itself. Children may demonstrate this obsession through play or speech, and it can present as fears or as a morbid curiosity. Anxiety regarding death can expand to include worry about other loved ones.
(American Psychiatric Association, 2013)

The third criterion comprises 12 potential symptoms that signify notable emotional distress, issues with identity formation and integration, or disruption of social relationships and activities. The individual in question must exhibit at least six of these symptoms over half the time and to a significant level. As with the previous criterion, these signs must persist for 6 months in a child for a minimum of 12 months in the case of an adult (American Psychiatric Association, 2013).

The list includes:

- Substantial hardship accepting the reality of the death. In children, we must consider the child's cognitive understanding of the concept of death and dying.
- Denial or emotional numbness in relation to the death.
- Inability to recall memories about the loved one in a positive light.
- Intense feelings of anger, injustice, or resentment about the loss.
- Misperceptions and extremely negative or harsh self-appraisals about the death, such as blaming oneself or focusing on regretful behaviors.
- Avoidance of reminders of the death or the deceased. This avoidance may become obsessive and involve elaborate methods to avoid any triggers.

Diagnosable Issues 101

- Desire to stop living to reunite with the loved one.
- Inability or difficulty learning to trust or attach to other people since the death.
- Intense feelings of loneliness and inability to connect with others.
- Difficulty finding meaning, purpose, or happiness in life. This symptom can manifest through beliefs that one cannot go on without the deceased.
- Identity confusion that the death triggers. For example, the bereaved may feel as though parts of her own identity are dead, or she may have difficulty dealing with role changes since the death.
- Lack of interest or enthusiasm since the loss. This includes a reluctance to maintain social engagements and relationships.

(American Psychiatric Association, 2013)

The fourth criterion involves the level of distress generated by the previous symptoms. To meet this standard, the level of discomfort and negative emotions is intense and substantially affects the person's normal performance in her daily life (American Psychiatric Association, 2013).

The fifth criterion places the symptoms within social, religious, and cultural contexts. To meet this requirement, the behaviors must deviate from what is acceptable or customary within given norms. Social groups can vary on what they deem appropriate grief expressions. This criterion leaves room for recognizing these variations and observing an individual within his social milieu (American Psychiatric Association, 2013).

We give a special consideration to the diagnosis of "traumatic bereavement." In this circumstance, the death has occurred from a homicide or other violent means. The focus of the sufferer's reactions is on the traumatic nature of the death itself, including imagining the loved one's last moments and levels of pain and suffering (Schupp, 2004).

Reading this long list of criteria, one can recognize the subjectivity involved in making the diagnosis. For anyone who has experienced the death of someone close, these signs and symptoms should be familiar. Most bereaved people will find their minds wandering to the deceased. Memories are easily triggered and often obsessive. Imagining the circumstances of the death, maybe reliving it in our own minds is a normal reaction. Feelings of guilt or remorse are generated in many mourners, as are conflicting preoccupations with the loved one and attempts to avoid the memories (Howarth, 2011). If an immediate family member died, the physical and role changes inherent in this loss are hard to ignore. Emotions are intense, and when so, are hard to push aside to allow interactions with friends or involvements in fun activities. The major issue when making the diagnosis of Persistent Complex Bereavement Disorder is assessing intensity against longevity of the symptoms. Most of us learn to cope after a little adjustment time. People with this diagnosis struggle to adapt for an extended period.

This last point is significant. We cannot diagnose Persistent Complex Bereavement Disorder, by definition, prior to the 6-month (for children) or 12-month (for adults) milestone following the death (American Psychiatric Association, 2013). Psychologists do not assign this diagnosis in the immediate aftermath of a loss. During this time, we probably consider grief more-or-less "normal."

102   Grief During Early and Middle Childhood

That may not always be the case. Nor is it prudent or appropriate to assume that intense grief is typical; therefore help is unnecessary. Mourners need support despite the lack of a label. Although professionals should be cautious in jumping to a premature diagnosis, sometimes therapeutic intervention should begin early in the grief process.

The most serious of these red flags are hints of self-harm. Select grievers desperately wish to join the deceased loved one, hoping to meet them in an afterlife. Others want to end their emotional and physical pain. Irrationality and lack of perspective are common consequences that follow psychological reactions, particularly in times of trauma. Worry that life will never be normal, that one cannot go on without the loved one, or that the pain will never cease, creates panic in the griever. This possibility is more likely if the person is new to the grief experience. Without this prior knowledge, a bereaved individual may struggle to believe that life will continue. The potential for self-harm in these cases is real, and we must pay attention to the warning signs. In these cases, mental health practitioners do not wait the allotted time before providing emergency help. Likewise, we should be concerned when negative behaviors impact physical health in other ways. Prolonged periods of refusing to eat can lead to unhealthy weight loss. Lack of sleep can impair cognitive and physical functioning. Older children and teenagers may resort to cutting behaviors or turn to substance abuse to dull their emotional pain (Archer, 1999). In these circumstances, parents and educators would be wise to intervene earlier rather than later.

That the official criteria define a 6-month timetable for children while dictating a 12 month for adults implies the vulnerable emotional nature of children. As their nervous systems are still under construction, the chance of permanent effects from any major emotional upheaval is real. If the child perceives the loss as a trauma which then triggers the fight-or-flight reaction, the chance is even greater. When we intervene proactively, we might circumvent negative consequences that can lead to neurological changes in the brain.

Some sources use the diagnostic labels of Prolonged Grief Disorder (PGD) or Complicated Grief (CG). Despite the name variations, these labels typically describe the same symptoms, and the tools used in diagnosis are the same (Spuij et al., 2012). Although there may be subtle distinctions among them depending on the source of the definitions, for our purposes, we will consider them as identical.

Persistent Complex Bereavement Disorder is not the only diagnosis available to those who are grieving. Sometimes, other mental health diagnoses are more applicable when the symptoms began before the loss, run genetically in a family, or persist for periods longer than a year. In these circumstances, the loss may be the impetus that triggers a disorder in a predisposed person. Although several diagnoses fit this description, there are common ones. Not surprisingly, these are often the ones we confuse with pathological grief reactions. While comorbid disorders commonly occur, there are distinctions among the classifications of grief disorders and other psychiatric diagnoses (Golden & Dalgleish, 2010). For example, suffers from grief disorders have demonstrated greater amounts of negative self-talk and devaluation than those from other diagnoses, and there are specific memory deficits unique to the condition (Golden & Dalgleish, 2012; Golden, Dalgleish, & Mackintosh, 2007).

To untrained observers, the differences may seem indistinguishable, but to therapists, these subtle factors contribute to the nature of treatment plans and their potential for success.

One related disorder is PTSD, or Posttraumatic Stress Disorder. Many laypeople are familiar with this condition via stories and movies that depict soldiers who return home after combat or crime victims recovering from violent ordeals. We now understand that other stressors can trigger this disorder, too. The technical criteria for this diagnosis include exposure to an actual death, severe bodily injury, or sexual violence perpetrated on oneself or others, or the threat of the same. This definition includes directly witnessing the event or vicariously experiencing it via informational sources. Exposure also encompasses repeated direct contact with reminders of the incident, such interactions with law enforcement or medical personnel. Interesting, knowledge obtained through forms of media (news, internet, social media, etc.) is not typically considered to be part of these criteria (American Psychiatric Association, 2013).

PTSD can be defined as Type 1, occurring after a onetime event, or Type 2, manifesting after repeated or ongoing episodes of a trauma. When we consider a child's cognitive interpretation of circumstances, the lines may blur between the types. Children may also show muted signs of PTSD, or symptoms that present in an uneven pattern or do not yet meet the criteria for the full-blown disorder (Keppel-Benson & Ollendick, 1993). While these kids may not technically have PTSD, their symptomology indicates the need for similar treatment.

After exposure, the individual must display intrusive symptoms, defined as negative reactions that intrude on one's daily functioning. These symptoms include repetitive, vivid memories of the event, recurrent nightmares, anxiety and other extreme emotional responses to environmental triggers, severe physiological reactions, and episodes of dissociation. This last condition refers to when we "zone out" during a flashback memory, losing awareness of surroundings for a brief time. Other signs of PTSD include avoiding reminders of the stressful event, repressing memories, and experiencing severe distress with a heightened state of arousal. The symptoms persist for at least a month and can begin shortly after the traumatic incident or after a long delay (American Psychiatric Association, 2013).

We must consider a few unique factors when making this diagnosis with a child under the age of 6 years old. For these young children, sexual abuse is traumatic even without the accompanying threat of actual violence. A few children will not react overtly to triggering stimuli but may express their panic via play, which is considered to be a reenactment of the trauma. Traditionally, we do not consider medical procedures as traumatic unless they are sudden and catastrophic, such as waking up during surgery or experiencing an anaphylactic reaction. Therefore, we do not include long, life-threatening illnesses in this definition. Also excluded are deaths by natural causes. Only violent or accidental deaths are deemed traumatic within this designation.

Although we may suggest valid arguments for excluding the earlier criteria, the rationale behind the DSM is that suddenness or aggression increases the level of trauma (American Psychiatric Association, 2013). Even if we accept that definition for adults, we realize that children's interpretations of events will differ. We can reasonably assume that a child will view trauma through a cognitively immature perspective. However, the DSM does not make such clear distinctions. As a result, diagnosing a young person is arguably more challenging than labeling an adult.

An individual can manifest PTSD in several ways, including displaying exaggerated fear responses (hypervigilance), moodiness on exposure to triggering stimuli, or aggression and anger (American Psychiatric Association, 2013). Because of these extreme behaviors, interpersonal relationships will likely struggle under the strain. Intense, inappropriate responses may appear randomly and without warning. The sufferer requires time and insight to process the trauma and learn to recognize the triggers. He should acquire effective coping techniques, too.

The characteristic pattern of PTSD involves prolonged responses whose onset can be delayed. When symptoms resolve in a month or less, the diagnosis is more likely to be that of Acute Stress Disorder. In children, this condition often involves repetitive play reenactment. Kids may utilize toys or dress-up clothes to act out traumatic events that influenced them. Other signs include inability to experience positive emotions, sleep problems, and lack of concentration. As with PTSD, the hallmark physiological responses occur when the sympathetic nervous system engages. Individuals may be in a constant state of hypervigilance, like the zebra walking across a lonely savannah ever wary of an approaching lion. Intrusive memories and dreams may be vivid, as if the experience is real in terms of sensory awareness. Catastrophic and irrational thinking is common is Acute Stress Disorder, often characterized by nagging fears or feelings of guilt. Impulsive behavior is also a sign of this condition. Children may express their intense anxiety through fear of separating or sleeping in the dark. Occasionally, individuals will suffer from full-blown panic attacks in either PTSD or Acute Stress Disorder. Panic attacks are short periods of time in which the individual reacts as if a life-threatening stressor is present. The sympathetic nervous system and accompanying hormonal responses initiate body-wide physiological responses, including quickened heart rate, hyperventilation, eye dilation, tension of skeletal muscles, sweating of the skin, and burning of glucose for accessible fuel. There are concomitant emotional and cognitive responses, such as heightened feelings of fear, tightness in the chest, and belief that one is dying. The person's reaction is severe enough as to prevent normal functioning, at least for a few minutes. Even with no specific treatment, the attack subsides within 15–30 minutes, although it may last much longer to the person in question. Sometimes the shortness of breath and chest pains mimic symptoms of a heart attack, and if this is a first-time occurrence, the individual requires medical attention to rule out serious physical conditions (American Psychiatric Association, 2013).

Another differential diagnosis is that of an adjustment disorder. These conditions have similar signs and symptoms as PTSD and Acute Stress Disorder, but to a lesser degree. These reactions can manifest after any stressful life event, not just to the ones defined previously. Essentially, a major negative reaction following any surgery or serious illness may be considered an adjustment reaction. In this category, distress follows (within three months) a specific event is disproportional to the actual threat involved (American Psychiatric Association, 2013). This distress is also maladaptive, causing significant disruption to daily activities.

Each of the mentioned disorders shares the common the diagnostic criteria of exposure to a traumatic event. Where the incident is obvious and the symptoms present soon after the incident, we can readily issue these diagnoses. In other cases, the connection between an event and subsequent mental health issues is less obvious. This is true, for example, if an individual labels something traumatic when others do not find it as distressing. When a response is delayed, the correlation between stimulus and reaction may be difficult to uncover. For example, a young child may be more likely to perceive the beeps and alarms of medical equipment as scary and threatening than an adult would. As we have learned, a child's reaction to grief may be delayed by years. If no one connects troublesome behaviors to grief, diagnoses can be missed. Comorbid conditions are commonplace, complicating the diagnosis and prognosis.

Major depressive disorder has close ties to grief. Depression is characterized by chronic feelings of sadness, hopelessness, and helplessness, severe enough to impact normal daily functioning. Other symptoms include sleep disturbances (too much, too little, nightmares), disrupted eating behaviors (too much, too little), lack of interest or enthusiasm for stimulating activities, withdrawal from social interactions, slowness of movements and speech, inability to generate positive emotions such as happiness (anhedonia), and suicidal thinking. These signs must be remarkable and persist for a minimum of two months. (Of course, potential suicidality trumps the 2-month guideline, requiring treatment at any point.) Depression may or may not have an obvious starting point or triggering event (American Psychiatric Association, 2013). Perhaps the delayed reaction of psychological responses prohibits connecting the dots.

Anxiety disorders are alternative diagnoses that a therapist might affix to a bereaved individual. For example, generalized anxiety disorder, or GAD, comprises a vague but persistent feeling of dread and worry. In GAD, the anxiety is unfocused. There is an ominous sense that a horrendous event is on the horizon. The ambiguity in this condition makes it difficult to treat, since the source of apprehension is unclear. Obsessive-Compulsive Disorder (OCD) involves repetitive nasty thoughts (obsessions) that generate severe anxiety and panic, resolved by completing specific behaviors (compulsions). For some, the rituals have a direct, but exaggerated, connection to the concern. (Consider repeated handwashing to avoid contamination with germs and catching a life-threatening illness.) For other sufferers, the ritualistic behaviors are irrelevant. (Insisting on flipping a light switch an even number of times or refusing to step on a sidewalk crack, all to prevent the crash of a plane carrying a loved one, are unrelated and irrational behaviors.) Although various theories suggest the root cause of OCD, sufferers have a strong desire to control events (American Psychiatric Association, 2013). After a loss, most people report feelings of powerlessness and loss of control; children may be susceptible to helplessness. Loss acts as a stimulus to creating a disorder which focuses on power.

Caitlin Doughty is a licensed mortician, author, and a host of a web series on death. As an 8-year-old, Caitlin witnessed the traumatic death of a toddler who fell from a railing in a shopping mall. Amongst other reactions, one of the aftereffects of this incident was the emergence of obsessive-compulsive symptoms. Caitlin's fears of dying or losing her parents were only lessened by her rituals, behaviors that others would find irrational but that seemed logical to her. She would feel compelled to jump into her bed from several feet away, circle her house three times before caring for her dog, repeatedly check the locks on the doors, and hold her breath when passing the dreaded mall. One of her more unusual rituals involved spitting into the neckline of her shirt, leaving a collar of spit that drew the attention of others. To her way of thinking, these odd behaviors were protective, controlling the "governing powers of the universe" and preventing further traumas from occurring (Doughty, 2014). While a percentage of OCD suffers outgrow their symptoms, others may need psychotherapy or perhaps medication to diminish the symptoms.

A few individuals will suffer from full-blown panic attacks during the grieving process. Panic attacks are an extreme form of the fight-or-flight response. In addition to extreme anxiety, the person will experience rapid heart and breathing rates. He may shake and sweat profusely. There are complaints of chest pains and shortness of breath, leading many to assume they are having a heart attack. Since the episode is accompanied by an overwhelming feeling of dread, symptoms of hypochondria are common (Wood, Wood, & Boyd, 2013). The sufferer truly believes he is dying. While we can become adept at hiding mild or even moderate anxiety from others, there is no easy way to conceal a panic attack. Others notice, and the attention can trigger more anxiety and embarrassment. After a sudden loss, it is logical to assume that some people will endure a panic attack. However, many individuals report having these spells long after the initial shock. In fact, the time lapse is often long enough to obscure the link between cause and effect (Smith, 2018).

Phobias are frequent responses after any trauma or grief experiences, and children are most vulnerable (American Psychiatric Association, 2013). Through egocentrism, kids become fearful of anything that reminds them their loved one's death. Typical phobias involve fear of germs and illness, which might surface after a peer passes from meningitis. A child's panic may be triggered by cars following an accident, and he may go ballistic at the idea of other loved ones driving. Sometimes kids become afraid of the monsters and the dark. These objects represent the unknown. The intensity of the phobic response creates major behavioral problems, such as inability to sleep alone or refusal to go to school. When the phobia is reminiscent of the death itself, the association will be obvious and easier for a therapist to confront. When fear projects onto something abstract, the connection with grief may be missed. We must remember the potential for early grief and anxiety to transform into a phobia after the fact. Recognizing the association is the first step in healing the problem.

Euphemistic language can inadvertently create phobias in young children. When we tell kids that a beloved pet was "put to sleep," bedtime causes distress. Phrases such as "going home," "expired," "bought the farm" or "receiving their great reward" may be taken literally, generating misunderstandings and unnecessary concern from kids who have not yet experienced this life event (Wass, 2000). The specific circumstances of death and related ceremonies have the potential to be scary for a little one. For example, witnessing a loved one's casket being lowered into the ground can generate images of being buried alive or eaten by worms. As educators know, vivid imaginations can overwhelm children under normal circumstances.

Diagnosable Issues   107

Stress and trauma heightens this response. Although we cannot avoid every challenge, recognizing the need for compassion and sensitivity can help us cope.

If the death was traumatic, or if the child interprets it that way, there is the potential for another acute psychological manifestation known as a Brief Psychotic Disorder. We refer to this as a brief reactive psychosis when we can identify the trigger. This client is out of touch with reality. Specific symptoms include delusional thoughts, hallucinations, or erratic behavior, and uncharacteristic speech. For example, a person in the throes of such a reaction may become convinced the loved one is not dead and that he can see and talk to them. Sufferers may be distractible and obsessed with the belief that the deceased will return to life. Sometimes distraction can be so severe as to create a trance-like state within the individual, known as catatonia, in which the person appears spacey and unaroused by external stimuli (American Psychiatric Association, 2013). Since there is a weak grasp on reality, this condition may be hard to diagnose. The lack of comprehension of death and fantastical thinking may trigger a youngster's insistence that a loved one is still alive. With psychotic reactions, however, the split from reality is intense and intractable. Related symptoms, such as odd speech and behaviors, are common. This reaction typically begins soon after a traumatic event and resolves itself spontaneously. The episode lasts for a few weeks to a month. The sufferer may then return to a normal functional state, maybe never again having such an episode. Although the duration is short, the symptoms are often severe enough to need hospitalization to prevent injury. A delusional child, for example, may be so distracted talking to the deceased loved one he walks into the path of an oncoming car. There is a risk of relapse, although spontaneous remission can occur again in later episodes (American Psychiatric Association, 2013).

Mental health issues are challenging to diagnose in children because kids naturally blur the lines between fantasy and reality. "Normal" for a 5-year-old is not the same as "normal" for a 10-year-old. (For instance, a preschooler with an imaginary friend is cute, while a teenager with the same buddy is odd.) Likewise, professionals can misinterpret behaviors when the link between a symptom and a loss is not obvious. For instance, let us consider 10-year-old Billy who has begun his fifth grade year in school. From the first day of class, Billy has not hit it off with his male math teacher. His annoyance is easily triggered, leading to frequent disrespectful outbursts. When the teacher corrects his behavior, Billy flies into a rage and becomes even more defiant. A less astute counselor may suggest that Billy presents with a conduct disorder such as Oppositional Defiant Disorder (ODD) or even worse, a personality disorder such as Antisocial Personality Disorder (American Psychiatric Association, 2013). With psychological investigative work, a therapist can discover that Billy's dad passed away three years ago, and the new math teacher bears an uncanny resemblance to him. Billy might hold unresolved anger toward Dad which he now projects onto the teacher. If true, Billy's lashing out is understandable. Not to suggest that we should tolerate such behavior, but correction may take a different course if adults realize the true nature of the problem. An inaccurate label for Billy can generate other issues later. This example provides another illustration of the importance for school personnel to exercise sensitivity and awareness.

108 Grief During Early and Middle Childhood

Although the causes and triggers of mental illness are multifaceted, we know these conditions run in families. Genetic predisposition may play a large role in determining whether one person develops a more serious psychological problem after a loss while others cope in a less extreme fashion (Wood, Wood, & Boyd, 2013). That genes may be partly to blame for psychiatric issues, these problems are no one's fault. There are so many variables that determine mental health conditions that definitive predictions are inaccurate. We should be sympathetic about the potential for serious mental health issues to arise after the death of a friend or family member. A diagnosis is not a sign of weakness, but our modern society continues to stigmatize mental illness. Myths and misconceptions prevent sufferers from receiving adequate help. As educators, we must refrain from judgment and spread accurate information to the other children and families. Teachers can make referrals to school psychologists or similar services. While not an easy topic to broach, the benefits to the students are huge. We should familiarize ourselves with signs and symptoms as a way to stay informed. Although this chapter is not a definitive list of potential diagnoses, it presents enough detail to allow school personnel to familiarize themselves with common mental health conditions.

Section 3

How to Help Grieving Students

Chapter 17

What to Say to a Grieving Child

The question everyone invariably asks is "What do I do or say to someone who is grieving?" There are comments that are *not* helpful. When we consider individual differences in mourning, constructing an itemized list of supportive, or at least appropriate, comments is a daunting task for sure. Nonetheless, I will offer a handful of guidelines and suggestions gathered from research and responses from the bereaved themselves.

It is important to keep in mind what your goal as a support person is. As Megan Devine suggests in her book, *It's Ok that You're not OK* (2017), losing a loved one is not a fixable dilemma. Death is final. It cannot be reversed. Things will not be "OK." A child will intuitively know that any statement that implies otherwise is an empty promise. True, the intense pain of an immediate circumstance may dissipate, but as Devine so poetically suggests, grief is something we "carry," not "get over." We learn a new normal, a way to exist in a drastically changed world. When we love someone, we miss them when we no longer can see, hear, or touch them. The finality is painful to accept, and no words of encouragement can alter the facts. To a mourner, comments implying that patience is all that is necessary for life to "get better" are dismissive at worst and missing the point at best—regardless of the true intent of the person delivering the statements.

The best course of action is to communicate to the child you recognize her feelings and are available for support. Although it may be awkward to mention the loss to a child who is just returning from bereavement leave, ignoring the issue is usually worse. Many of the respondents in our interview study broached this topic, saying that the lack of acknowledgement from educators and peers was painful. To the grieving child who has experienced a major life change, the fact that others do not mention the event implies a lack of caring or recognition of the seriousness of the child's feelings. Teachers should be sensitive to a child's privacy, and they should recognize that comments should be made privately. Educators can take a minute and speak to the child quietly to make a brief acknowledgment of the child's grief. Even a simple "How are you?" can be enough to express concern and validate the significance of the issue.

Like adults, children will vary wildly in their need to talk over their feelings and tell their stories. This is true not only from person to person but can vary within a single individual. As a teacher who may have a solid understanding of a student's personality and behavior patterns, you may guess which a pupil will be willing to share and who will keep thoughts to herself. Do not be surprised if your predictions are incorrect. Grief often changes the usual responses, so be ready to "go with the flow." If a child shows a desire to talk, let them do so. It might be best to find a quiet time when the student can speak privately. This will allow you to understand what information the child wishes to share and evaluate the appropriateness of expressing these ideas to the other children. A few pupils may ask to speak with the class, and the instructor should be prepared to handle the nature of the child's comments. Other times, a child may not wish to speak even in a private conversation. You might take the student's lead, allowing him to share as he wishes. Acknowledging grief is not the same as forcing conversation. Even if a child responds to a simple "how are you?" with an obviously untrue "fine," the message of caring and concern will be conveyed.

Why do we, as supporters, find bereavement so uncomfortable and awkward? When a youngster falls and skins a knee or shows up in a class with a cast on a broken arm, no one hesitates to ask the hurt child about the physical injury. When a student returns to class after a long illness or recovery from surgery, most people, even peers, find it easy to inquire about her health. After a loss, however, the case is very different. This is true for several reasons. First, watching someone in emotional pain can trigger similar responses in us. Their grief may remind us of our own losses. We have an underlying worry that death is contagious; "there but by the grace of God go I." Most people fear losing their loved ones to the point of disassociation. We ignore the possibility by avoiding the subject at all costs. Observing others mourn is painful, not only because of our ability to emphasize but because of our need to pretend that grief cannot happen to us.

Second, the emotional part of grief is hidden from view, leaving well-meaning supporters clueless to the effects of their helpful attempts. Opening the door for Jimmy, who is on crutches as he recovers from a broken leg, is an obvious course of action unlikely to have negative consequences. When we say the wrong thing to a grieving child, we worry we will create more pain and suffering. Our fear of saying the wrong thing leads to our silence.

Third, our society holds the view that death and grief are failures of sorts, problems that need to be fixed (Devine, 2017). We may consider a crying person to be weak-willed, and we want the grieving individual to "get over it" as soon as possible. We crave normality for ourselves and for everyone else who touches our lives. Their pain and discomfort disrupt us, too, and we may do whatever we can to fix the glitch in our everyday existence. One way we act on this motive is to offer advice and practical solutions to those who are hurting (Devine, 2017). Most of us are kind-hearted, and we wish to ease suffering. We are sincere in our efforts to mend their broken hearts, and our comments and advice are intended to lessen their pain. But grief is not fixable, and although we may have useful ideas, we cannot solve the "problem" of losing a loved one. The perception of futility and ineffectiveness generates learned helplessness, which most of us will go to great lengths to avoid. As a result, we may unconsciously "blame the victim," assuming that the bereaved individual is at fault for their own distress. This scenario unfolds through avoidance of the mourner or insensitive comments like "suck it up" and "be strong." Moreover, a grieving person knows that the loss will not resolve. Suggestions on courses of action, such as cleaning out the deceased's clothes or going to a movie to distract oneself, are likely to be interpreted as unwanted commands that miss the mark. At worst, these types of comments may isolate the mourner further, forcing them into silence to avoid further unsolicited advice. However well-intentioned and practical this advice may be, a person in the throes of new grief is in no real position to hear or accept it.

Connection is most helpful and desired by a person who has suffered a loss. Grief isolates us and generates loneliness. It denies us the opportunity to believe that others empathize with our pain. Sometimes we may even doubt that concerns voiced by others are genuine. While the details of grief are unique to personal circumstances, all of us can relate to the pain of loss. Supporters should be available to listen, to help with mundane tasks, to give a hug, to just "be present and sit with grief" (Devine, 2017). As helpers, we must first acknowledge of the loss. Ignoring reality does not erase the grief. A next step is showing support through a simple statement such as "I am here if you wish to talk." This comment requires follow-up in terms of action. Check in with the bereaved and offer opportunities for the grieving child to seek help. Be sensitive to the potential for overextending the offers. Your job is not to commiserate. Student in our study reported that too much attention by school staff, especially in front of other children, was extremely unhelpful. Our grieving kids want their distress to be accepted but not in public or dramatic ways, and they certainly do not want pity. Children are intuitive and will balk at comments that appear condescending or patronizing. Pity and fake sympathy are to be avoided. If you are sincere in your questions, then be prepared to hear the answers and respond with honesty.

Active listening is a technique used in humanistic therapies and taught to laypeople. Psychologists teach this technique in trauma coursework, giving class attendees ways to broach sensitive topics with people who are trauma-impacted. To be honest, active listening is a skill we can use in everyday life. Concern and empathy are conveyed through this method. This technique allows for communication and support without asking probing questions or pressuring the respondent to divulge details that are too uncomfortable. Sometimes referred to as reflection, the goal of active listening is to concentrate on a person's comments and then "reflect" their essence. The goal is to clarify, affirm, and validate what the individual has said without judgment or elaboration. This technique requires the listener to pay attention, and by reflecting the ideas, misunderstandings are eliminated.

One way to learn this technique is to become familiar with common sentence starters that promote its goals. Here are a few examples of reflective responses:

- "It seems like you are thinking. . . ."
- "It sounds like you are saying. . . ."
- "That must make you feel. . . ."
- "You would like to. . . ."
- "That might make anyone feels. . . ."
- "It must have hurt when. . . ."
- "You did not expect. . . ."
- "You might want to change. . . ."

114 How to Help Grieving Students

- "You don't know why. . . ."
- "You wish things would be different about. . . ."
- "You are upset about. . . ."
- "You are scared about. . . ."
- "You are angry about. . . ."
- "You are sad about. . . ."
- "You seem confused about. . . ."
- "It must seem unfair to you that. . . ."
- "A solution you seem to be considering is. . . ."
- "It must be challenging to deal with. . . ."
- "It is tough when. . . ."

Through active listening, an educator shows compassion by engaging with a student in need. When you reflect the student's comments and feelings, you supply acceptance and validation. The child not only learns that his emotions are acceptable, but that others recognize and appreciate his hardship. Since no judgment is made, the stage is set for an individual to share freely, without fear of condemnation. The listener offers no advice, since the speaker can perceive this as criticism. Therapists focus on allowing grievers to access their emotions. This method demonstrates to the griever you can handle their pain and are not intimidated by their reactions to the loss.

Active listening is an excellent way to create a safe space for kids to share their experiences. It can promote an empathetic bond between the communicants. Obviously, some discretion is needed, since there are times when this technique may be inappropriate. For example, if a child asks a specific question that requires a definitive answer, reflecting the question could be inappropriate. ("When should I turn in this late assignment?" is not answered by "It sounds like you are wondering about the due date.") If a child's comments are self-destructive or violent, mere paraphrasing the aggressive intention may be insensitive. ("It seems as if you'd like to cut yourself" may be empathetic but may be interpreted as granting permission.) In these cases, we can use active listening to acknowledge the pain behind the threatened behavior while suggesting a more appropriate way of expressing the negativity. Frequently, a child may genuinely need reassurance, and active listening may just sound placating. (The anxiety of a student who asks, "Am I going to die, too?" will not be ameliorated by a comment such as "I hear how worried you are about your own health and safety.") Of course, when a child is asking for reassurance or a boost of confidence, adults must not lie. In the previous example, for instance, stating definitively that the child will not pass away is a claim no one can make with 100% certainty. A child who has suffered the death of a loved one will recognize the lie, having proof positive that deaths can and do occur. What the caring adult can say, however, is the actual truth: although no guarantees exist in life, chances are small that a child will die in her early years. Practical information, such as reminding the child that she sees a doctor regularly and wears a seatbelt, can also provide some reassurance—assuming those facts are true. Hollow promises and blanket reassurances will only reinforce to a child that adults are not being honest with them.

What to Say to a Grieving Child   115

Reflecting conversation requires the listener to focus on the speaker, setting aside one's own issues, opinions, and values. This is easier said than done, and the technique will be ineffective if the listener interjects too many ideas or expresses an arrogant attitude. A novice might invoke the sentence starters in such a way as to sound scripted or phony. The method takes practice until the responses can flow naturally and elicit open reactions. The technique can be utilized almost anywhere, anytime, and with any person, allowing for a multitude of opportunities for honing this skill.

When speaking to a grieving child, be careful about the use of too many questions, resorting to lecturing, or providing too many suggestions. When the pain of a loss is new, the bereaved individual first requires connection and validation. By asking for details, the listener may encroach upon personal space and trigger more pain. Using the event as a topic for an information-disseminating session avoids the emotional aspect of the situation, and by offering advice or coping strategies, the listener implies that the griever just needs to "get better" soon. Avoid the human tendency to share too much of one's own personal experiences. It is natural to compare and relate others' circumstances, and it may appear helpful to commiserate by sharing similar events. In these cases, a blanket statement such as "I've been there" or "I lost my mom, too," may promote empathy and help the listener understand that she is not alone in her grief. But too many details divert the focus from the grieved to the listener. No two losses are identical, and these comments create the implication that comparisons are being made. The point to communicating with a grieving child is to express empathy and concern through acceptance of pain and emotional suffering. By keeping that goal in mind, an educator can approach this student with compassion, humility, and respect.

Children and adults both yearn for permission to feel their own emotions. One of the most helpful actions a support person can take is merely to be present and witness the person's grief (Martin & Ferris, 2013). Kids may be embarrassed to cry or express emotions, and they may be suppressing their reactions at home. Giving students a safe space in which to unload and express themselves may be the best thing you can do for them.

Humor can be helpful in adjusting to loss, too. In studying individuals who have been coping well with bereavement, Bonanno (2009) reported that the majority retained their ability to laugh and smile. In certain instances, these reactions related to positive memories of the deceased. Other times, the interviewees had managed sadness enough to find respite in laughing. Naturally, adults should not find humor in anything directly related to the death or loss. However, many adults fear it is inappropriate to focus on anything humorous while someone is in the midst of grief. This is usually untrue, and the majority of people use laughing as a way to feel better or distract themselves momentarily from their pain. While humor may not be well-received immediately after a loss occurs, with a little time, grievers might jump at the chance to find something funny in their lives.

It is helpful to remember that you are not required to offer answers to every child's questions, and it is OK to admit that you do not know everything (Granot, 2005). No correct way to grieve exists, and none of us always knows what to say. Although kids may look to you for knowledge, advice, and solutions, the better choice is to acknowledge an uncertainty rather than to lie or feign insights with which you have little confidence. You might consider using your own lack of answers as an opening to honest discussions or a guidepost on the path to further learning you and the student can do together. Perhaps the class, as an entity, could benefit from a group project designed to explore issues that grief can generate. Children need your strength and wisdom, and they can learn from you how to search for answers to the tough questions.

Chapter 18

What Not to Say to a Grieving Child

Even though most of us have suffered through a loss in our lives, connecting to someone else who is grieving is often awkward. Sometimes we shy away from the bereaved, afraid that what we say might upset them. Being a witness to someone in intense pain is uncomfortable and often mortifying; we cannot help but think "there but for the grace of God." A great number of us will try to avoid any contact, rationalizing and concocting excuses for not attending funerals or visiting the houses in mourning. Although this behavior may be insensitive, it is understandable that others' grief hits a nerve with us, reminding us of our past pain or creating apprehension about the future. Sometimes, we can keep the bereaved at arm's length, sending along a condolence card or submitting a message to a social media page. Teachers of grieving children cannot avoid face-to-face contact. The child may look to you for comfort and consolation. As a role model, you may have a major influence as the bereaved student turns to you for stability and healthy reactions. Although there is no perfect thing to say, many comments are decidedly unhelpful. Here are statements that create pain and discomfort in students on the receiving end.

- "I know exactly how you feel." It is fine to commiserate and acknowledge that you have lost loved ones too, but since every relationship is unique, you cannot know *exactly* how anyone else feels. You can empathize, however, and share in someone's pain. But it rings false when you claim to comprehend the nuances of another person's emotions. This is particularly true when you have not lost a similar person in your life. For instance, we can distinguish between losing a pet and losing a parent. Even if you have experienced a similar loss, avoid sharing too much of your experience when the mourning period is new. People immersed in grief do not have the emotional time or energy to listen to your stories. Children are not prepared to hear too many details of another's losses. The educator-child relationship presumes a level of emotional distance. Be careful not to divulge intimate details.
- "Everything happens for a reason." This comment has several flaws. First, it is not a fact. This opinion is a matter of faith for those who hold specific views. Second, whether we can find a grand purpose life is a subjective point. For some people, happenstances seem to be part of a master plan. For others, events occur randomly. This statement triggers guilt and incompetence, implying that the

listener does not understand meanings in his own life. Listeners may perceive this statement as presumptuous and self-righteous.

- "Your loved one is in a better place." Again, this comment stems from faith, not a fact. Everyone holds different religious views, and you may have no clue if a child or her family subscribes to this belief. This claim does not diminish the pain of loss, anyway. Although it may reassure us to have faith that a loved one is safe in a happy afterlife, the pain of living without him or her is still real. A child who hears this may experience guilt for missing their person when that individual is potentially happy, safe, and secure in an afterlife. Young kids may not even be considering the fate of the object of their grief; they are focusing on their own experience. To the child, the egocentric effects of the loss are most salient.
- "You will be reunited someday." Be cautious when suggesting this idea, even if you sincerely hold this belief (Hone, 2017). As a child's teacher, and not a family member, you are not familiar with the details of your students' spiritual views. This statement can backfire when a guilt-ridden child harbors doubts regarding his own goodness and frets over his potential eternal fate. None of us have factual knowledge of what awaits us after death, so do not make comments that suggest that you know better. Acknowledge the child's beliefs and be respectful of differences.
- "It could be worse." In saying this statement, the speaker is diminishing the child's right to be upset. The implication is that the student is grieving in a manner disproportional to the event. Grief is subjective, and no one may challenge whether a person is sufficiently or excessively sad. Pointing out how circumstances could be more traumatic not only sounds like criticism, but this comment feeds on fears. Telling a child whose dad died in a car accident that "at least his mother survived" not only triggers a sense of guilt for grieving too much and not being grateful for mom's presence, and it may remind the child that his other parent could die, too. It is fine to remind a bereaved child of the positive aspects of her life, but not in a way that minimizes the current feelings.
- "You must be brave for _____." It is not a child's place to buck up and be strong for the adults in their lives, or even for their siblings. Remaining stoic and holding oneself together is a taunting task for grown-ups, so asking this of a child is unfair. This comment might cause a child being pressured to support those around them, along with pangs of guilt and failure and if they stumble in this endeavor. Children are learning how to grieve and repressing their feelings is not a good lesson for the present or the future.
- "Everything will be OK." Some things in life are never "OK." Although the stabbing pain of a recent loss may recede and become less sharp over time, the deceased is not coming back. There is a hole in the child's life that cannot be refilled. People are not replaceable, and no one "gets over" grief. As Devine (2017) says in her book, we carry grief. It is important for a grieving child to realize that life continues and that there will be a new normal, but the missing piece remains absent. Grievers of any age will sense that this comment is intended to comfort but rings hollow.

What Not to Say to a Grieving Child   119

- "It was their time." This, too, is an opinion, and an irrelevant point to a griever. The loss is painful, regardless of whether the loved one was ready, prepared, or cosmically destined. This presumptive idea is unhelpful to a bereaved person. This comment is abstract and hypothetical, and young kids are not cognitively mature enough to contemplate this idea.
- "_____ would want you to be happy/cheer up/move on." Do not speak for the deceased individual. This comment, even if true, will make a loved one bristle, even a child. This statement intrudes on the child's relationship with their loved one and assumes that you know what that person might want. It is impossible for someone to cheer up on command. There is a danger that the child may believe this comment and feel even worse for suffering. Grief does not disappear just because we wish it away.
- "Are you still sad?" This question sends the message that the griever is abnormal or weak for continuing to grieve. It also forces a person to deny their feelings (Hone, 2017). Rather than promote healthy communication and connection, this comment encourages repression of emotions and slams the door shut on conversation. Death is a sad event for those left behind, with no deadline for feeling better.
- "Time heals all wounds." This claim is a common response, but most of us recognize its inadequacy and inaccuracy. Although the intensity and frequency of our pain may lessen over time, losing a loved one hurts for the long haul (Dyregrov, 2009). While we may find it easier to remember the deceased with joy with time, good thoughts are often tinged with at least a hint of sadness. Typically, time alone is insufficient; we must also work to express our emotions and deal with unfinished business (Martin & Ferris, 2013). If we assume that love never ends, then sadness over losing it persists, too. The wound may no longer be in an acute condition, but the scar is permanent.
- "Just think happy thoughts." Asking a bereaved individual to ignore or repel negative thoughts and feelings is not only impossible when grief is intense, but it might actually encourage negativity. While focusing on positive memories may be a good strategy eventually, trying too hard *not* to think about something usually results in greater attention being drawn to it (Cacciatore, 2017). Distraction is fine, but do not pressure a child to cheer up.
- "God does not give us more than we can handle." Although the truth of this statement depends on one's own faith and experience, this remark is not comforting to most people in pain. They are aware only of their distress. It may even depress confident people to hear this comment. Moreover, the implication of this statement is if you are strong, you will receive more pain. This is a frightening concept! Although meant to compliment and encourage, kids can interpret this remark negatively.
- "Let it go." Grief does not just go away. While we need to cope and move on with our lives, asking someone to release their pain prematurely is useless (Cacciatore, 2017). This well-meaning piece of advice may be popular because of Disney's movie, *Frozen*, but a bereaved child may interpret this comment as dismissive and insensitive. We need to experience grief fully in order to process it, and although the intensity may lessen with time, memories and love do not sail away like a released balloon.

Many adults have the mistaken idea that children will forget their losses, or perhaps they do not care as much as adults do. Likewise, grownups assume that kids do not need facts and are better without complicated information (Granot, 2005). Although we must recognize a child's developmental maturity, hiding the truth or neglecting to recognize the impact on a young person can only deprive kids of the support they need during stressful times. Information should be age appropriate, and adults would be wise to check for an accurate understanding.

Euphemisms are never a good idea, since it is too easy for a child to misinterpret them. Some, such as "sleep forever" or "put to sleep," may scare the child into equating death with actual slumber. Others are confusing, such as saying the love one "departed" or "expired." Trying to make the situation sound positive by saying the loved one went to this "great reward" creates inaccurate perceptions and does nothing to lessen the sting of loss (Wass, 2000). Kids need to hear the truth, since a fact of this magnitude can never be completely hidden from them. Be clear in the language you use without providing unnecessary details.

Avoid asking too many questions, especially about the death itself. Refrain from preaching or sounding like you have all the answers (Hone, 2017). Limit questions to general inquiries, especially about the family. Follow the child's lead and do not tread into areas with which you are uncomfortable. Comments that hit a raw emotional nerve may not generate an overt reaction, but students remember how they sting, despite the best of intentions.

Chapter 19

What to Do for the Grieving Child

Besides listening, an educator can do more to support a grieving child in the classroom. Some appropriate responses involve a direct acknowledgement of the loss, while others can aid in academic and social ways. Cacciatore (2017) suggests that traveling the road of grief is a learning experience. If this sensitive situation is ripe with teachable moments, who better to navigate this journey but an educator? We might find it useful to have specific goals in mind. What are we trying to accomplish? Baker, Sedney, and Gross (1992) described the major tasks a grieving child will need to tackle when coping. In the early days, the focus is on understanding what has occurred but with protection from unnecessary or age-inappropriate details. The middle phase involves accepting the reality of the loss and adapting to the resultant changes. Last, the child will need to reestablish a sense of identity and continue to develop within the framework of the loss. If we are mindful of this grief map, we know where the child is heading on the path while remaining aware that the speed of the journey varies from person to person.

When preparing for working with the grieving child in your classroom, the overarching principle is to establish a sense of safety. Death creates instability, but we need to feel secure in our surroundings. There are many ways to build a stable environment, such as through routine, openness, empathy, and reassurance. Maintaining trust is essential, along with providing a nonjudgmental environment (Corr, 2010). By keeping our eyes on the ultimate goal—being a solid support for the child—we direct our good intentions in helpful ways.

Communication with the child's home is essential to understanding how the child is coping and expressing concern to the family. As educators, we must incorporate teamwork when working with students. For kids to learn, teachers and parents or guardians must cooperate. Adults must share essential information for the benefit of the students. Instructors may find these discussions awkward and worry they are intruding on a family's privacy by making a phone call. If so, an email or letter to the home is appropriate (Cohen & Mannarino, 2011). The goal is to connect, and any method of communication can work. Although a few parents may initiate the contact and reach out to their children's schools soon after the loss, at other times speaking to school personnel is the last thing on their radar. It does not hurt for a teacher to send off a quick note expressing condolences and asking how the child is doing. Educators should keep in mind that the adults are grieving too, and sensitivity to their reactions is essential for helping the affected child by

122 How to Help Grieving Students

the reactions of adults in his life (Granot, 2005). This empathy opens the door for the adults to express any concerns and offer a heads-up regarding any problematic behaviors. Practical matters such as absences and late assignment and then agree upon solutions.

If staff members have built a solid relationship with the child's family, it may be reasonable to offer direct help beyond the school setting. Besides the phone call or a condolence note, willingness to help with the grieving child will be welcome (Cohen & Mannarino, 2011). Do not make empty promises, however. Many people will make blanket statements such as "Call me if you need anything," and they may be sincere in the offer. A bereaved child rarely asks for help directly. A mourner may be embarrassed or needy and answering the phone may exhaust him. He may not know what to say or ask, as grief has a way of alienating us from our own needs. Therefore, try to make specific offers. "I can bring dinner tonight for your family" is a more concrete and palatable offer rather than a vague "Let me know if I could bring you food." The same thing goes for a student in your class. If you can make a helpful offer, such as providing homework help, be sure to follow through.

Teachers and other school personnel may wonder whether they should attend the funerals when a student's loved one dies. There is no hard-and-fast rule for this circumstance. Factors such as closeness to the family and the student must be considered. Keep in mind your own comfort level with such action. Let us be honest: no one enjoys going to funerals, and many of us find that these ceremonies make us uncomfortable and may trigger our own history with grief. If you believe that your reaction and discomfort may be too extreme or obvious, it might not be the best course of action for you to attend. If you are close to the child and think your presence might be comforting, then it is appropriate to attend a funeral as a sign of caring and support. Be open and show emotion; kids learn by watching others cope with sadness. Be mindful, however, that intense expressions can challenge a vulnerable child.

When the child returns to school, adhere to a normal schedule as much as possible. Although acknowledging the loss is important, special treatment should not be overt. Many of our student respondents admitted that in their time of grief, school became a welcome distraction. Routine and structure provide a sense of familiarity that is comforting (Samuel, 2018). Many reported that they preferred school to home for a while, as they found it helpful to get a reprieve from the grief-saturated atmosphere on the home front. Many claimed that they threw themselves into school-based activities to distract themselves from their pain. Sometimes, a child may welcome a special project or other concrete task in which to engage (Granot, 2005). Although too much preoccupation with tangential activities and other forms of avoidance may not be the best course of action all the time and in every case, the need to have a semblance of normalcy is reassuring. The child's performance in the classroom and in extracurricular activities may not be up to par, but educators should recognize the desire for life to remain the same, despite the contradictory signals a child may give. Loss is confusing, and mixed emotions and irrational behaviors may be normal in the immediate wake of the event.

Educators can help a grieving child by giving them time to regroup following the loss. If they miss several days of school, be sure to give them extensions on the

What to Do for the Grieving Child   123

work they need to complete. Remember, even when the child returns to school, he will be distracted. Many of the comments made by our interviewees related to this issue. Students in the Ursinus study reported that their teachers were not flexible in accepting late assignments and did not offer sufficient catch-up time. Many interviewees admitted that they had substantial difficulty concentrating and paying attention for weeks or months after the loss, but their teachers were unaware and unaccommodating. One astute respondent stated that the grief process is "not linear, and teachers need to stop acting like it is." Remember that children grieve uniquely, and their mourning will ebb and flow. Be cognizant and flexible regarding the difficulty many kids have in focusing on schoolwork. It may be next to impossible to study vocabulary words when thoughts of a missed loved one intrude into consciousness. Perspectives change after a trauma or loss, and the small things become unimportant (Cacciatore, 2017). Students may be unmotivated, avoiding studying and putting forward little effort. Be patient with the grieving child and offer support. Do not judge the child's journey through grief and do not assume he "should be over this by now." Grief has no established timetable, and none of us are qualified to tell another when he should be back to "normal." There could be times when the grieving process is taking a negative turn, and they may require outside help. Even in this case, understanding and leniency regarding schoolwork may be necessary. This may be a good opportunity to offer extra tutoring or help with homework, either from you or perhaps a trusted, empathetic peer. Flexibility with assignments and school performance were the most common needs suggested by our respondents when asked how teachers can help a grieving child.

Some bereaved children may wish to recount their experience and share memories of the deceased. Staff may resist hearing their stories and feel awkward listening to personal information. But allowing the bereaved to express their thoughts and emotions can be positive steps in coping. One task of grief is maintaining a bond with the loved one, although in within a new context. Sharing our stories is useful in this regard (Kosminsky & Jordan, 2016). Teachers should be sensitive and encourage appropriate conversations. The discussion can shift to a private talk and counselors may be included. These talks may be uncomfortable for the adults, but we should not discourage children from sharing their narratives.

Play is helpful to a child who is struggling with grief. For kids with limited vocabularies, play allows for acting out and expressing feelings. Stressful events can be reenacted, helping the child to process what has happened. Because of stigmas surrounding grief and intense emotional reactions, older children can use games and dramatic play to adjust to loss. Play may be distracting, too, and kids may find it easier to discuss their problems while busy rather than through a direct conversation (Gonzalez & Bell, 2016; Hooyman & Kramer, 2006). Simulations and role-playing exercises have been shown to work well in allowing children to practice their reactions to dilemmas and problems related to death and loss (Klingman, 1983). Physical activities are outlets to dispel energy healthily. (Bazyk, 2007). And of course, recess and other free time periods are refreshing and calming, allowing kids to reset before returning to serious work. Creative projects, whether visual and literary arts, musical expression, or dramatic endeavors, can allow for catharsis of emotions that are difficult to express directly (Hilliard, 2001). Nonverbal means of expression are extremely useful when working with a special needs child who has a limited vocabulary or poor communication skills (Zakreski, 2017).

Bereaved pupils have reported that school staff acted as if they had forgotten the loss after a time. For instance, one student recalled how her teacher asked the class whether anyone had lost a loved one. This occurred only two weeks after the death of the student's brother! (The instructor was aware but oblivious to the potential pain her question might generate.) The girl inferred that her instructor forgot the loss, implying a lack of significance that hurt her deeply (Dyregrov, 1991). Students in the Ursinus study indicated that staff expected them to be back to normal quickly, refusing to extend any flexibility after a limited time. While we should not patronize a grieving child, patience, compassion, and understanding are crucial.

A few children may resist a teacher's attempts to reach out. Sometimes, the student does not know how to accept this help, so they may act disinterested. Pupils may reject new attachments to avoid the risk of losing them. Other students, particularly older ones who crave of peer acceptance, may fight against any sign of perceived weakness or reaching out for help. No one can force a child into an attachment. But the realization that someone loves them may motivate them to cultivate new relationships. And outright avoidance or ignoring the elephant in the room can send the message of disinterest. Even when they put up a brave front, kids notice how those around them respond. Do not be fooled into thinking otherwise!

Classroom teachers can offer support in ways that involve the rest of the class. When a student experiences a death in their family, this reality will affect classmates vicariously. In today's world of social media, information passes at a rapid rate, and even if a child does not share details herself, it is a safe bet that rumors and other bits of news will soon make their way around the school. When the grieving student is absent, the instructor has an opportunity to discuss the topic openly. Without offering too much personal or confidential information, the instructor or school counselor can clarify the facts and make sure the other students at least know of the plight of their peer. This may be a good time to dispel any misconceptions of death without being too graphic or providing unnecessary details. It might be a good idea to inform the students' families of the upcoming discussion to allow for parents to voice concerns. In a public school setting, refrain from too much religious-based talk, although students may broach this topic. Be receptive to diverse ideas and express a tolerance of various views. The point to this open conversation is not to preach but to ensure that rumors are not rampant and encourage empathy toward their classmate. One helpful activity is role playing, as pupils can practice ways to approach and talk with the grieving child. Take advantage of teachable moments so the group can learn hard life lessons, building the foundation for their own future coping.

Another valuable idea is to incorporate relevant topics into actual lessons. For example, learning stress-relieving behaviors such as deep breathing, guided imagery, and relaxation techniques will benefit any student. Teaching healthy coping skills is a vital part of any wellness curriculum. Instructors can introduce cultural ideas and varieties of social customs in academic coursework such as social studies. Teaching tolerance for strong emotions and support for mental health problems are additional ways teachers can help any child who is struggling with tough issues (Cohen & Mannarino, 2011).

What to Do for the Grieving Child   125

When a teacher starts a class discussion, she should be mindful of triggering fears and anxieties. It is natural for children, young ones in particular, to internalize information and relate it to themselves, in a typical self-centered fashion. Their first reactions and thoughts may not be for the well-being of their classmate but may relate to possibilities in their own lives. Hearing the news of Billy's dad may create concern for one's own father. Learning that Sally's sister died from pneumonia may create fears that one's own cough predicts the same fate. To an adult, comments that reflect this egocentrism may appear inappropriate and insensitive, but these are normal thoughts and feelings. Try to be reassuring and nonjudgmental as you acknowledge these worries and yet steer the conversation back to the child who experienced the loss. We can quell students' fears and encourage empathy at the same time.

Teachers should take special care when involving the class in group activities or discussions when a particular group of students has a history of being unsupportive, or if the issue at hand is divisive. The point of including the class is to allay fears and allow positive expression of feelings. If the classroom has a hostile atmosphere before the traumatic incident, the heightened emotions of the stressor will not improve things (Johnson, 1998). In these cases these, an educator might separate the class into smaller groups to address concerns effectively. While not every negative reaction can be predicted, good judgment is needed regarding specific students' ability to respond appropriately.

Unfortunately, a minority of kids may use the information of a classmate's loss as fodder for bullying the griever. Though unbelievable, cruel treatment can and does occur. This possibility has a greater likelihood in cases of suicides and drug-related deaths. For example, one child related how a peer told her that "if her mother wasn't already dead, she would kill herself because of having a child like you." Although students often become adept at hiding bullying from the view of their teachers, educators need to pay close attention to nip any such behavior in the bud. By establishing a strong rapport with a grieving child, teachers can create an environment in which the victim of bullying agrees to share such actions with you. Staff can prevent this behavior through honest communication with the class, a no-tolerance policy that involves swift consequences for the perpetrator, and positive role-modeling from the adults in the school. Teachers should encourage interactions and try to minimize attempts to ignore or ostracize the griever.

Other times, hurtful comments may be inadvertent. Students have reported that uninformed children may ask about a parent they do not know is deceased, putting the grieving child in the awkward position of having to explain the situation. Young children naturally exhibit morbid curiosities and ask for details about the death or the funeral, triggering painful memories and requiring difficult responses. The likelihood of these types of dilemmas is why honest discussion with a class prior to the child's return may be beneficial.

If such conversations take place after the child returns, try to be transparent in addressing the issue. If possible, include the grieving child in plans (Dyregrov, 1991). Many of our student respondents stated that they did not wish to be the subject of rumors and secret conversations. Although this behavior will undoubtedly take place to some degree, and may even serve a useful purpose (teachers collaborating on ideas to help a child, for example), no one wants to overhear others talking behind her back or observe people hush as soon as they enter a room. Tact is the rule of the day.

Teachers should be mindful of their own comments, too, after a pupil returns to school. For instance, reminding students to ask their mothers for help with a bake sale may present as insensitive to the motherless student. These statements are not intentionally hurtful and may be unavoidable. At a certain point, a grieving child will need to learn how to deal with comments that hit a nerve. A level of sensitivity can go a long way, particularly when the child has not yet built up defenses and refined coping skills.

One concrete suggestion for teachers is to involve the class in a project designed to show support to the grieving child and her family. My first-grade teacher did just such an activity, and the effect on me was so positive and so strong that it remains a vivid memory to this day, over 50 years later. My class had been preparing to make a Christmas mural for the classroom before my absence. During my days away from school, the teacher directed the students to decorate the mural for me, and each child made a personal card which they affixed to the giant sheet of paper. Later, the teacher hand-delivered this to my home. Even as a 6-year-old, I remember being in awe that this elaborate work of art was meant for me. Every one of the individual messages written by my classmates in the typical scrawl of beginning writers touched me. Not only have I preserved the mural, I still recall the sense of love and compassion expressed when I felt isolated and misunderstood. I am forever grateful to my teacher for having the foresight to know how meaningful this act was. I realize she helped not only me, but she also performed an invaluable favor for the class by allowing them the opportunity to express empathy and concern. Creating cards or pictures takes little time and effort, but the rewards may last a lifetime.

Online platforms are another vehicle to honor the deceased and empower students to express their feelings. This project can take many forms, from simply commenting on established pages or creating a unique memorial site. The nature of the endeavor and level of involvement by children will depend on their ages and appropriateness of the sites involved. If the pages are public, hurtful comments and posts are possible, so be mindful. However, done responsibly, online memorials can be effective ways to share grief, receive support, and honor the loved one (Mitchell et al., 2012).

Your class may find it therapeutic to raise money or gather donations to help the family. Projects that raise awareness for causes may be relevant, if the age, level of maturity, and circumstances call for this. Physical action can be cathartic and help the other students believe they are doing something constructive. Death and loss make us powerless; concrete action can mitigate this helplessness.

On a larger scale, educators can opt to offer support group services or to acknowledge the loss in ways that involve the entire school. Educators can create ways to incorporate death education into curriculum designed to encourage social and emotional learning. Specific courses of action may be warranted, and even necessary, where the deceased was a student in the school. In cases of school-wide violence, specific courses of action might be useful. I will address this topic later in this book.

Whatever you do or say to the grieving child, his family, or to the class, remember that you do not walk this path alone. Your school should have counselors or psychologists who can support you, and other adults who may have traveled this road previously. Unfortunately, even licensed mental health professionals may have limited coursework in this area and are unprepared to offer formal training. Personal experience can be an adequate prerequisite for coping with loss and grief, if individuals keep in mind that every bereavement period is unique and that individuals cope and react differently. Team up with other teachers or staff, if for no other reason than to bounce ideas off them and to serve as a support system for you.

That last point bears emphasizing. Helping a grieving person to navigate the waters of hurt and loss after a death is difficult and drains our own emotional reserves. Hearing details of another's experience may trigger memories and feeling we thought we had processed. Watching another suffer, especially a child, yanks at our heartstrings and can exhaust us psychologically, mentally, and physically. While expressing emotions is healthy, be careful not to react in extreme ways in front of students who are looking to you for support (Johnson, 1998). Be aware of your own sense of vulnerability and fulfill your own needs throughout this process. Whether that means exercising and eating right to maintain health and strength, distracting yourself via activities you enjoy, or reaching out for help from a friend or a professional, be sure to take the time to replenish your own coping skills. It may be clichéd, but the idea is correct: you cannot help anyone else if you are in falling apart yourself.

Remember that your students look up to you, for information and support, and as a model of acceptable behavior. They are discretely studying you, and they note your actions and reactions. It is often useful to join in class discussions and present your experiences, but this must be completed as a "controlled sharing" (Klingman, 1989). Showing emotion is fine and can help normalize expressions of grief, but intense reactions may scare young kids. Monitoring your own responses and serving as a role model may be heavy burdens when undertaken within the context of grief, but your job is to comfort, not scare. You have a unique opportunity to help not only the grieving child through their pain, but to teach other students how to be supportive and cope through loss. The experience may even be personally beneficial. We learn best by doing, and though sad but true, learning how to cope with loss is a lesson we must learn at least once in our lives. You can be the teacher who guides this subject—none of us want to tackle it. Unfortunately, we do not always pick our own curriculum; we just learn the best way to make the lessons stick.

Chapter 20

Sublimation, Catharsis, and Finding Meaning

So far, we have discussed specific ways to approach a grieving child in your classroom, along with suggesting ideas for support. Teachers can provide structured or impromptu casual information on death and dying, offering positive coping strategies. Many schools have courses in mental health or personal adjustment, or educators can incorporate ideas into an established wellness class. Students will benefit from learning ways to cope with the inevitable stress they will encounter throughout their lives. Other ways of expressing feelings and keeping anxiety at bay may be proffered indirectly. Educators can weave creative outlets into their regular lesson plans. As modern educators, we understand that our role is no longer limited to disseminating facts and ideas. We will be required to provide emotional and psychological support at times. Learning positive coping skills is a life lesson we can deliver through modeling admirable behaviors, teaching related coursework, and suggesting activities that encourage resilience.

Freud surmised that when emotions become too overwhelming or anxiety-producing, our psyche uses defense mechanism techniques used to lessen and indirectly express our negative impulses. In his view, most of these methods merely mask the urges, further shoving them into the unconscious mind, where they fester until emerging later in life as a mental health disorder or behavioral problem (Freud & Breuer, 2004). For example, an addict may deny his problem with alcohol through rationalization, blaming his behavior as the natural consequence of a horrible childhood. An employee angry at his boss may suppress his rage and force a smile at work but then displace his hostility upon returning home by yelling at his wife and punching the wall. A preschooler, jealous of his newborn brother, transforms his aggression into regressive behaviors, such as bedwetting and baby talk. Defense mechanisms include not only denial, rationalization, displacement, and regression but also projection (attributing one's own negative motives onto another) and reaction formation (acting passionately in a manner opposite from one's true unconscious feelings). Another defense mechanism is sublimation, Freud's term for finding a socially acceptable way of expressing emotions. For instance, we may channel a negative urge, such as aggression, into healthy behaviors such as writing or painting (Freud, 1961; Freud & Breuer, 2004). These activities are cathartic, serving as outlets for the expression of painful feelings. We can easily incorporate relevant exercises and projects into the school environment.

Sublimation, Catharsis, and Finding Meaning 129

Physical activity is one of the most obvious ways to release internal anxiety. Stress creates an emotional milieu that is unbalanced. Emotions like fear, anger, guilt, and sadness necessitate expression, but outlets for direct catharsis may be hard to find. As we age, we learn that it is often socially inappropriate to wear our emotions on our sleeves, but young children may be less reluctant to let their feelings show. Occasionally, painful emotions are challenging to express without creating additional problems, as what might occur with anger. Rage can be displaced healthily by hitting a punching bag, batting a ball, or swinging a golf club. Sports and other physical exercise are ideal ways to expend energy created by grief. Allowing children time to be active during "brain breaks" in the classroom can be a great way of incorporating physicality into the typical academic day. Encouraging active play during recess and ensuring regular gym classes or after-school sports participation will benefit students. We are familiar with how exercise prompts our bodies to release endorphins and improve our mood, along with our physical wellness.

Conversely, meditation and other techniques designed to calm our bodies are healthy methods that teachers can use. Today, we often hear the term mindfulness. This word refers to a heightened awareness of one's body and mind, allowing for the appreciation of the here-and-now. Methods that encourage this practice include yoga and transcendental meditation. Progressive relaxation is another easy technique. This exercise involves systematically tensing and then relaxing the muscles of the body from the feet to the top of the head. Although masters of these techniques spend long hours learning and practicing, abridged training and informal use can be appropriate for anyone. Techniques like deep belly breathing and guided imagery help us focus our minds and relax our bodies. Even for a teacher who is unfamiliar with these activities, they are easy to learn and enact. (Refer to Appendices for specific ideas.) Taking a few minutes to guide students through focused breathing or relaxation exercises can help all students, including those who are anxious, depressed, or bereaved. The benefits of calming oneself are known to all of us, as we can usually recall times when this technique improved our performance on a task.

Additionally, we can learn to channel negative ideas and emotions through artistic expression. Endeavors such as creative writing, painting, drawing, and making music can serve as indirect ways of expressing our inner conflicts. There are numerous examples of famous artists that sublimated their inner demons. Consider Edgar Allan Poe, who could not legally, ethically, or morally construct a torture device in his basement. However, he could express his pent-up rage and pain through *writing* about this project in *The Pit and the Pendulum* (Jamison, 1993). Recall musicians like Kurt Cobain from the band Nirvana or classical genius Wolfgang Mozart, both of whom expressed their emotional turmoil into musical creations such as *Heart-Shaped Box* and *Requiem in D Minor* (Goldberg, 2019; Jamison, 1993). Reflect on the beautiful artwork of Vincent van Gogh, whose psychic turmoil is palpable in his paintings such as *Starry Night, Rain,* and *Couple Walking in Forest* (Jamison, 1993). Plenty of artists used grief in their art. Listen to the emotional pain so eloquently expressed by Beatle John Lennon in his odes to his dead mother, *Julia* and *Mother.* Lennon previously described the agony of grief through the lyrics to *In My Life,* a song that describes memories of lost loves (Connolly, 2018). We can encourage children to write in a journal, paint a picture, listen to or play music. These activities

130 How to Help Grieving Students

are effective ways to acknowledge emotional pain. These projects are integrated into a regular classroom schedule or incorporated into a grief support program. Play, too, can foster the sublimation of intense emotions generated by trauma. For young kids, pretend play that uses themes of power, like dressing up as a superhero, helps instill a sense of control over their lives.

Another example of sublimation is engaging in deeds connected to one's individual circumstances, thereby attaching meaning to the loss. A few ideas include volunteering at a local hospital, investigating a career in medicine, and organizing fundraising events for a charity. We can involve kids in these activities, which may create a sense of goodness and control in life while acting as outlets for repressed thoughts and feelings.

In *Man's Search for Meaning* (1984), Holocaust survivor Viktor Frankl insists that suffering can be the impetus for discovering meaning in our lives. Bouncing back from adversity involves not only accepting the negative, but uncovering something positive in our heartbreaks and struggles. We may become motivated through tragedy. In *Untimely Meditations* (1987), Frederick Nietzsche suggests that life implies suffering, and finding purpose in the hardships is the key to living fully. Primo Levi, in *The Drowned and the Saved* (1988) emphasized that each of us has untapped strength within us, unleashed only when we are face to face with adversity. Levi, Frankl, and Nietzsche refer to methods of grief expression that acknowledge the intensity of our pain but appreciate the chance to learn from experience, too. Knowledge gained from confronting and surviving challenges is crucial to healthy personality development. The ability to find meaning and direct our behaviors in positive directions aids healing as we believe that our loved ones did not die in vain. When we find purpose within our mourning, we achieve a sense of control, allowing grief to relinquish its hold over us. Our students can learn the lesson of empowerment, too. As educators, we play a role in this process by directing activities and suggesting positive methods to express the pain of grief. Adults make a tremendous impact as role models. If you learn from your own life's lessons, your strength and resilience will be clear to others. Sharing your own coping strategies can be an effective way to support our youth and encourage character building through adversity.

Chapter 21

Starting a Grief Support Group

One positive action school personnel can take is to organize a grief support group for students in the school. There is strong evidence that these groups are helpful to attendees. Adult facilitators provide support, as do peers who can offer advice and comfort (Graham, 1999, 2004; Marino, Thornton, & Lange, 2015; Spuij, Dekovic, & Boelen, 2015; Schwartz, 2000; Tillman & Prazak, 2018; Tonkins & Lambert, 1996). School counselors or other trained individuals (including teachers and parents) can do this informally, or they can make plans to start an actual nonprofit program. This chapter will present advice and guidelines to help with these endeavors. The Appendices provide sample letters, ideas, and lesson plans that can be used by group leaders. Please keep in mind that the information provided in this book is meant for informational purposes only and should not be considered legal advice. Founders would be wise to do their own research and consult with an attorney for answers to specific questions.

It is crucial to keep in mind that the purpose of a school support group is to do just that—offer support. Parents and other teachers should be informed that no formal counseling is being conducted. Discussions will touch on mental health issues as topics include the emotional, cognitive, and behavioral aftermath following a loss. Facilitators are not diagnosing or analyzing group members. Since many grieving students, including those in our interview study, report that feeling alone is one of the major issues when in mourning, the point of this group is to build a community of fellow bereaved kids. In this setting, it should be easier to talk and share, since everyone is in the proverbial same boat of grief. Sharing one's personal story helps in processing and adjusting to loss (Neimeyer et al., 2002). Group sessions provide a natural opportunity to talk over experiences with others who understand.

Although the group schedule will need to be loose in order to "go with the flow" as students discuss what is on their minds, facilitators will find it useful to have planned activities prepared. There are excellent curricula for such groups, and the Appendix includes sample lesson plans and related projects. Organizing each session around a specific well-developed theme can set a framework for constructive group meetings.

Forming a good support group is basically more of an art than a science. It is important to have prior knowledge of the kids who make up such a group. Factors such as age and grade and type of loss should be considered. There are no definitive rules, merely ideas to keep in mind.

132 How to Help Grieving Students

Groups are typically most effective when children are of similar ages. Although the curriculum for the group activities is flexible and student-directed by necessity, we cater the lesson plans to specific age groups. Stories and suggested creative projects may be most appropriate for particular grade levels, although an experienced group facilitator can adapt these. A wide age difference may interfere with discussions and projects. Preschoolers may find it fascinating to learn about butterflies and enjoy making paper insects out of pipe cleaners, coffee filters, and clothespins. Teenagers will more likely find that topic boring and the art project too simple. Vocabulary and knowledge may be so variable between students of extreme age differentials, and therefore, group chats may create confusion or miscommunication. On the other hand, it can often be beneficial for older students to learn by supporting younger ones, and you could recruit them to help in a peer-mentor arrangement.

It is unnecessary and often impossible to create groups that comprise children who are experiencing the same loss. Within a school, there may be a few kids who have lost siblings or mothers. Since experiences vary from person to person, gathering a group with different losses is usually not a problem. The same thought is valid and relevant regarding the details of the losses themselves. These kids can find common ground via similar emotions and challenges despite the differences in the details of their loss. We can discuss any differences when group members connect. Since the primary purpose of the group is to cultivate a supportive environment in which to share with like-minded peers, the exact details may not hinder pursuit of this goal.

More important are personality factors of the students. It might be helpful to allow guidance counselors or principals, or others who know children from various classrooms, to help create the groups. Too many talkative students, for example, may fight for the floor or may overwhelm the shy members of the group. An entire grouping of quiet students may create uncomfortable meetings in which no one wants to take part. Be cautious when including children with severe behavioral issues, unless an added adult is present who works with this child, and remove him if he becomes too disruptive to the others.

Gender may or may not be a consideration in the group's makeup. While mixed groups are more common, and diversity is usually an advantage in learning new ideas, some people may believe that males and females react to grief in different ways. For example, many assume that males struggle to express emotions while females are too open with their feelings. Studies have not borne out these variations, however. In fact, individual coping style may trump gender and even age as the determining factor in how a person grieves (Zonneblet-Smeenge & DeVries, 2003). For most school children used to coed environments, heterogeneous groupings should present little difficulty.

The total number of students in a group can vary depending on the age of the children, their personalities, and needs of the school, but limiting a group to fewer than ten or 12 members is wise. Large groups can become unwieldy with an insufficient opportunity to hear everyone and may create a less intimate atmosphere that is not conducive to sharing.

Where and when the groups meet will depend on the availability within the school setting, but organizers should keep a few ideas in mind. For a proper setting, a smaller area where the children can sit close and face each other is best. It may work well to avoid congested areas with distractions. A small conference room may be ideal, with seating either around a table or pushed to the side to allow for a circle configuration. Young kids can sit on the floor, while older teens may prefer sitting in chairs. Facilitators can distribute snacks for the members to enjoy, putting them at ease. Be careful to note any allergies or other health concerns.

Members should be told about the group's purpose. Informed consent is essential; no student should be pressured to attend group meetings. Facilitators should inform parents of the goals, too, and give consent before the program. Facilitators should answer questions to confirm that participation is voluntary and informed.

Most groups run for eight to ten weeks, with one meeting per week that lasts between 30 and 60 minutes. Organizers can adjust these stipulations to meet the needs of specific students and individual schools. Group participants may ask to continue the sessions beyond 10 weeks, while other groups reach an endpoint sooner. Since students may need to get a few sessions under their belts before benefiting from the program, a trial run of at least four to six sessions makes sense. Regardless of the duration, facilitators should set a definitive end-date. Closure is crucial and acknowledging the end of the sessions allows for expression of ambivalent feelings. Facilitators can refer students requiring additional support to other services. A group operates best with an established time limit to allow the processing of the experience.

Group time may work best when conducted toward the end of the school day. Returning to class shortly after a session may be distracting. As a former group member stated, "It was hard to concentrate on class lessons when dealing with the memories and feelings triggered during group." The facilitator should be observant and notice if any student is struggling with issues. In most cases, sending group members immediately back to class may not give them the chance to clear their heads after the relative intensity of the session.

The beauty of informal groups with a flexible curriculum is the potential for accommodating the uniqueness of the students involved. Discussions can focus on specific circumstances of the deaths, such as suicide (Dyregrov, 2009). Staff must ensure that the curriculum encompasses the needs of various ethnic, racial, and religious groups (Arman, 2014; Baggerly & Abugideiri, 2010). Special education teachers may adjust lesson plans and steer discussions to include children with disabilities, such as autism spectrum disorders (Sormanti & Ballan, 2011; Zakreski, 2017).

Since the purpose of these meetings is to support, not counsel, facilitators do not need extensive, formal training in mental health. They should be knowledgeable in issues of child development and basic grief responses, but this information is accessible through resources such as this book and related trauma-informed trainings that are becoming more available. It is helpful to have the guidance of a mental health professional, such as the school psychologist or other licensed counselor. This individual is not required to attend the meetings but can be available as a support person for the facilitator. In addition, school counselors should follow up with the students after the group has concluded. Remember that the facilitator's job is to conduct the actual meetings, not to engage in ongoing care or supervision for the children.

Should a child be invited immediately after a loss occurs, or should some time have elapsed? While here is no definitive rule, guidelines are useful. When a death is recent, a child's emotions may be too raw and group sessions too overwhelming, especially when other members have more distance and objectivity. Also consider including pupils whose loss occurred long ago. Grief has no shelf life! Children whose loved one passed before the child's birth could learn from a support group, too. For example, a few participants in my bereavement groups lost parents or siblings they never knew personally. But these losses left gaping holes in the family, affecting the kids indirectly. These children are also mourning and have a rightful place in a grief support group.

Confidentiality issues are essential to the success of a group, so it is vital that facilitators ensure that both students and their guardians understand this concept. It is helpful to have both consent and agreement forms signed by both parties. Kids will need thorough explanations and frequent reminders. In general, confidentiality in this situation refers to keeping all shared information within the setting. Exceptions are made, however, when the safety of an individual is at stake, such as in the case of potential suicidality. Additionally, facilitators are mandated reporters who are required by law to report suspected abuse in children. In these special circumstances, adults should be the designated individuals to share sensitive information with the proper individuals. For more clarification, do some research on the legal requirements in your area.

Working through our pain with others who empathize is the key to healthy coping, and support groups serve an important role in this endeavor. Various species of animals, including elephants, dolphins, dogs, and cats, demonstrate behavior that is best interpreted as mourning. Elephants visit the dead bodies of their family members, while dogs have guarded his deceased owner's casket. While these creatures may incorporate social aspects to their grief, we humans are unique in the way we use language to help us cope. Sharing our stories, possibly over and over, helps us to deal with the events and connect to others who care. We also benefit from ritualistic behaviors that allow us to remember and honor our dead (King, 2013). Group settings are an ideal place for these coping mechanisms to occur. Telling our tales and memorializing our lost loves helps us express our feelings in a supportive environment, creating bonds within the context of grief. Storytelling helps us to process our grief, allowing the rational part of our brains to connect with the emotional areas. Left and right brain communication is enhanced, too, which facilitates a neurologically integrated perspective of the loss (DiCiacco, 2008). The social aspect of grief keeps us from falling too far into the abyss. Watching my middle school group members, most of whom would never have associated with each other prior to group, call out and smile to each other in the hallway is a testament to the power of connectedness. Facilitating relationships is the reason-to-be for grief support groups.

Chapter 22

Founding a Nonprofit Organization

One project that individuals can undertake is forming a nonprofit organization to provide support in the community. Each state in the United States has different specific guidelines; you will need to be mindful of specific processes if you go this route. State and federal websites should give you legal details, and books are available to offer step by step guidelines. The Appendices provide some examples that may be useful. Please keep in mind, however, that it is beyond the scope of this book to provide legal advice. Consult an attorney for specific information relevant to your own circumstances.

The first step is to determine what needs exist within an area. What inexpensive services are accessible to grieving children? Contacting local school administrators and asking their protocol with cases of student bereavement is an excellent first step. Many districts have no plans specific to this situation, treating grief as they would any other mental health issue. If a bereaved child is coping adequately and does not exhibit negative behaviors, no intervention is offered. If a student is having problems after a loss, the recommended support services relate to the specific troubling behavior, such as tutoring for academic difficulties, punitive or restorative practices for rule infractions, or referral to a therapist for depression. When a child exhibits negative behaviors a year or more after the loss, adults may not make the connection. Many students are struggling with grief, even when adults do not identify them. Do not be surprised if many administrators deny the presence of a large population of grieving kids. As the educator, you can gain insight by paying close attention to the responses regarding available and affordable services.

Once a potential founder determines that only sporadic direct grief support is offered in a school, the next job is planning for the role of the nonprofit. Should the organization concentrate only on providing support group services to the students in need? Or should it consider expanding its work to include spreading awareness and education to the community? The answer not only depends on the needs of a specific locality but also on the knowledge and comfort level of the organizers. This last task will involve providing in-service presentations to teachers and other school-based professionals. Presenters should be comfortable in delivering these messages and have some level of experience or training in relevant fields. This last point is essential to add credibility to the information being disseminated. If the group's founders do not have this background, they might consider reaching out to professionals such as counselors, psychiatrists, or other mental health workers in the area who may offer their time. The role of these individuals can be significant since they perform public speaking tasks, or they may merely serve as consultants or resources. Even if a group limits its focus to support services only, recruiting a mental health professional to serve as a clinical director is a good step to take. His or her role can be minor but having a knowledgeable individual on board provides validity and trustworthiness. Moreover, he or she can answer questions and address concerns that founders are unable to answer adequately.

There are pros and cons to consider when forming a new nonprofit. Most times, it might be more convenient to join forces with an established program or agency, such as the local YMCA or a community mental health service. This way is less expensive, and starting actual services may be quicker. The drawback is that any action the group wishes to undertake may need approval by the larger agency, and this procedure may be laborious (Mancuso, 2015). If the host agency is funding the grief support process, there may be a great deal of micromanaging and oversight on its part. When group members have a high level of trust, knowledge, and cooperation, there may be few problems. When the lead organization is controlling or uneducated on grief topics, however, involvement becomes a hindrance. Which route originators of a grief support program take depends on the specific circumstances, including funds' availability.

After founders establish the need for the organization and define the goals, they can begin the tedious task of filing paperwork. Consult your state's website for specific instructions, but the first step in establishing a nonprofit is to decide upon a name and then file Articles of Incorporation. This application, once accepted, gives your nonprofit status as an official organization of the state. Your nonprofit will need by-laws and a board of directors who must meet at least once a year. The advantage of installing your group as an official nonprofit is that although the founders are listed as part of the group, it remains an entity of its own (Mancuso, 2015). In practical terms, this means that the financial aspects of the organization are separate from those of the individuals in the group. Being a documented, independent entity provides a level of security to show that an organization does not have access to a person's assets.

Part of the incorporation guidelines may include advertising in local publications (Mancuso, 2015). There are fees involved with many of these steps, which vary from state to state. It is difficult to obtain grants prior to the group's formation, but founders can perform internet searches to determine if there are any options in their area. Likewise, they can explore the possibility of enlisting a financial backer, whether an individual or business, who might donate money to the cause. If several organizers are involved, they may chip in and pool the money for the start-up fees. Since the costs are sequential and not simultaneous, it might be possible to fund this endeavor, eventually. You might find it useful determine all the costs prior to starting the process so that there are no surprises. Information is easily accessed online through government websites.

You will need a federal tax number, or EIN number, for your organization. Applying for this number is a simple process you can complete online. At the present time, there is no fee for getting this number, and once you submit the form, the system generates the organization's number (Mancuso, 2015). The charity should request or print the approval paperwork with the EIN number to include in the paper file. You will need this information when completing the paperwork for 501(c)(3) status and for opening a bank account.

Once the state recognizes your organization's name, you can offer services. If members hope to offer support groups involving children, purchasing liability insurance is essential. Shop around to get the best deal. Many agencies will work with you on costs, understanding that nonprofits have limited funding. Inquire about payment plans, which allows time for the group to fundraise to help finance the insurance costs.

Organizers must decide whether to apply for that federal 501(c)(3) status. This is a government designation of an organization as a national nonprofit, allowing for donations to the group to be tax deductible. If founders intend on any fundraising, this is an important label. Individual donors may wish to deduct their donations from their federal taxes, and they require the 501(c)(3) designation for this action. In addition, if the group plans to hold public fundraisers at other businesses, such as a family night at the local restaurant, those hosts will need the 501(c)(3) information for their own tax purposes. Applying for this federal status can be straightforward or confusing, depending on the size and complexity of the organization (Mancuso, 2015). Although the steps can be expensive and challenging to novices, being granted this nonprofit status improves the potential for successful fundraising and grant-securing and lends credibility to your charity.

The last step in becoming an official nonprofit is to register with your state. This gives you the green light to raise funds. Once again, regulations vary from state-to-state, so founders will need to check their state's requirements (Mancuso, 2015). If the organization plans to remain small (at least in financial terms), the group may be exempt from certain steps. Members can gather most of the needed information on the state's government website.

This chapter merely provides a brief overview on how to create a nonprofit; it is not meant to be specific advice. Although any ordinary citizen can acquire the pertinent information to start a charity organization, beginners can find it to be a complex and daunting task. Consulting a local lawyer is a great idea but be sure to choose someone familiar with your state's nonprofit laws. You might search for other citizens who have related skills. Many towns have local groups who will work with new endeavors, often free of charge. Willing people should be available and excited to help. Volunteers are necessary for all aspects of this endeavor, especially for performing the services once your organization is ready to go. Do not be reluctant to reach out for help and look for others who can further your mission to support grieving children and the adults in their lives.

Chapter 23

When Grief and Loss Hits the Community

On rare, unfortunate occasions, school personnel confront a situation in which the deceased individual is a student or adult within the actual school. In these cases, staff will encounter many children who are grieving, sometimes even an entire class. This circumstance is challenging because the large number of bereaved children involved and the variety of individual differences in coping styles create an overwhelming scenario. When the kids are of different ages, such as in a K-8 setting, the challenges are even greater.

In 1985, an Israeli Junior High School sent four busloads of seventh graders on a field trip to celebrate the end of the school year. An oncoming train tragically hit the first bus, killing 19 children, a parent chaperone, the teacher, and the driver. Another 15 students were critically injured. Passengers in the other three busses witnessed the deadly crash, while nine other busloads of classmates were in a separate convoy who overheard news of the crash via the bus radio. Four students were members of the class comprising the first bus occupants, but they remained at school instead of accompanying their peers on the trip. Needless to say, this situation required the need for intensive grief support and became one of the models studied by psychologists (Klingman, 1987).

In this circumstance, the school quickly found themselves forced to manage a large group of professionals and volunteers both from within the school and from the surrounding community. Some of those offering help, while well-intentioned, were not prepared for the enormity of the tragedy and could not emotionally distance themselves. Lack of coordination in the immediate aftermath created duplication of services and conflicting approaches. To handle these issues, officials established a command center and placed a local psychologist in charge of the support efforts. The first job was to triage and determine which groups needed immediate assistance, such as students injured in the crash, children who witnessed the accident, eighth and ninth graders back at the school, and so forth. Volunteers were then assigned to specific tasks, such as sitting with various groups of parents or talking to students. Staff members were provided with information and guidelines on how to react. They were taught signs of normal grief reactions and red flags signaling high-risk students. While the services were helpful, prior planning would have been extremely beneficial (Klingman, 1987). No one wants to consider this tragedy affecting their school and we readily avoid the topic. However, this Israeli case demonstrates how advanced preparation is a good idea. Moreover, this event illustrates

When Grief and Loss Hits the Community   139

that the effects of grief can persist over time, as some students reported difficulties months after the accident. However, this number was lower than expected, a fact attributed to the intensive support services made available to them immediately after the disaster (Milgram, Toubiana, Klingman, Raviv, & Goldstein, 1988). Individuals involved in such a tragic circumstance will vary in their needs, and helpers should be assigned specific tasks, such as advising classroom staff or offering mental health treatment to children or adults (Klingman, & Ben Ali, 1981; Toubiana, Milgram, Strich, & Edelstein, 1988). This level of organization requires forethought, especially when the heightened emotional atmosphere following a sudden tragedy will create confusion, not only in those who are helping but also in the grievers, who may not willingly seek help (Klingman, 1988).

Rather than be overwhelmed, educators who find themselves in this unenviable position should recognize the fact that grief on such a large scale can provide opportunities to teach lessons on loss. School-wide activities such as presentations or services can foster a sense of cohesion among the student body. Students may come together to meet a shared goal. They may raise money or support a cause related to the individual or the cause of death, like holding a bake sale or 5K race to raise money for Alex's Lemonade Stand or Mothers Against Drunk Drivers. We can involve kids in decisions on constructing a memorial project, such as planting trees or creating a garden on the school grounds. In these circumstances, children will not be alone in their grief, and they should realize that others are struggling with the same thoughts and feelings. We can use class time for group discussions, understanding that social and emotional learning facilitates academic time. Classroom rituals, such as an impromptu memorial ceremony or picture display, may meet with approval (Dyregrov et al., 1999). When grief distracts a student, learning about fractions or the victories of Revolutionary War generals are pointless tasks. Instructors can incorporate teachable moments and allow for constructive expression of feelings. The teachers can even maneuver these practices into the actual lesson plans. For example, studies of death customs may be relevant to a social studies unit or explored through reading or a book on in a language arts class. (Suggestions for age-appropriate books are listed in Appendix D.) Music and art classes can be valuable settings to suggest cathartic ways to cope. By approaching a school's collective grief head-on instead of trying to side-step it, educators can use the natural salve of shared grief to help everyone heal.

It is vital to remember that although grief may be communal, individual children will cope in unique ways depending on their cognitive maturity level, experience, personalities, and relationship to the deceased. We need to recognize children's uniqueness while helping them find common ground in their grief. Group discussions can be immensely helpful. By creating a social environment of acceptance and tolerance, teachers can encourage children to discuss the variety of thoughts and feelings they may be having. In a large group, at least one or two other participants can relate. Kids can suggest ideas for coping and sharing stories of their family's customs and ideas, this exchange of ideas disseminates information and promotes unity. Cohesion might decrease bullying and teasing. We need to explore and consider a variety of ways to encourage empathy.

140 How to Help Grieving Students

Teachers and other adults should be cognizant of the possibility that a few children isolate themselves. Bereavement often forces us to retreat into our own private shell. Withdrawal is borne from our fear or suspicion that our feelings are different, perhaps greater, than that of others. It is human nature to compare ourselves to others, even in grief. We may believe we are not grieving similarly to others in our midst. When we rank our expressions of grief and come up short, we find ourselves alienated. Kids are not immune to this cycle of perception, and wise educators can be sensitive to this grief "competition." Although this propensity is difficult to eliminate, encouraging sharing of feelings and group cohesion activities such as fundraisers and memorials can create a stronger sense of community within a classroom or school, the goal is to share the burdens, not create more sources of alienation and pain.

With public losses such as these, students may view the event egocentrically and develop worries and fears over their own safety. A classmate's death from a sudden illness, for instance, may generate concern over one's own health and well-being. If a popular lunch lady expires in a car accident, youngsters may be reluctant to be a passenger in their own cars. These are good opportunities for educators to discuss topics such as safety and preventive measures for various activities. For example, we can share information on illness transmission and methods to prevent the spread of germs. We can offer programs on driving and bicycle safety. School systems can offer courses in substance abuse and mental health. Bereaved children are emotionally vulnerable, and even if they do not express their fears, they are most likely worried that death is imminent for themselves or their loved ones. Although we should refrain from blanket promises or fake reassurances, helpful and truthful information cannot only ease fears but must also become a way to promote positive health and safety habits.

A student's suicide presents another unique circumstance. Many of us realize that there may be a copy-cat effect after such an event. The actions of other people may enable or encourage individuals who are struggling with depression and contemplating self-harm. Educators should know of this potentiality, watching for red flags. Suicide prevention services and education in schools are crucial, yet few schools offer them (Wass, Miller, & Thornton, 1990). Studies have suggested that when suicide strikes a school, strengthening the sense of community is crucial. If possible, students can be informed as a group to facilitate peer interactions. Disseminating information publicly decreases the chance for rumors or inaccuracies to spread. Routine and structure can provide a sense of normalcy. Helpers should focus on the emotional well-being of staff and children, since suicide creates a variety of mixed emotions in survivors (Klingman, 1989). When districts offer a death education curriculum, a unit on suicide and other forms of self-harm should be an essential part. Likewise, every staff member, including support personnel, should learn the warning signs of potential self-destructive behaviors following suicides or any other tragedy.

Occasionally, an event in the community at large may rock the entire school population. For example, natural disasters such as floods, storms, or earthquakes may have generated tremendous numbers of casualties near a school. Studies that have investigated events such as Hurricane Katrina emphasize the need for school-based

When Grief and Loss Hits the Community 141

supports after such a tragedy, including peer group formations and classroom discussions (Salloum & Overstreet, 2008; Salloum, Garside, Irwin, Anderson, & Francois, 2009). Tragedies like these will impact students in a variety of ways and on a multitude of levels. They may lose homes, belongings, or family members. Other kids may know friends who have experienced loss, vicariously connecting to grief. Regardless of the circumstances, youngsters may be anxious, sad, confused, and traumatized. The tendency to view negative events through the lens of "will this happen to me?" can create fear and panic in many school students as the town struggles to cope. Insecurity can multiply when a child witnesses the intensity and variety of adult reactions.

If the tragedy involved a violent event, responses may be significant and impactful on children's development. Researchers who studied kids after the Oklahoma City bombing discovered, unsurprisingly, that grieving children reported increased feelings of anxiety, arousal, fear, and other post-traumatic stress symptoms. The researchers discovered that these emotions persisted over time and predicted later psychological issues. Students reporting greater distress at the time of the death had more mental health issues over the years. One factor that contributed to the intensity of reactions was the media response to the event. Media attention was not always positive, and the reporting influenced how children remembered and processed the event (Pfefferbaum et al., 1999). Once again, the need to recognize children's reactions and attention to ways to support their grief is paramount in mitigating negative consequences surrounding death and loss. School-wide support services were useful in New York City after 9/11, those undertaken and led by trained personnel (Cohen, Goodman, & Brown, 2004)., the same service is helpful for any location exposed to violence or similar tragedy involving great numbers of losses.

Fears and anxieties are likely when the deaths follow a violent attack at the school itself. Mass shootings have occurred repeatedly in our society over the past few decades. The students experiencing an attack firsthand have a strong possibility of PTSD after hearing gunfire or seeing victims' bodies. Even kids without direct experience may find it easy to imagine being in the line of fire. When violence intrudes into our daily life by invading our physical environment, we find reminders of the horror everywhere. Children who attend a school that was a target of a school shooting are struggling over the loss of their friends, along with fear and anxiety that reemerges each time they revisit targeted areas. Survivor guilt may plague children and staff, and kids may regret words they said or actions they took. Students may wonder why they survived while others did not. If those "others" included a close friend, the chance or guilt increases. It is no wonder that many schools shut their doors and move to a different building after a mass shooting within their walls. It is difficult, if not impossible, to rebuild the sense of physical security necessary for students to thrive in a learning environment. Even in the new setting, much time, effort, and patience will be necessary, as many kids will find it hard to feel safe even in their new classrooms with blackened windows and double locks.

The sad truth of our world is nothing is guaranteed. No matter how much time, energy, and cash we spend trying to make our environment safe, we cannot ensure this. That does not mean we abandon our efforts. Preventative measures such

142 How to Help Grieving Students

as seat belts, smoke detectors, and vaccines have saved many lives. But even with today's knowledge and technology we will die and leave this material world someday. None of us are ever completely safe, and no one lives forever.

A death in the school drives home these truths to a young child. Teachers should not dwell on these anxiety-inducing truths, but it makes no sense to lie. In fact, lying does nothing but fosters distrust and drive a wedge between the liar and person on the receiving end. Vigilant teachers will make an enormous impact by encouraging support for their class, particularly when a peer has died (Dyregrov et al., 1999).

Although honesty is the best policy, reassurance is necessary, too. An adult does not have to dwell on every danger inherent in the world to recognize their accuracy. After losing a loved one, children know that death is a harsh reality. But it is comforting to understand that dying at a young age is *likely*. Telling a kid that most people recover from the flu is not a lie, while stressing how children are typically strong and healthy is an accurate statement, too. Without making false promises or empty guarantees, adults can focus on the optimistic side of things. In a school affected by violence, telling students that such an incident can never happen again is vague reassurance with no basis in reality, and the children see through this. Explaining that school shootings occur rarely and are even less likely to happen twice at the same place, is an honest statement that can be comforting. After loss, "mildly reassuring" may be the best you can offer.

How far should schools go in providing reassurance regarding safety after a violent event? This is a tricky question with no definitive answer. On the one hand, it is beneficial to secure the building and provide a solid measure of protection, such as installing locks and video cameras. School personnel should brainstorm about vulnerable areas and come up with ideas to improve those issues. Children's safety, along with their perception of their safety, is crucial in creating an environment that promotes their well-being and ability to learn. By going to extreme measures, however, a school may risk sending a message diametrically opposed to what is desirable. Metal detectors, locker and bag searches, and police officers patrolling the halls may make some students feel safer, while serving as constant reminders to others that danger is lurking at every turn. Most educators strive to make their school settings warm and welcoming, not intimidating like a prison. True, these protections may deflect trouble, but they also may remind us that school is unsafe. Moreover, the effectiveness of these measures is questionable. For example, many schools have instituted ID card systems for entering school facilities to make it difficult for intruders to gain access. Although this system may screen potential villains, most school shooters are students themselves, who will have their own ID and be able to use it to enter any area of the school they desire. Not that ID cards are a bad idea; the practice is harmless and easy to implement. The risk is being lulled into a false sense of security by enacting a multitude of security practices that may have limited value, and we need to be cognizant of the message we are sending to students through our attempts to keep schools secure. We want our kids to feel safe but not by shoving constant reminders of violence in their faces at every turn. It is a fine line to walk.

An example of this issue is the modern day's stranger or intruder drills. While earlier generations learned how to hide under their wooden desks from atomic bombs or how to react during a disaster such as fire or tornado, today's kids grow up practicing what to do if a dangerous person enters the building. This training is sadly necessary in our world today, as preparing children for this event has the potential to save lives. This drill has the potential to scare children, too (Quindlen, 2002). The teacher sets the tone of these practice sessions, and her pupils will look to her for guidance not only about what actions to take, but how to handle the stress. Some teachers of young children may opt to make this activity a game, ignoring the true purpose and avoiding giving kids that information. Others are more forthcoming about the rationale, but they can explain the odds of ever needing such information and model a calm demeanor. Adults struggle with the same balancing act between promoting vigilance and preventing unnecessary fear when teaching life lessons on stranger danger and inappropriate touching. We strive to protect our children and keep them as safe as possible, but we do not want them paralyzed with fear. The same dilemma is inherent in collective grief. Teachers will need to acknowledge the truth and create a climate of acceptance, while teaching skills and providing ways to vent feelings without overwhelming the students' emotional defense mechanisms. This is challenging but can be achieved through honesty and positive role modeling. We must tell children the truth, but disclosing gory details is unnecessary and unhelpful. Likewise, they need tools for coping and for protecting themselves, without focusing or exaggerating the negatives of life. Keeping these main ideas in mind when dealing with a school of grieving kids will be helpful but relying on the bonds of many is the best suggestion. Talk, share, and lean on each other for support. Grown-ups who handle grief and pick up the pieces after a devastating loss serve as strong role models for the children in their lives.

Chapter 24

When the Deceased Is a Pet

Suppose a child in your classroom is grieving, but the object of their heartbreak is a beloved pet instead of a human. As adults, most of us can empathize with feelings of despair that result when pets die. Children are no different, reacting with sadness when Rover or Fluffy pass away. This is a unique scenario, however, worthy of specific discussion. Pet grief is considered disenfranchised (Cordaro, 2012). When our animal friends pass on, we frequently mourn in silence and isolation, embarrassed by the extent of our feelings and worried about how others will react to our distress. Yet, those of us who are pet lovers can emphasize with the pain and emptiness one feels when a beloved companion leaves our world.

As a society, although we mourn the loss of our animal friends, we hold an implied assumption that furry, scaled, or feathered creatures are not as important as humans, and their deaths should not elicit the same level of emotional pain. Although many pet owners might disagree with this, it is implicit in our societal view of grief. When a family member dies, no one bats an eye at the bereaved taking time off from work or school. When a pet passes, bosses and principals might not be as understanding. There are usually no official funerals for our deceased pets, and most people do not send flowers, cards, or meals to families who are grieving a dog or cat (let alone a bird, or a snake, or a gerbil). The bonds we have with our animal friends, however, can be immensely strong. We attach to pets just as we connect to people, and children are no exception. (Gage & Holcomb, 1991; Hart, Hart, & Mader, 1990). As a child grows up, animals in the home occupy a special place in the child's heart. Spot can be a good listener when a child needs to vent; Whiskers is a loyal friend who loves and comforts. Children who help care for the pet may develop a level of mutuality and describe Fido and Kitty as their "best friends." The relationship we form with animals ensures that when they die, our grief can be traumatic or complicated (Packman, Bussolari, Katz, Carmack, & Field, 2017; Packman, Field, Carmack, & Ronen, 2011). Many of us remember losing a childhood pet. The loss hurts immensely, but with time, our memories usually become happy ones. A recently bereaved child is not yet able to recall Whiskers or Spot with a smile.

In accordance with many adults' beliefs that pet bereavement is not as valid as other types of grief, many parents will underestimate and misinterpret a child's reaction. Adults might consider dealing with the death of the family dog or cat as a mere "rehearsal for the real thing" that will happen when a human dies (Corr & Corr, 2007) Taking this view does a disservice to a child who cannot see the

When the Deceased Is a Pet   145

distinction; losing a loved one is just that—the absence of an attachment object. Parents need to understand that this loss can be just as intense as others, and the level of sadness can be because of the same factors, such as level of bonding, frequency of contact, and specific role the animal played in the child's life. Although it may seem inappropriate to us adults, a child may be more distraught over the death of the family canine than the loss of a grandmother who lived far away. Keep in mind that our role as grief facilitators is not to judge but to empathize and help the child cope. The first part of this task is the awareness of how a loss of a pet can create emotional upheaval for a young person.

As is true in cases of other losses, factors such as cognitive understanding of death, emotional resilience, family structure, and history of coping with previous losses can influence a child's reactions. But the death of a pet has unique circumstances. For example, adults may believe it to be acceptable, even preferable, to lie about what happened to Buddy or Sassy. Many parents may tell the child that their furry friend just ran away or rehomed to a "farm" out of town. Although well-intentioned, these falsehoods are not doing the child any favors in the long run. Kids may fear they failed their pet, in that the dog or cat was so miserable at home that they left, abandoning them. They may worry that the animal is alone or not cared for properly. Guilt and confusion complicate bereavement. The child must cope with the loss of a friend in any event, but believing that the animal is happy and healthy in a new environment without him may magnify a child's sense of pain and hurt surrounding the pet's absence. Ambiguity does not allow for any sense of closure.

Euthanasia is a unique situation. As the child's educator, you will not play a role in this decision, but you may need to handle any fallout. If children were present when their dog or cat was put down, they may struggle to cope. Others may have the pet's fate explained to them euphemistically, with parents using terms such as "put to sleep." Because of the tendency interpret language literally, kids may never understand what truly happened to their pet. If the child was present when the pet was euthanized, he may be struggling with a host of questions, since an animal that dies in this manner truly looks as if it is merely sleeping. As their teacher, you may find it useful to touch base with a child's parents so that the adults can be on the same page with helping a child cope. Realizing that a young student may have no familiarity with euthanasia will help you empathize with a child who has lost a pet in this way.

In Western society, there are few mourning rituals for pets, at least when compared to the established ways we grieve for humans. There may be no ceremony or official chance to say goodbye, creating more guilt and emotional distress for kids. The lack of rituals means fewer chances to accept the loss. Adults are likely to hurry a child through the bereavement after an animal dies. Backyard funerals may be rushed and off-the-cuff, if they occur at all. Ambiguity can surround the fate of the animal's remains, since we do not care for pets' bodies with the same level of respect as we do for humans. Often the deceased pet is not buried or cremated, so no formal resting place or memorial is available for paying respects. Even worse, the body may be treated irreverently, perhaps just thrown in the trash. This is very common when the pet is a rodent, reptile, or fish. Grown-ups may see no problem with flushing Fishy down the toilet, but a preschooler may cringe as their loved one departs

146 How to Help Grieving Students

to an undignified gravesite. Adults need to respect their child's point of reference in helping with the grief.

The lack of meaningful rituals can interfere with any sense of closure, increasing the difficulty for some kids to accept the reality of the pet's death. The sense of impatience and intolerance of grief for pet hamsters and goldfish create feelings of alienation and guilt in young children. A preschooler may not understand why Mom and Dad are not upset about the death of Slimy the snake. A third-grader may have trouble comprehending why a teacher gives a failing grade on the homework that was incomplete because of mourning for Hoppy, the family bunny. Kids, if not the adults in the home, consider animals as bona fide family members (Kaufman & Kaufman, 2006). The deaths require no less time to acknowledge, mourn, and accept.

A child mourning their doggy or kitty cat may exhibit the same signs and behaviors as a child coping with any other loss of a loved one. The major difference is the lack of acceptance of this grief by others, and adults who overlook the intensity of this loss will ignore the effects on a child's emotional and cognitive well-being. Older kids may consciously attempt to hide their sadness, feeling embarrassed by the magnitude of their reaction. Teachers should realize how deeply the death of a pet may affect a child. As in cases of other types of grief, support and empathy can go a long way in helping a child handle the heartbreak when their beloved dogs, cats, hamsters, and other animal friends die. Validating someone's grief may be enough to provide a bit of comfort. Remember that this grief reaction is the real deal, not just a trial run. Coping skills learned in this circumstance are transferable to later encounters with the loss of a loved one.

Chapter 25

Grief During the Holidays

In their book entitled *The Empty Chair: Handling Grief at Holidays and Special Occasions* (2001), authors Susan Zonnebelt-Smeege and Robert De Vries describe grief as a "firestorm." They equate grief with the devastation and destruction caused by the whirlwind of flame and heat that occurs in the natural disaster that is a wildfire. To take this analogy a step further, we might consider grief that is often smoldering after the intense and obvious first wave of fire first strikes. Any wind that stokes the dormant blaze can rekindle the embers of a fire. Such is the case with grief. After the initial blaze has wreaked its havoc, the raging fire may diminish, at least on the surface. But as any bereaved person can attest, a spark can reignite the fires of pain and loss. Holidays can be one such spark, and as educators who work with students through a long year of special occasions and events, we must realize that innocent comments and activities can trigger a grief "flash point" in a child.

Grief intensifies during holidays for several reasons. The extended winter holidays are especially challenging because reminders of the season are ubiquitous. We find it hard to avoid the inundation of commercials or decorations that appear before Halloween. There are scores of holiday shows and movies. People perceive pressure to spend good times with family and friends. This time of the year may generate nostalgia in even the most stoic of us. The myriad of reminders of our youth and our past are too strong. For a bereaved person, the loved one's absence is glaringly obvious. Reminders of the loved one everywhere, from the empty seat at the holiday dinner table to the extra money in our pocket resulting from one fewer present on the gift list. Watching others, real or fictional, immersed in family fun and exuding happiness and joy, only serves to remind us how much we are hurting. No matter where we turn, something triggers painful memories.

To make matters worse, we may experience guilt when having fun. Society places a subtle pressure on us to enjoy special occasions, and when not in the proper mood, we may resemble Scrooge for not wanting to join in the fun and camaraderie of the season. The pressure to be joyful is intense. Consider how at Thanksgiving, for example, the emphasis is on gratitude and appreciation for what we have. This is a noble ideal but one that is immensely difficult for someone who is coping with a devastating loss. It is impossible to see past grief long enough to recognize the remaining things for which to be thankful. In time, the griever will appreciate the positive aspects of life. Gratitude usually returns, but it takes time. The insistence of others to "look at the bright side" and remember that "at least you have X, Y, Z" only serves to magnify the guilt the person already feels.

148 How to Help Grieving Students

Teachers and educators should realize that holidays are likely to be very difficult for a child who has experienced a loss. He imagines how different his holidays will be, and the upbeat moods of classmates frustrate him. Adults may be sensitive with children who are grieving a close family member, but other losses may also trigger painful emotions and memories. For instance, first-grader Claire can ignore Grandma's death for most of the year, but her absence is obvious at Thanksgiving dinner. Reminders will bombard bereaved child, both at home and in school.

School staff should expect that even minor holidays can trigger grief. Special care is crucial in a class when students are discussing holiday plans or making gifts for family members. The child whose father has died may become upset when the rest of the students are decorating pencil holders for Father's Day gifts. Even when the death occurred years before the current date, the loss is still real and there is no recipient for the gift. Bereaved kids can join in these discussions and projects; most children have another person in their lives who can serve as a substitute. The truth is obvious to both the child and the other kids, however. Making the gift for Uncle Steve instead of Dad certainly allows the child to take part in the art project, but this switch may emphasize how different this child's life is from the others, magnifying the hole in his life.

Does the desire to avoid triggering a grieving child mean that teachers should avoid discussions of special holidays or change lesson plans? Not necessarily. It is an unfortunate fact of life that the bereaved child must learn ways to cope with reminders. There is no way to avoid this circumstance in everyday life, even if a sensitive educator excludes the topic from her classroom. In fact, avoidance typically does the child a disservice, since he or she will need to learn ways of handling these issues. Sensitivity is the key to supporting the child through the special days of the year. Teachers should know that holidays intensify feelings of grief and be mindful of the specific circumstances of the child's loss, altering projects and comments to accommodate bereaved students. If the teacher knows that Sarah has lost her dad, for example, she can suggest that students choose a "special man" in their lives as the recipient for the Father's Day pencil holder. Not only does this allow Sarah to take part without singling her out, but it has the added advantage of allowing other children with varied relationships to choose which man is filling the role of "dad" in their lives. This approach is helpful in allowing inclusion of kids whose losses might have occurred years ago, including ones of which you, as the teacher, may not even be aware. Remember, holidays can stir up memories of losses that are not recent. Sometimes, they can remind kids of loved ones who died before they were born or had little to no relationship to them. Although these kids may not experience the loss directly, they are still affected by the reminiscences of others. Their loss deserves respect, too.

One other potential problem relates to comments made by the other children. A class discussion on Mother's Day plans may remind the students that Karen has no mother, emphasizing Karen's plight. Unfortunately, kids can be brutally honest and may be quick to comment. Sometimes others make those remarks innocently. For example, 4-year-old Tommy is not intending to cause pain by posing an honest question to Karen ("What do you do on Mother's Day since you don't have a Mommy?"), but she will sense the sting, nonetheless. Karen is too young to realize Tommy's motivation. Other times, kids purposely inflict emotional harm. A few may find the circumstances funny and use this as fodder for teasing Karen about making her Mother's Day vase for Aunt Jenny instead of a mother. As educators know, children who are harassing a fellow student often know how to do so clandestinely. As unthinkable as it sounds, teachers need to realize that a minority of children will make negative comments or even resort to bullying a grieving child. Whether this behavior results from projected fear, lack of knowledge, or just meanness, the teacher's job is to intervene and protect the target of such inexcusable behavior. The child reeling from this painful interaction may not be in any emotional place to defend himself.

Holidays can be an excellent time to broach the subject of diversity. In today's world, children come from a variety of family structures. Children's varying cultures will create differences in views on death as well as on the holidays themselves. Discussing alternate viewpoints can not only generate attitudes of tolerance but can open the umbrella of inclusion. These circumstances are a great opportunity to teach correct information, too. Bullying results when kids do not adequately understand someone else's view, or when they are scared or intimidated. By disseminating facts, teachers can help children learn the truth about the world. Instructors can then encourage students to better understand the perspectives of others. Loosening the reins of egocentrism is an arduous process but one that adults can help by asking the right questions and suggesting ideas that encourage empathy.

For example, we can consider Karen's third grade class. Karen's mom died a few years ago from cancer, and the other children know she is now motherless. Several of these peers may react negatively to Karen out of fear that they, too, will lose a mother. Others are just not adroit at standing in Karen's moccasins and understanding how life is for her. An upcoming special day like Christmas or Hanukah opens the door for general discussions on alternative family structures and the positives qualities found in all of them. A teacher can ask students to role play scenarios, placing themselves in unfamiliar settings and dilemmas. While it is not the teacher's place to discuss Karen's specific case or promote theological points of view, ensuring that kids have good information is an appropriate course of action. Truth dispels rumors, which, in turn, limits false information and lies that generate teasing, bullying, and other forms of emotional mistreatment.

Anniversary dates are often triggering events for a grieving child, too. Similar to traditional holidays, these dates evoke feelings of nostalgia. These anniversaries are typically birthdays and death dates of the deceased, and the emotions that are generated can run the gamut. Unlike reactions to major holidays, though, these special dates are often known only to the griever and her family (Zonneblet-Smeenge & DeVries, 2001). While some children may share information, others will probably refrain from telling anyone that today is Mom's birthday or the anniversary of when Dad suffered his heart attack. Nevertheless, these times are meaningful to a bereaved child, and she may seem distracted, withdrawn, or overly emotional. As a nonfamily member, you may never know the true significance of such a date to a child, but it would be wise to keep this possibility in mind when a mourning student suddenly has an uncharacteristically bad day.

As professionals with a background in child development, the family may seek you out as a resource for helping their child through the holidays. Included in Appendix L is a list of tips to make available to parents who ask for practical advice.

Chapter 26

The Need for Grief Education, Planning, and Training

Having familiarized themselves with information on grief and childhood development, educators may realize they unprepared to apply this knowledge in their schools, especially on a widespread level. Doing so may be a daunting task, given the plethora of information and the variety of circumstances in which a teacher may find herself. Psychologists rely on patterns to form theories and proceed with research. Although we can discuss general patterns of grief responses, we must consider the variety of individual differences in scenarios and reactions. Breen and O'Connor (2007) focus on this "paradox" within the grief literature. They argue that sometimes professionals may recognize that grief is individual but still try to force this reaction into a metaphoric box of "normal grief." They suggest that one way to mitigate the ramifications of these dueling perspectives is to broaden the scope and availability of death education.

Research has supported the positive effects of a death education curriculum, even among preschoolers (Bailis & Kennedy, 1977; Galende, 2015; McClatchey & Peters, 2015). Since the experience of losing a loved one is a universal life lesson, it makes sense to include suggestions for effective coping skills and practical information as a topic in a health and wellness course or a unit in a biology class. School districts are increasing their focus on social and emotional learning, working with students to improve ways of regulating feelings and behaviors. Countless high schools offer psychology coursework. Grief education fits naturally into lesson plans for any of these offerings, yet we often ignore or de-emphasize the topic (Busch & Kimble, 2001; Wass, 2000, 2004). We need not discuss this topic within the format of a predetermined course but can incorporate it into related topics. We do not assume students can handle other life challenges without a little background knowledge, so it makes sense to tackle grief and loss similarly.

Educators themselves have acknowledged the need for preparation to support grieving students. In several surveys-based studies, teachers reported that they did not feel qualified to help bereaved kids (Reid & Dixon, 1999). Most teachers admit to having little to no training, either during their formal education courses or via in-service programs (Densen, Lansworth, & Siegel, 2012; Jenkins, Dunham, & Contreras-Bloomdahl, 2011; Ober, Granello, & Wheaton, 2012; Potts, 2013; Rosenthal & Terkelson, 1978). More astonishingly, many school counselors, psychologists, and nurses also claimed to have little to know exposure to grief work during their training (Dillon, 2012; Riely, 2003; Rosenthal, 1981; Seadler, 2000). This situation

Grief Education, Planning, and Training   151

is a travesty, given that the guidance counselor is often the first stop for both parents and staff when a psychological issue is at hand. The need for more effective preparation for these individuals is crucial (Glass, 1990). Teachers are on the front lines in the interaction with grieving students, and we should make any attempt to educate and increase their comfort level with bereavement. Pupils may be reluctant to seek help or start painful conversations, and the adults will appreciate support and guidance to help them step up and meet the needs of the students (Atkinson, 1980; Barry & McGovern, 2000; Glass, 1990; Lowton & Higginson, 2003). Studies have shown that professional development can alter death attitudes in staff, increasing their comfort level in discussing the topic and easing death anxiety (Molnar-Stickels, 1985). Moreover, knowledge about grief reactions encourages patience and understanding so that the bereaved student is not perceived as a mere behavior problem (James & Friedman, 2001).

Unfortunately, most professionals who could use this education have not, historically, been provided much opportunity. Studies show that less than 20% of students in health fields were offered significant death education during their training. Other research found that most students in relevant fields claimed that information on this topic was limited in scope and relied too heavily on models that emphasized "normal" grief patterns (Dickinson & Field, 2002; Dickinson, Sumner, & Frederick, 1992). School psychologists, too, report inadequate training in grief counseling. Even when these individuals are well-trained, overburdened schedules do not always allow for much grief work. Society needs to do more to prepare professionals and support staff for their work with the bereaved. Educators, classroom teachers in particular, are professionals who need this information and guidance. Although teachers-in-training rarely consider that the advantages from learning ways to interact with grieving students, the law of averages suggests that eventually they will come face to face with this unfortunate life lesson. Recognizing the lack of preparedness has rallied calls to action in creating, offering, and expanding trainings for school-based professionals.

Schools and communities typically ignore grief education for students and staff until the need arises immediately after a traumatic event. Too often, personnel merely react to a tragedy within a specific building, making grief counselors available for a limited time after a student or teacher dies. This plan has limited use, and we must remember that young people may have delayed reactions that occur long after the imported grief counselors have returned to their normal schedules. Students in a state of shock in the immediate aftermath of a crisis may not be in the best position to ask for help or recognize the importance of support. Although materials, services, and information should be readily available to everyone after a tragedy, the emotional vulnerability makes it difficult to offer a lengthy grief and bereavement in-service training. Experts have recommended that school districts be proactive in formulating a grief plan, just as they have protocols for other contingencies, such as natural disasters and violence in the buildings (Dyregrov, 1991; Lima & Gittleman, 2004; Wass, 2000).

Preparations should be thorough, but do not need to be time consuming. Professional development is essential, but training can be limited in scope, provided by in-house staff familiar with the topic or by inviting local counselors or therapists to the school. Disseminated information should focus on topics such as children's perception of death; manner in which young people might express grief both at home and in the classroom; ways in which to interact with the grieving child, his peers, and his family; recognition of the immediate and long-term effects of grief; understanding red flags that might indicate severe or problematic reactions; and knowing specific behaviors and practices that educators can use to offer support. While death is not a comfortable topic, keeping the subject taboo creates a state of silence, ensuring that teachers may find themselves unprepared and ill-equipped to teach a grieving child. Districts should make resources available, including fact sheets and a directory of community members who could offer support. Administrators could reach out to other organizations or individuals, creating a network that is ready when needed (Dyregrov, 2009). If an entire in-service time is unavailable, a brief session at a teachers' meeting can offer enough information to improve sensitivity and increase the comfort level of school personnel.

Specialized trainings should be targeted to support and auxiliary staff, too. For example, Bazyk (2007) suggests utilizing occupational therapists in ways that help children who are grieving. Speech therapists, music and art teachers, and other itinerant instructors bring unique skills and perspectives to the school. Paraprofessionals should be included in trainings for awareness, too. A grieving child may comment to any adult whom they trust, including lunchroom staff and custodians. Sensitivity trainings are invaluable, and information sessions can be short and to the point.

Organizations such as the American Red Cross suggest that people learn how to give psychological first-aid after a tragic event, just as many of us learn physical first aid. This approach stresses that in the immediate wake of a trauma, victims require certain things. First, they need to feel safe and confident that their physical needs will be met. A brief plan for the next steps should then be discussed, and support systems should be made available. Focus on factual and complete information is crucial so that informed decisions can be made (Vernberg, 2002). No one can cope with reality when the details are unclear or inaccurate.

As for death education aimed at the students themselves, we can incorporate the material into traditional health courses. Similar topics. such as coping with stress and recognizing mental health problems, are typically included in the physical education coursework, so expanding the topics to include the issues of death and dying is not a big leap. Even young children can be taught the meaning of grief and given tools for coping. (Most students in one of my middle school support groups admitted they were completely unfamiliar with the word "grief.") For older students, we can introduce existential questions such as why death occurs or the existence of an afterlife, triggering the expressions of honest opinions and attitudes (Ulin, 1977). Even if the need is not immediate, this information will be useful at some point during one's lifetime. Learning coping skills to handle negative emotions is a valuable part of any school's emotional and social learning curriculum.

Several published curricula are available, and I have included many in the in the Appendices. Educators can broach the topic informally, too, via classroom discussions that allow for controlled venting of feelings and a forum in which to ask questions. Bibliotherapy is useful, and a large selection of stories, books, and poems focus on the topics of death and grief. (An annotated bibliography is in the Appendices.)

We can teach children via role-playing activities or simulation games, techniques that are highly effective (Klingman, 1983, 1988). Regardless of the specific method used, grief education should be nonjudgmental and nonthreatening.

Training is not the only requirement in a grief preparation program. Staff members need personal support services that are quickly in place in times of tragedy. Survey responses indicate that educators rely on other professionals to assist them. Whether this help is in the form of information, advice, or support, classroom teachers admitted that coping with bereavement in school is challenging and emotionally training. Patience is necessary as students' behaviors will vary from child to child, and from time to time. Respondents also emphasized that programs and policies should be proactive, not reactive (Hart & Garza, 2013). They understand the importance of planning and having a protocol in place before the need arises. When it comes to confronting grief in our educational institutions, it is a matter of when, not if. It behooves us all to be prepared.

As with sex education, educators should keep parents informed about when and how they will present this material. Most of the time, staff should refrain from emphasizing religious ideas and welcome the diversity of viewpoints. Educators, at least in a public-school setting, should be neutral on sensitive topics, keeping in mind that students come from a variety of spiritual backgrounds. Although we should never ignore students' questions, teachers should avoid becoming too dogmatic or preaching subjective views. It is better to use such inquiries as teachable moments on diversity and tolerance, recognizing that different individuals have varying opinions on this topic. Students may have strong opinions, and educators might struggle to allow alternate viewpoints from being ridiculed or squelched. If a class is interested in this topic, this might be a good opportunity to incorporate cultural variations regarding death and dying into a social studies unit.

For death education and support services to be successful, both teachers and parents need to buy in to the endeavor. Through training and their own personal experiences with bereaved students, educators should recognize the potential value of grief support (Alisic, 2012). Once teachers are on board with the program, their enthusiasm can help elicit approval from parents. Through informational meetings, written material, and social media outlets, we can enlighten parents and guardians about the benefits of these supports (Jones, Hodges, & Slate, 1995; Barry & McGovern, 2000).

The goal of death education in the schools is not to eat up valuable academic time but to foster emotional growth and social understanding. As we know, distressed children will be distracted and unfocused. Whatever educators can do to foster their psychological development will undoubtedly affect academic performance in ways both direct and indirect. According to Wass (2000), the most important need of bereaved children is to feel safe, assured that their needs will be met with empathy and concern. Coping and support skills are not innate, we learn them. Death, dying, and bereavement are universal experiences. We become stronger from instruction on these topics and related curricula should have a place in our schools.

Chapter 27

Resilience

In addition to the terms trauma and attachment, the word resilience has become a buzzword recently. In trauma courses, we learn how to help people become resilient. The term refers to the ability to overcome challenges, adapt to hardships, and bounce back from adversity (American Psychological Association, n.d.). To an extent, everyone is resilient. If not, any little challenge or setback would defeat us, preventing us from trying or even living, depending on the challenge. If psychologist Rollo May is correct in his assumption that we "do not become fully human painlessly," then challenges in life are to be expected (Cacciatore, 2017; May, 1978). It stands to reason that we are programmed to not only overcome but thrive in the face of adversity (Hone, 2017; Rasmussen, 2019). The same is true with grief: most of us will rebound, moving on with our changed lives. But does resilience mean forgetting our struggles, or surviving with no effects? A bird with a broken wing may very well survive, and he may even thrive in the best of circumstances. But he will not fly again. His life has been irrevocably changed.

Semantics is the problem when contemplating issues such as resilience. What does it mean to adapt and move past our hurt? Some researchers claim that the majority of people, children included, navigate bereavement well. They explain how mourners take time to grieve but then move on, picking up the pieces of their lives. A term like grief recovery indicates a state in which the individual has overcome emotional pain. To illustrate this point, researchers have provided examples and statistics indicating that most individuals return to their normal activities after a reasonable period. They deny feelings of continued intense sadness or psychological symptoms, and most can speak of happy memories involving the deceased (Bonanno, 2009; Bonanno & Mancini, 2008; James & Friedman, 2009; Sprang & McNeil, 1995). Parents add children to their family, spouses remarry, and friends form new relationships. All of us encounter grief and loss, and we usually do "recover" enough to go on with our lives without living in eternal sadness. If this is our definition of resilience, then our actions fit this well.

But just as grief is unique, resilience is, too. While life goes on after a loved one dies, it does so in novel ways that can be uncomfortable or intimidating. We adjust, largely because we have no choice. It is human nature to survive, and the will to live contributes to our ability to move past grief. The question is whether there are permanent changes. When we have a sinus infection and the doctor treats us with antibiotics, we say we have recovered. Usually, we mean that the virus or bacteria

Resilience   155

is gone. We are now healthy and symptom-free, having returned to our pre-illness state of normalcy. However, if we lose a limb through amputation, do we completely recover? While the wound itself may heal, we will not grow a new arm or leg. Our bodies are permanently altered. We will learn new ways of living, and we could consider these adjustments as recovery. After a time, the "new normal" becomes merely "normal"—for us. We have adapted to the stressor, but it forever changes us. The issue does not disappear or resolve. We learn to cope. And we remember how things used to be.

The potential problem inherent in books that discuss recovery and resilience lies in interpreting the terms (Kauffman, 2008). A few authors claim that most people "get over" their grief, implying pushing it into the past and preventing its intrusion into the present (Bonanno, 2009; Kauffman, 2008). As we have seen with children, experiences with loss early in life may rewire neural connections. Relationships transform and environments change. Unexpected course corrections in life are not always negative, but they require adjustments. To imply that people who recover from grief do not feel its sting may frustrate kids who continue to hurt for the long term, triggering guilt and inadequacy. Other experts admit that owning our sorrow and speaking of our pain may not prolong our grief but help us cope. We need to give our children permission to experience their emotions without judgment or worse, condemnation. We should respect individual differences in coping (Johnson, 1998; Mancini & Bonanno, 2009; Smith, 2004). Once a person understands that there is no definitive right way to grieve, a load is lightened.

Moreover, the effects of tremendous grief may not manifest for years. By that time, making connections may be difficult. Although many people claim to be back to normal eventually, how can we be sure that residual effects will not surface? For example, the results of my Ursinus study showed significant differences in GPA, anxiety level, and hypochondria between groups who suffered a traumatic loss from those who did not. These findings validate other studies that have described fallout from grief occurring ten years or more after the death. When the loss occurred in childhood, consequences such as substance use may begin during the volatile teenage period (Walter & McCoyd, 2015). Other research has suggested prolonged physiological responses, including altered levels of stress hormones (Saavedra Perez et al., 2017). In many cases, a loss affects an individual's sense of personal identity (Kauffman, 2008; McCoyd, Walter, & Lopez-Levers, 2012). This dynamic may manifest through new interpersonal roles ("Now I am an orphan) to one's perception as an experienced mourner ("I always feel sad but have to act brave"). Since the events occurred years prior to these studies, we cannot definitively connect these differences to the loss. We cannot prove cause and effect with this self-report data, and so we can never be sure whether a problem or symptom that first appears in adolescence had its roots in a loss from years ago. But it is very possible. Without falling into the trap of blaming every issue on our childhood experiences, we must remain open to the potential for an early loss to affect us years down the road. These effects can be positive or negative. One of my sons, at the age of 10, experienced the death of a beloved teacher. He was sad and struggled with his grief for a few weeks as he gradually accepted the loss and continued with his daily activities. He rarely spoke of this teacher over the years, but when he did, the accompanying emotions

156 How to Help Grieving Students

were positive. His memories were good ones. Years later, though, as a young adult, he now acknowledges how her death affected him more intensely than he realized at the time. A decade passed until he recognized the anger and sadness, and those emotions likely triggered issues in adolescence. On a positive note, her death generated a strong sense of empathy and connectedness in him. This painful experience left indelible marks on his psyche.

It is therefore important to stress resilience not as a way of forgetting and acting as if the loss never occurred or does not still hurt. Remember that a person's response to a specific loss depends on many factors, including the relationship to the deceased, attachment style, manner of death, history of other losses, accumulation of other stressors in the environment, personal characteristics such as age and personality, and social factors such as support systems (Worden, 1996). Cultural and religious experiences, too, contribute to resilience (Cox, 2013; Mancini & Bonanno, 2006). Although we understand that grief is unique, we must be mindful that resilience is, too. While certain reactions to loss, such as major depression, substance abuse, and suicidality are clearly negative, positive responses are not as easy to describe or even recognize. For example, one survivor may take solace in attending to a gravesite; for another, this activity generates pain and sadness. A bereaved family member may find it helpful to raise awareness for a cause, while others cope better by focusing on unrelated activities. While finding meaning and purpose after a loss is important, the exact nature of that task will vary from person to person (Hooyman & Kramer, 2006). We each have our own way, and the same is true for children.

We should recognize the positive changes that grief can generate. Some individuals refer to the "gifts" they have received as they struggled to reorganize and reconstruct their lives during the bereavement process (Bush, 1997). After losing a loved one, many survivors report increasing levels of empathy and kindness toward others. Learning the reality of life's transience can foster an attitude of gratitude and appreciation for the present. Those of us left behind often report a new sense of purpose, whether to fulfill the ambitions of the deceased or to achieve personal goals. We may focus on our "bucket lists" with renewed urgency. We develop continuing bonds with the deceased through positive memories. Our relationships may others may become stronger. Children may incorporate the loss into their life plans, including a choice of career (Attig, 2000; McCoyd & Walter, 2014; Neimeyer, Baldwin, & Gillies, 2006; Packman et al., 2017). For many years, I considered a future in medicine as a direct reaction to my brother's death from leukemia. Although I abandoned those plans, my focus on psychology and grief research is obviously an alternative method of finding meaning and purpose out of my loss. Grief can sometimes paralyze us, especially when new and raw, or when it is prolonged or triggers mental health issues such as PTSD or major depressive episodes. Conversely, it may serve as a great motivator. Loss, grief, and trauma can be considered the source of much of our personal development (Bush, 1997; McCoyd et al., 2012). Currier, Holland, and Neimeyer (2012) suggest that the potential for learning and growing after traumatic grief varies with the level of our suffering. Too much or too protracted a grief period may be detrimental to the psyche, and less intense bereavement is not significant enough to leave a big impression. Moderate levels of grief, however, were shown to stimulate high levels of psychological growth. Maybe the phrase "no pain, no gain" applies mental and emotional hardiness just as it refers to physical strength.

Sometimes, the greatest gift we receive from the pain of loss is the knowledge that we can, in fact, survive. We learn how to tap into our internal reserves and continue with life and fill our toolboxes of coping skills. Most of us discover new ways to meet tough challenges, and we realize who are friends are. Even losing a pet generates psychological growth after a mourning period (Packman et al., 2011; Packman et al., 2017) With the passage of time, it becomes easier to remember our loved ones with positive feelings along with the painful ones. We figure out how to continue our bonds with the deceased without drowning in sorrow and heartache. Unfortunately, there is no other way to learn these lessons but to experience loss firsthand.

As educators who support grieving kids, we know grief is a rocky road for our students that must travel it. Each loss, and each surviving loved one, is unique. The goal is to meet reality head on, change direction if needed, and continue our life's journey. When we use the term "accept" in terms of loss, it should not mean that we become complacent about it. Freud's idea that grieving involves breaking the bonds and separating with the deceased is typically impossible and, most likely, not useful in learning to cope (Freud, 1986). Death of a loved one is really not OK, it just *is*. Being resilient and "recovering" from grief does not mean "getting over it" with the implication that the event, and the loved one, will never again generate feelings of sadness. Although most of us have within our psyche a natural resilience, we need support to hasten our healing from the pain of loss (Dilworth & Hildreth, 1997). In the book, *The Other Side of Sadness*, the author describes grief as a wave, not a step-by-step, stage-oriented process (Bonanno, 2009). Feelings of sadness ebb and flow, sometimes with little warning. While we ride dramatic dips in the waves, crests can create a positive force, too. For some of us, the tides of grief may be low, while others, the tide is high. The goal of coping with grief is to build a secure boat to ride the waters, both up and down the waves. If our vessel is sturdy and flexible enough, we will survive the tide and make it to other shores. Of course, storms and winds may make our waters rough at any time. True resilience means understanding that fact, having confidence in the fact that our boat will keep us safe, regardless of in which sea we find ourselves. Moreover, it means that we learn from our experiences, building a lifetime of memories. As supporters of young people, your job is to help them stay afloat by providing support and empathy, so they know they have help along the way. Being a good captain takes many skills and the ability to change course when needed. Know as much information as possible and then trust your instincts. Your experience matters, and so will your natural concern for children. Sailing the seas together is infinitely better than navigating on your own.

Chapter 28

A Few Final Thoughts

Gone are the days in which society ignored the emotional lives of children. Today we assume that the childhood environment molds and directs the person we become in adulthood. The ACE study (Felitti et al., 1998) has opened our collective eyes to the concerns of chronic childhood trauma. Psychologists such as William Worden have helped to shine a spotlight on how children grieve. I hope we have come a long way toward knowledge and enlightenment from his 1996 book, *Children and Grief*. His work opens with the question "Do Children Mourn?" as if implying that in years past, the conventional wisdom was that kids were immune from the effects of a loss in the family. Today, we are sensitive to the emotional and psychological needs of young people. We recognize that although the event that starts the grief process—the death itself—may be just one event in a child's life, the consequences of the loss have no expiration date. The pain of loss is a constant ache, a reminder of the lost love. It is therefore reasonable to assume that grief, too, is a chronic source of stress. Research has shown that mourning refers to a lost attachment, so strengthening other relationships can help to lessen the pain of loss (Ludy-Dobson & Perry, 2010). With this thought it mind, our focus should turn toward cultivating bonds with students that encourage personal growth along with academic achievement. It is time for us to be cognizant of how grief can invade a child's life and create issues at home, school, and wherever else the child ventures. As guardians of the place where children spend a great part of their lives, educators have a responsibility to empathize with the ways in which children grieve. We should be mindful of how bereavement manifests in school. School staff form strong attachments to our youth and have an incredible influence on their lives. By acting with knowledge and sensitivity, we can be life preservers. We have the chance to help students navigate the rip tide of grief.

Appendices

Appendices

Appendix A

Statistical Results of Childhood Traumatic Loss Survey Study, Ursinus College (2016)

We performed independent sample t-tests to analyze responses, focusing on the relationship between perceived trauma level and other variables. Data was split on trauma level in order to form two groups. The high level included losses reported as 5 or greater in severity on a Likert scale (with an upper limit of 7), while the low level included losses rated less than 5 or no loss at all. Several statistically significant findings were found in the following areas, with participants in the high trauma group demonstrating (with the high trauma group listed first):

- Lower GPAs [M = 3.1566, SD = .422, M = 3.3168, SD = .432, t (310) = 3.250, p = .001].
- Higher levels of anxiety [M = 30.91, SD = 12.29; M = 28.03, SD = 11.91; t (303) = 2.046, p = .042].
- Increased levels of hypochondria, including a greater focus on illness and increased worry about potential health problems [M = 20.91, SD = 2.519 M = 22.03, SD = 2.296; t (301) = 4.017, p = .000]
- An external locus of control, exhibiting the tendency to view life events as out of their personal control [M = 9.14, SD = 1.157; M = 8.88, SD = 1.135, t (306) = 1.989, p = .048].

A Pearson correlational analysis was also conducted, and results demonstrated a significant negative correlation between trauma level and overall health. [r (314) = −.207, p =.000]

A significant relationship was found when considering the identity of the deceased. Subjects who experienced the death of a mother (M = 35.45, SD = 8.323) reported more feelings of anxiety than those who had lost a sister (M = 18.67, SD = 3.055). [t (12) = 3.348, p = .006].

Appendix B

Childhood Traumatic Loss Survey, Ursinus College (2016)

Here is the survey sent via email to Ursinus College students. The results are presented in Appendix A.

Survey for Trauma Research

1. Age:

2. Gender:

3. College major:

4. During childhood (under 18 years of age), did you experience any of the following losses? Check any that apply.

Death of mother? _____
Death of father? _____
Death of brother? _____
Death of a sister? _____
Death of close platonic friend? _____
Death of a romantic partner? _____
Death of another person with whom you emotionally close? _____
If yes to above question, please indicate relationship to you: _____
Divorce of parents? _____

5. If you experienced a *death* listed above, what was the cause? Skip if no loss.

a. Long-term illness _____
b. Sudden illness _____
c. Car accident _____
d. Other type of accident _____
e. Drug overdose/substance use _____
f. Suicide _____
g. Violent act _____
h. Other _____
If other, state cause: _____

6. What was the age of the individual at the time of death? N/A if no loss _____

Appendix B 163

7. What was your age when the loss (any listed above) occurred? N/A if no loss

   _____

8. Using a 7-point scale where 1 = not at all traumatic, 4 = somewhat traumatic, and 7 = extremely traumatic, how traumatic do you feel this experience of loss was for you *at the time*? Please define "traumatic" as intense emotional upset or psychological reaction as the result of the event. N/A if no loss _____

9. Do you currently suffer from any of the following physical symptoms on a regular basis (once a week or more)? Check all that apply.

   a. Headaches/migraines   _____
   b. Digestive problems   _____
   c. Insomnia   _____
   d. Extreme fatigue that interferes with daily routine   _____
   e. Asthma   _____
   f. Nightmares   _____

10. How would you rate your current state of physical health compared to others of your age?
    1: Chronically ill 2: Frequently ill 3: Average 4: Rarely ill 5: Almost never ill

    _____

11. Compared with other people of your age group, how do you rate in terms of being mindful of your own state of health (e.g., exercising regularly, refraining from excessive substance use, eating healthily, getting appropriate medical care, etc.)? Choose the statement that best describes you: _____

    1-I am very negligent about my health.
    2-I am somewhat negligent about my health.
    3-I am about average in terms of health habits.
    4-I am moderately conscientious of my health.
    5-I am extremely conscientious about my health.

    Using the scale below, rate yourself after each statement:

    1-------2------3-------4--------5
    Not at all characteristic of me   Very characteristic of me

12. I find it difficult to allow myself to depend on others.   _____
13. I find that people are never there when you need them.   _____
14. I find it relatively easy to get close to others.   _____
15. I am nervous when anyone gets too close.   _____
16. I want to merge completely with another person.   _____
17. I find it difficult to trust others completely.   _____
18. I often worry that a romantic partner won't want to stay with me. _____
19. I connect quickly with new people.   _____
20. I feel very close to my immediate family.   _____
21. I usually have few close friends.   _____

Indicate with an X which statement in each pairing best describes how you feel.

164 Appendices

18.
___Many of the unhappy things in people's lives are partly due to bad luck.
___People's misfortunes result from mistakes they make.

19.
___The idea that teachers are unfair to students is nonsense.
___Most students don't realize the extent to which their grades are influenced by accidental happenings

20.
___No matter how hard you try, some people just don't like you.
___People who can't get others to like them don't understand how to get along with others.

21.
___In the long run, people get the respect they deserve in this world.
___Unfortunately, an individual's worth often passes unrecognized no matter how hard he tries.

22.
___One of the major reasons why we have wars is because people don't take enough interest in politics.
___There will always be wars, no matter how hard people try to prevent them.

23.
___When I make plans, I am almost certain I can make them work.
___It is not always wise to plan too far ahead because many things turn out to be a matter of luck, anyway.

How often has each of these symptoms disturbed or worried you during the last seven days?

Use the following scale to rate each symptom:

0	1	2	3	4
Never	A little	Moderately	A lot	Extremely

24._____Nervousness or shaking inside
25._____Nausea, stomach pain or discomfort
26._____Feeling scared suddenly and for no reason
27._____Palpitations or feeling your heart beat faster
28._____Significant difficulty falling asleep
29._____Inability to free yourself of obsessive thoughts
30._____Tendency to be easily irritable or bothered
31._____Feelings of loneliness
32._____Poor performance at work or school
33._____Anxiety about the future

Agree or disagree with the following statements using the following scale:

1 = I agree a lot
2 = I agree a little
3 = I neither agree nor disagree
4 = I disagree a little
5 = I disagree a lot

34. In uncertain times, I usually expect the best. _____
35. It's easy for me to relax. _____
36. If something can go wrong for me, it will. _____
37. I'm always optimistic about my future. _____
38. I enjoy my friends a lot. _____
39. It's important for me to keep busy. _____
40. I hardly ever expect things to go my way. _____
41. I don't get upset too easily. _____
42. I rarely count on good things happening to me. _____
43. Overall, I expect more good things to happen to me than bad. _____

Answer Yes or No to the following questions:

44. I worry more than most people I know about having a serious illness, disease, or medical condition. _____
45. I am very aware of sensations occurring in my body and notice many aches, pains, and/or other symptoms of what I think may be illnesses, diseases, or medical conditions. _____
46. I frequently check my body for signs of illnesses, diseases, or medical conditions. _____
47. I sometimes check others for signs of illnesses, diseases, or medical conditions, and/or ask them to check themselves. _____
48. I own special equipment for checking my body (i.e., blood pressure cuff) that was not ordered by a doctor. _____
49. I often ask friends/family to reassure me that I do not have an illness or disease. _____
50. I frequently wash or shower in an effort to make sure I do not get an illness or disease. _____
51. I own medical texts or other health-related books, and/or spend a lot of time researching in books or on the internet about specific illnesses, diseases, or medical conditions. _____
52. I often visit or call doctors because of concerns that I have a serious illness, disease, and/or medical emergency. _____
53. I often worry that doctors have not correctly diagnosed me when they are unable to find something wrong with me. _____
54. If I hear about a disease or illness (through the media, or from someone I know), I worry that I have that illness or disease. _____
55. I suffer from an extreme phobia that interferes with my life. _____

Appendix C

Comments From College Students Obtained Via Interviews and Online Surveys, Ursinus College (2016–2019)

- "Reach out rather wait for the child to come to you."
- "Don't expect them to be immediately alright when they come back to school, as family issues may persist after they return."
- "The loss of a grandparent is unique, just like every type of loss is different. (It's) so hard to understand without going through it."
- "Seeing others upset (bothered) me the most."
- "My whole world changed. (I) jumped into reality. It's still difficult to deal with."
- "(Other students told me) to get over it."
- "It was hard to be the same person after going through something completely different."
- "People acted like they were my best friend (when they weren't)."
- "Tough to understand when you are young."
- "(Some kids) didn't want to hang out with you anymore."
- "Don't sugarcoat things."
- "(People) could have talked to me more. It was swept under the rug."
- "(Everyone) just trusted I was OK."
- "Talk directly; don't talk behind (child's) back or ignore it."
- "Kids made jokes (about the loss)."
- "I thought all were sad, so I shouldn't cry. I needed to be happy."
- "(Others) kind of have to experience it to get it but can still help."
- "Friends who never lost (anyone) don't get why I am upset since it happened so long ago."
- "(I) will not forget, keep in back of head and use as a positive thing and not a crutch."
- "Understand that any reaction is OK. It's not wrong because (child) does not do something."
- "(It was) traumatic to see parents and grandparents upset."
- "(I was) not actively paying attention—physically there but not my mind."
- "Don't say 'I understand.' Just listen."

Appendix D

Online Sources of Support and Advice

www.newyorklife.com/foundation/bereavement-resources; New York Life has been a huge supporter of grief services for children. The organization offers grants and provides excellent resources on their website, offering information and practical advice.

https://childrengrieve.org: This is the website for the National Alliance for Grieving Children, a large nonprofit whose sole purpose is to offer advice and support on the subject. Their site offers practical information for professionals and laypeople. Additionally, they sponsor an annual conference each year that brings together individuals involved in griefwork from all perspectives.

www.comfortzonecamp.org/about-us: Comfort Zone Camps host bereavement camps throughout the country. Their website gives details regarding upcoming camp experiences as well as general information for educators and parents. Results from their own grief research study are provided.

https://elunanetwork.org: Formerly known as the Moyer Foundation, this group funds support services for children impacted by loss and addiction. One of their offerings in Camp Erin, a weekend-long bereavement camp held each year at various locations throughout the country.

www.grievingstudents.org: This is the website for the Coalition to Support Grieving Students, a conglomeration of school personnel and professional organizations that have the common goal of helping grieving students. Their website is full of suggestions, handouts, worksheets, and other information that is useful for any educator.

www.aft.org/childrens-health/mental-health/supporting-grieving-student: This page is part of the website of the American Federation of Teachers and suggests ideas for teaching bereaved students. Data from their study conducted with New York Life Foundation is also included.

www.centerforloss.com: This website includes resources that can be utilized in a classroom setting or with grief support groups. Materials include worksheets and other printed materials appropriate for use with preschoolers, elementary schools, preteens and teens.

www.compassionatefriends.org: An online site for survivors of all kinds; there are also local chapters for face-to-face meetings.

www.griefnet.org: Another site that can connect readers to various specific, topic-related groups and sites. They ask for a small fee to join, but they refuse no one and help people who cannot pay by using "angel" donors.

www.griefwatch.com: This site provides information and contact details regarding specific groups throughout the United States that hold meetings for family and friends struggling to cope with the loss of a loved one.

www.dougy.org: The Dougy Center is an organization founded as a support network for children who may feel alone in their grief. Their website is a wonderful source of support not only for parents but also for the children themselves. There are links to activities, resources, and explanations for any aged readers. There are even connections specifically designed for teens and young adults.

www.dailystrength.org: This is a site that members can join to connect and share with others via an online forum.

www.healingheart.net: This site not only provides information and presents a collection of writings from sibling survivors.

www.childtrauma.org: Dr. Bruce Perry's site that provides information and other sources relating to the biological and psychological effects various traumas can have on children.

www.MADD.org: Although this website's primary focus on drunk driving, serving as the online home of Mothers Against Drunk Driving, the sources page has links to informative articles which can relate to bereavement of any kind.

Appendix E

Annotated Bibliography of Children's Books That Deal With Death, Loss, and Grief

Anne and the Sand Dobbies: A Story about Death for Children and their Parents (1964, reprint 1986) by John B Ste. Coburn (New York City, NY: Seabury Press). This out-of-print book can still be found in used condition and is worth seeking. It is a poignant story of parents and surviving children coming to terms with the coinciding deaths of a baby sister and the family dog. This is a chapter book, but it could be read to younger children. When Tim died so many decades ago, this is the book my parents read to me over and over. It left an indelible impact on me, and I treasure it still.

Mick Harte was Here (1996) by Barbara Park (New York City, NY: Yearling Press). A book for intermediate readers, this story recounts the fictional tale of a sister dealing with the accidental bike death of her only brother. This story is intense, but it takes the reader through the conflicting, confusing, and powerful emotions felt by the surviving sister in the story.

The Fall of Freddie the Leaf: A Story about Life for all Ages (1982) by Leo Buscaglia (Thorofare, NY: Slack, Incorporated). This wonderful but deep children's story explains death by using the allegory of a falling, dying leaf from a tree in autumn. This book is geared toward younger children but could be appreciated by all generations of readers.

The Invisible String (2000) by Patrice Karst (New York City, NY: Little, Brown and Company). Although this story abstractly illustrates the emotional connections we have with loved ones, it has an obvious relevance to the topic of missing and remembering someone who is gone. This picture book is useful for preschoolers and young readers.

Tear Soup (2013) by Pat Schwieber and Chuck DeKlyen (Chicago, IL: Acta Publications). A beautifully written allegory, this richly illustrated work equates the grieving process to a recipe for soup. This book is specific in its references to deaths of children, so it may not be appropriate for young children. But for older kids and even adults, the portrayal of a person's unique method of grieving is touching.

I Miss You: A First Look at Death (2000) by Pat Thomas (Hauppauge, NY: B.E.S. Publishing). This is a concise picture book for toddlers and preschoolers that explains death and loss in terms a young child can understand and appreciate.

When Dinosaurs Die: A Guide to Understanding Death (1998) by Laurie Krasny Brown and Marc Brown (New York City: NY: Little, Brown and Company).

170 Appendices

Written by the creator of the character Arthur the Aardvark, this similarly illustrated book for preschoolers and early elementary-aged children explains not only death, but practical issues that will be encountered by families suffering loss. The pictures are reminiscent of Arthur and his family, so kids will find the characters comforting.

Sad isn't Bad: A Good-Grief Guidebook for Kids Dealing with Loss (1998) by Michaelene Mundy (St. Meinrad, IN: Elf-Help Books for Kids). This book, geared primarily for readers 6–10, provides a practical and no-nonsense advice for coping with a death in the family.

The Tenth Good Thing about Barney (1971) by Judith Viorst and Eric Blevgad (New York, NY: Atheneum Books). Focused on a child's loss of a beloved family pet, the book suggests positive ways to remember the positive aspects of those we have loved and lost. Written in simple terms, the ideas can be applied to humans as well as animals.

What's Heaven? (1999) by Maria Shriver (Crawfordsville, IN: Golden Books Publishing). Although this book is more spiritually based, it is written by a Kennedy family member, which lends obvious credence to her ideas in discussing death with children. It is a picture book that preschool and early elementary school children would enjoy.

When a Pet Dies (1998) by Fred Rogers (New York, NY: Puffin Books). In his humble and honest style, Mr. Rogers gently explains death and loss of pet to young children. This book is replete with photographs rather than illustrations, lending realism to the situation. On his TV show, Mr. Rogers had a knack for letting children feel supported, comforted, and understood. He does no less in this book.

Where's Jess? For Children Who have a Brother or Sister Die (1982) by Marvin Johnson (Omaha, NE: Centering Corporation). Designed as a picture book for preschoolers or even toddlers, this work is directed to kids who have lost a baby sibling either before, during, or shortly after birth.

Lifetimes: A Beautiful Way to Explain Death to Children (1983) by Bryan Mellonie and Robert Ingpen (New York, NY: Bantam Press). This short picture book artistically describes death by discussing its role in nature, especially in the animal kingdom. Preschooler and young school-aged children would relate most to this book.

The Memory Box: A book about grief (2017) by Joanna Rowland (Minneapolis, MN: Sparkhouse Family). This beautifully illustrated story of a young girl provides a concrete way to cope with loss. The picture book explains that by keeping memories, we hold the loved one in our hearts. The author provides practical suggestions for helping a bereaved child.

Ocho Loved Flowers (2007) by Anne Fontaine (Stoneleigh Publishers). This is a charming story about a child who must come to terms with the illness and eventual death of her beloved cat, Ocho. As she struggles with her grief, she learns to remember the good times with her best friend, including his love of flowers. Eventually, she can use a bouquet as a happy reminder.

Always Remember (2016) by Cece Meng (New York City, NY: Philomel Books). This picture book for early readers recounts the tale of an old sea turtle

Appendix E   171

whose life has ended. The other sea creatures remember his influence in their lives and realize that he will never be forgotten. The adorable illustrations emphasize the wonder of memory in helping heal grief.

I have a Question about Death: A Book for Children with Autism Spectrum Disorder or Other Special Needs (2017) by Arlan Grad Gaines and Meredith Englander Polsky (Philadelphia, PA: Jessica Kingsley Publishers). This is a nonfictional book that answers kids' common questions regarding death in simple and practical terms that are easily understood. The book assumes special needs, but the descriptions of death are written so clearly that it could be read to any young child who is dealing with his first experience with loss.

A Terrible Thing Happened (2000) by Margaret H. Holmes (Washington, DC: Magination Press). This story follows the experience of an animated raccoon who witnessed an event that upset him. The fact that the incident is not described in detail allows for readers to project their own encounters with trauma into the story. The protagonist struggles to cope until he learns that sharing his feelings with a trusted adult helped him feel better.

The Dragonfly Story: Explaining the Death of a Loved One to Children and Families (2018) by Kelly Owen and Helen Braid (Independent Publisher). In a different twist on the butterfly transformation analogy, this story uses a tale about how brown bugs transform into dragonflies. This example is used to explain death, along with a view of heaven, to the main characters who were trying to cope with the death of a sister.

Goodbye Book (2015) by Todd Parr (New York, NY: Little, Brown Books). This basic picture book, illustrated by simple drawings of a bereaved fish, takes a very straightforward approach to teaching kids about death. The words are simple and sparse, but they clearly explain the concept of death and describe common feelings. There is no plot, and its simplicity makes this most appropriate for toddlers and young preschoolers.

Ida, Always (2016) by Caron Levis and Charles Santoso (New York City, Atheneum Books). If anyone reads *Ida, Always* and not shed a tear, they will be in the minority. This beautifully illustrated picture book depicts the true story of male and female polar bears at the Central Park Zoo in New York City. As art imitating life, the story follows Gus and his best friend Ida, with whom he spends his time during the long, fun days in the zoo. One day, their happy days are interrupted when Ida gets sick, and they realize she will not recover. The tale follows the two as they come to accept that although the body may die, our loved ones can always be felt nearby.

Nana Upstairs & Nana Downstairs (1973) by Tomie dePaola (New York City, NY: Puffin Books). This tale, based on dePaola's childhood experiences, describes a young boy's relationship with two of his grandmothers and his attempt to understand loss when one of them dies. The story is simple and honest while still being uplifting. Readers of any age will identify with losing an elderly family member.

City Dog, Country Frog (2010) by Mo Willems (New York, NY: Hyperion Books for Children). With watercolor illustrations, the story does not mention death directly. Instead, it tells the story of a dog and frog friendship

172   Appendices

through the seasons, and the dog's sadness when his friend is no longer present. Preschoolers and young elementary school kids will relate to the adorable dog in the story.

Badger's Parting Gifts (1984) by Susan Varley (New York City, NY: HarperCollins). This picture book tells the tale of Badger, who realizes his time is limited. After his death, his woodland friends manage their sadness by sharing memories of him. The book deals honestly and directly with death, and the story is longer than similar picture books. This story should be appreciated by older preschoolers and elementary school-aged children.

Sadako and the Thousand Paper Cranes (1977) by Eleanor Coerr (New York, NY: Puffin Books Publishers). The main character in this book is terminally ill from the aftereffects of the Hiroshima bomb, and the story confronts anticipatory grief along with community grief. Personal and universal themes of loss and hope are explored in this short but achingly beautiful story. While the book is short, the themes are most appropriate for school-aged children.

A Monster Calls (2011) by Patrick Ness (Somerville, MA: Candlewick Publishing). A young boy struggling with his mom's terminal illness and imminent death confronts his guilt in the form of a monster. By telling tales that are symbolic of the boy's situation, the monster helps the boy to recognize the truth of his ambivalent feelings and cope with the pain he is feeling. While the monster may be scary for very young children, older kids should be able to grasp the abstract aspects and symbolism of this book.

The Thing about Jellyfish (2017) by Ali Benjamin (New York, NY: Little, Brown Books). This middle-grade chapter book follows the story of a young girl whose ex-best friend dies in a drowning accident. The story grapples with the concepts of regret, denial, and guilt as the protagonist comes to terms with the finality and reality of the death.

The Poet's Dog (2016) by Patricia MacLachlan (New York City, NY: Katherine Tegen Books). In this simple chapter book for beginning readers, two young children are alone in the cold woods until the narrator of the story, an Irish wolfhound, leads them back to a cabin in the woods. The dog, grieving the loss of his owner, takes care of the children and can communicate with them. The story follows the animal's journey through grief and his finding a new purpose, and a home, with the children's family, who is grateful to him for saving the little boy and girl.

Remembering Mrs. Rossi (2007) by Amy Hest (Somerville, MA: Candlewick Press). This intermediate reader book recounts the first-person experience of Annie, a small girl whose mother dies unexpectedly. Her mom was a teacher whose class presents Annie and her father with a book of memories, which helps Annie grieve. The story is unique in that it presents bereavement from the viewpoints of the daughter, husband, and students.

Five Lives of Our Cat, Zook (2012) by Joanne Rocklin (New York, NY: Amulet Paperbacks). This story is aimed at middle-level readers, and its chapters tell the story of pet loss in an achingly beautiful way. In addition to tackling the topic of grief, the book allows readers to identify with the main character and empathize with her reluctance to experience happiness after the death of her beloved cat. Moreover, there is a younger brother in the story, so his reactions are explained along with those of the older child. This volume is relatable and honest.

Love that Dog (2001) by Sharon Creech (New York City, NY: HarperCollins). Written entirely in a modern poetry style, this book tells the story of the protagonist's experience with the loss of his beloved dog. The poems are a school assignment and they follow the young boy's attempts at completing the project. Throughout his rough drafts, the writer takes us on a journey through his grief and describes the loving bond between him and his canine best friend.

Counting by 7s (2014) by Holly Goldberg Sloan (New York, NY: Puffin Books). In this heartbreaking middle-grades chapter book, the protagonist is an adopted child who learns about a car accident that took the lives of her parents. Struggling not only with grief for her adopted mom and dad, this girl has the additional challenges of being separated from her biological parents and being uncertain of her new living arrangements. Through everything, she remains strong and finds true friends that support her, as well as a new, loving home in which to reside.

Mockingbird (2011) by Kathryn Erskine (New York: Puffin Books). This ambitious and touching book tackles two issues: that of dealing with a death by school violence as well as grief as experienced by a child with autism. The main character in the story is autistic, and she lost her big brother in a school setting. The story is an honest portrayal of how someone with special needs may have specific challenges dealing with grief. The book is written for intermediate readers.

If I Stay (2009) by Gail Forman (New York City, NY: Speak Publishers). This young adult novel recounts the story of a severely injured accident victim who struggles with returning to her life as she realizes the rest of her family is dead. She struggles with intense grief and the uncertainty of life without those she loved, experiencing thoughts and emotions like those who yearn to join their deceased loved one. Ultimately, this is a story of hope as the protagonist chooses life despite knowing her journey will be difficult.

Looking for Alaska (2005) by John Greene (New York City, NY: Penguin Books). This haunting young adult novel recounts the narrator's romantic feelings for a girl at their co-ed boarding school. When his friend dies in a car accident, he struggles with guilt and pain of the loss. His struggles are honest and painful as he works his way through his grief.

The Sky is Everywhere (2010) by Jandy Nelson (New York City, NY: Speak Publishers). When the protagonist of this young adult novel, Lennie, loses her big sister from a sudden heart problem, she finds comfort in her relationship with the new boy at her school. At the same time, she experiences confusing feelings toward her sister's boyfriend, who is the one person who truly understands her suffering. Complicating things further, she struggles to relate to her grandmother, who has raised her since her mother left the family. This book's strength is its focus on complicated human relationships and the power of love to strengthen us.

Appendix F

Family Movies That Depict Loss Sensitively and Honestly

Movies can be an excellent way of learning about loss and experiencing catharsis if the viewer is aware and prepared for the film. Children's movies often touch on the subject of death, even when it is not a major theme. Many of them contain references or scenes of a loved one's death. It is easy to pop in a DVD or go to a theater thinking a movie will be a diversion for a grieving child, only to find that painful memories are elicited during emotional scenes in movies. As educators who may occasionally show films, you should be familiar with the content before sharing with a class. Adults should be proactive and know of scenes that might trigger grief. Even when we cannot avoid a trigger, fair warnings can help. Consider these recent and classic children's films that refer to mourning in some way, shape, or form.

- *Bambi:* With his mother dead, Bambi sets off to grow up and cope with grief with the help of his friends Thumper and Flower. A sad story for sure, but one filled with hope and a sense of wonderment.
- *The Mighty Ducks 3:* In this third and final installment of the hockey series, the characters learn to cope with the death of their older friend and team supporter.
- *The Lion King:* Not only does Simba witness his father's violent death, but he is also forced to cope with feelings of guilt and responsibility as he tries to follow in his dad's paw prints as king of the jungle.
- *Dumbo:* The hero in this story is the sad little elephant with the big ears that must learn to cope not only with the loss of his beloved mother and strongest supporter but also with bullying and teasing from unsympathetic characters. Dumbo's remains strong and perseveres, finding happiness and meaning in his young life as he discovers the purpose of his large ears.
- *Nestor the Long-Eared Christmas Donkey:* In a similar plot to that of Dumbo, Nestor's mother dies after sacrificing herself to save him from the frigid weather. Nestor struggles with grief and loneliness while adapting to abnormal ears that cause him to trip through life. Ultimately, he finds joy and redemption in using his ears to help others. This story is warm and touching but has religious themes, as it portrays the Biblical Christmas story.
- *Up:* These children's film depicts a widower's grief and the transformative way his child friend helps him to come to terms with his loss. The interesting twist in this story is the power given to the young character as he plays the role of teacher to the older gentleman.

- *Old Yeller:* This classic Disney movie includes the gut-wrenching scene in which they must put down the rabid dog. Although emotional to watch, there is nothing graphic about this old-time film, and it includes lessons from a wise father on how to cope with loss and its consequential grief.
- *Bridge to Terebithia:* Inspired by true events, two young children form a close friendship after being bullied at school. They create a fantasyland in which they can escape. When one of the pair dies, the survivor must learn how to live without his best friend.
- The *Harry Potter* and *Batman* movies: Death is an underlying theme throughout these movies, whether directly or indirectly. Both storylines involve main characters whose parents are dead, and both possess powers symbolic of ways to overcome the negative effects of the loss. These movies follow the leads over a long time, demonstrating how grief can persist throughout life but still endured.

Perhaps I should include a special mention of the fantasy film, *The Neverending Story*. This movie includes a relatively lengthy scene depicting the slow death of Artax the Horse. Although the demise of the equine is symbolic of giving up in the face of depression (he dies in the aptly named Swamp of Sorrows), it portrays traumatic loss and guilt cathartically when seen from the vantage point of Atreyu, the child who valiantly, but futilely, tries to save the horse by encouraging him to continue his struggle. The lesson learned is that often, we can do nothing to prevent the loss of someone we love, but we cannot let this stop us from living. However accurate and resonant that message is, many viewers find the death scene to be too emotionally charged. Reviews of this movie are replete with comments from adult viewers who can vividly recall this scene many years after the fact, and others who claim it was traumatizing. Because of these mixed reviews, it might be a good idea to view this scene before allowing a grief-impacted child to watch the film.

There are people who hold the opinion that depicting death in children's movies is just mirroring reality. Death is a part of the life cycle, and we cannot shield little ones from this fact. We can refer to an interesting article by Cox, Garrett, and Graham (2004–5) that discusses the incidence of death scenes in Disney movies and the possible repercussions. These authors note the potential benefits if the films encourage frank discussion or comprehension of the topic. The researchers describe valid points, but we should consider whether these potential advantages are more likely to manifest when a child is on firmer emotional ground. I mention these movies not as a critique or as a suggestion to avoid at all costs. Parents may need reminders that death is a topic in these films and that grieving viewers may be ultra-sensitive. As always, remain vigilant, get informed, and use your best judgment as the caring adult working with a hurt child.

Appendix G

Lesson Plans and Ideas for a Grief Support Group

It is best to enter a grief support program with a lesson plan. By necessity, these guidelines will need to be flexible, as the best sessions follow the natural course of the students' needs. However, a simple plan will keep the group on track and provide ideas when the members require a little encouragement. A facilitator should become familiar with several options for each session, and adjustments can be made as required. Educators with classroom experience are familiar with how to switch gears quickly. This ability to roll with the punches will come in handy when directing a grief group. No collection of students will think, feel, or react the same way.

Most formal curricula on this topic organize ideas around a specific theme for each session. There is a great deal of similarity among these curricula despite the differences in the number of sessions suggested. For the sake of convenience, the ideas presented here are organized similarly, with themes that are universal. These themes can be adapted to any program. For example, topics can be combined into one session, while others could be split into two related concepts. The order of topics can be rearranged depending on the needs and characteristics of the group members. Activities and topics can be tweaked to fit various age groups and the interests of the students involved. For instance, one group may become engrossed in arts and crafts projects, while others may prefer physical activities. The ideas presented in this book are mere suggestions and may trigger new ideas. They are an amalgamation of several published curricula (Lehman, 2000a, 2000b, 2000c, 2000d, 2000e; Lowenstein, 2006; Morrissey, 2013; Wolfelt, 1996). If more information is desired, these original curricula serve as excellent guidebooks.

Week 1: Getting Acquainted and Sharing Our Stories

The goal of this week is to introduce everyone and to provide some basic information regarding the loss that brought each student to the group. Ice breaker activities can help to encourage participation. Although each child should be encouraged to participate, no one should be forced into sharing. The facilitator should pay close attention to nonverbal cues that might indicate a member wishes to talk, as well as ensure that no one person has the floor at the exclusion of the rest of the members.

During this initial session, it is important to discuss the guidelines and ground rules for the group for this and all subsequent discussions. The most important of these is confidentiality. Even very young group members can be taught the meaning of this concept. Children should be aware that what they share is personal and needs to stay within the group's circle. Gossip and rumormongering have no place in a grief support group! Of course, any comments that indicate the chance of danger to self or others are exceptions to the rules. The facilitator clearly needs to pursue these comments, and children should be informed of this issue during the first session. It might be important to suggest that specific information may be shared with other school personnel if this collaboration will help the child.

Rules for emotional safety also need clarification. Children should realize that participation is voluntary, and they will need to discover "safe spaces" if strong emotions are triggered. Continency plans for "escape" should be discussed at this session. These plans can include leaving the room for a break, shutting one's eyes and going to a "happy place," or reserving the right to not speak. Another option is to have members write down a description of a happy place or list safe words on an index card. Completed at the first session, this card is kept in the child's possession during all meetings to be used when it is needed. Kids feel secure when they can know they have permission to withdraw if truly overwhelmed.

It is important for the facilitator to ensure fairness in speaking times. While no one student should be able to dominate the discussions, discretion and flexibility are needed. Techniques such as "talking sticks" and ball tosses are good ways to give each child a turn, some students may require more time than others. For example, if Louis is sharing an intense detail of his story, cutting him off would clearly be insensitive. On the other hand, allowing anyone to monopolize the time prevents others from sharing. Moreover, students will vary in their willingness to share on any given day. Facilitators should be sensitive and aware of the needs and reactions of the kids, not only of the speakers but of the listeners as well.

Week 2: Learning About Grief and Death

Most students are inexperienced with death and loss. They may not know exactly what the term "grief" means, even if they have heard it before. During this session, definitions, emotions, and behaviors can be discussed. Very young children may not have an accurate appreciation of the concept of death itself. Group facilitators can offer examples of what creatures live and die, and children can be encouraged to share their ideas about dying actually means. This may be an opportunity to emphasize the finality of death. Children can talk about experiences with viewing dead bodies (people and animals) and their families' customs and ceremonies. Many young people have an abstract idea of these concepts, but reality can still be eye-opening. Due to the emotionally laden nature of the topics, group leaders can introduce them through simple means such as True-False or brainstorming tasks. Some published curricula include card game and worksheets that can be used in this manner (Lehman, 2000a–e).

Week 3: Feelings

Once children understand the reality of the loss, they can focus on the feelings that death can generate. Sadness will undoubtedly be a common emotion that kids recognize, but facilitators can steer discussion to other feelings that loss can uncover,

178 Appendices

such as anger, fear, and guilt. Children can answer sentence starters ("When I see a picture of my loved one, I feel _____") or use flash cards to stimulate discussion. The goal of this week's session is to express emotions and understand that reacting in a variety of ways is both normal and understandable. This is a good session in which to sublimate these strong feelings, perhaps through art activities, creative writing, musical expression, or physical activity. Another discussion point is determining positive and negative ways of channeling feelings, with emphasis on the distinction between emotions and behaviors.

Week 4: Changes

Regardless of the actual nature of the loss, a death of a loved one always generates a degree of change in the lives of the survivors. In some cases, the disruption to normalcy involves changes in normal routine, such as eating dinner with an empty place at the table or utilizing an alternate ride to school. In other circumstances, changes are major, such as when a child may be required to move to a new home or school. Facilitators should be mindful not to be judgmental or allow other group members to compare levels of changes. To the individual, any alteration to the routine of daily life can be perceived as a major stressor. Some children have not had the opportunity to share their feelings about the disruptions to their lives. Participants can be made aware that not all changes are necessarily negative, and that the mixed feelings generated by this situation are entirely normal and expected. Connecting change with its inevitable emotional reactions should be used as a path toward acceptance of the mash-up of feelings that occurs after a loss generates a hole in one's life.

Week 5: Unfinished Business

When we lose a loved one, we typically have unfinished business in our relationship with them. We may regret things said or left unsaid (including goodbye), lost time and experiences, fractured relationships, and inadequate final communications. Many mourners may harbor nagging thoughts that if they had done something different, the death could have been avoided. Most of the time, ruminating on the "what-ifs" leads to a cascade of negative emotions that interfere with the grief process. In fact, sometimes unfinished business prevents the griever from recalling positive memories and prolongs the pain of intense reactions. Some researchers have suggested that extended, and potentially pathological, grief reactions are due to the potency of these lingering thoughts. The first step in dealing with these cognitions is recognizing their existence. One way to do this is by introducing the sentence starters of "woulda, coulda, shoulda." Kids can finish the statements and uncover unresolved issues. Reflecting on unfinished business brings to light deep-seated perceptions and provides a clarification. Young kids may mistakenly believe that something they did or said may have contributed to the death. They frequently exaggerate their transgressions or idealize the person who died. Airing regrets and the pain generated by lost opportunities helps feelings to the surface where the light of objectivity can shine on them. Other members of the group can provide reassurance and commiserate.

As mentioned earlier, broaching sensitive subjects through light-hearted methods can balance the strong emotions these topics can generate. Lehman (2000a–e) suggests a post-it note activity in which each group member completes a note for "woulda, coulda, and shoulda" sentence completions. These three notes are then affixed to the shirt, and then each griever has an opportunity to rip the note off as she states the unfinished business indicated. This action is a symbolic way of ridding oneself of the thought.

This week grants an opportunity to explore other common methods of "letting go" of grief and saying goodbye to the loved one. Releasing butterflies or writing notes to the deceased are two options. (Butterfly kits are available online, which provides buyers with larvae which quickly form cocoons and then emerge as beautiful winged-adults, ready to be released.) Talking to the lost loved one in a role-playing scenario can serve a similar purpose. Facilitators should be cognizant of the potential for powerful emotions to be generated during the discussion of this topic. Remember not to push group members; all participation needs to be voluntary.

Week 6: Memories

As the grief process unfolds, there should come a time in which memories can bring joy along with pain. Sharing recollections is useful for children and teens, especially if they are reluctant to speak to other family members for fear of negative reactions. Likewise, friends who are not mourning may find it difficult to relate and may hastily change the subject, annoyed by what they perceive as ramblings or living in the past. Group is an excellent place to allow time and space for contemplating former experiences with the deceased.

Children can bring in pictures or other mementos to share. They can engage in craft projects that incorporate the items, such as picture frames. Another option involves drawing pictures or writing a journal entry about a special memory the child made with the lost loved one. If this week's session falls around a holiday, the memories can focus on this event or time of the year. There are limitless possibilities. It should not take too much prompting to unfurl a host of recollections.

This session is a great time to hold a remembrance ceremony. One idea is for the students to make battery-operated tea light luminaries out of white paper bags anchored with a handful of sand. Students have freedom to create their bag in any way they desire. After candles are lit, facilitators can conduct a short ceremony. Readings can be offered, and each child should have the chance to share if they wish. This ceremony is likely to trigger intense emotions in some grievers, so be ready with tissues. A moment or two of silence at the end is helpful as everyone takes a minute to regroup. Afterward, allow a little time for the kids to reflect on the experience. It might be a good idea for everyone to mention a positive quality of their loved one, or perhaps express gratitude for having known them. Facilitators should be sensitive to varied reactions and be cautious regarding the comfort level of the kids. However, even though this may be a difficult exercise, experiencing the emotions of grief are necessary for its processing.

Week 7: Coping and Self-Care

In this week's session, focus is on the importance of maintaining ones' physical and emotional health. Terms such as "stress" and "coping" are useful to define. Positive methods of stress-reduction can be explained and encouraged, such as physical

180   Appendices

activity and creative pursuits. Children and teens can be reminded about maintaining good health habits, such as a healthy diet and sufficient sleep. If children are unclear about how anxiety and other emotions affect the body, this is a good opportunity to teach that information. Negative ways of coping like self-medicating and self-harm are relevant topics, too. Facilitators must avoid sounding judgmental or preachy and should not pressure or generate feelings of guilt. The goal is to spread correct information and encourage healthy options.

In this session, be sure to emphasize the role of social supports. Students can describe people in their lives that offer help and strength. The option of turning to professional sources of support can also be addressed. Kids need to know that asking for help is not a sign of weakness, and most are unaware of their options. Support is available in schools, in church families, and throughout the community, even when the family is unwilling or unable to help.

Keep in mind that building a "grief toolbox," filled with ways in which to cope with loss, is an essential purpose of the support group. No one escapes life without loss, and although many students will be facing their first encounter with grief, it will most assuredly not be their last. Learning the facts and building positive and healthy coping mechanisms will serve them well in the future. Use this session to build a foundation for students to fall back on as they deal with grief and loss throughout their lives.

Week 8: Saying Goodbye

In this last session, students will process the reality that the formal meetings have concluded. Kids can share their feelings about their loss while being reminded that the actual relationships can continue. This is an excellent opportunity for kids to share what they have learned from each other.

For an art project relevant to this session, the kids will create some type of memorial item. Student can make beaded bracelets or necklaces that can remind them not only of the group, but of their loved one. Names and/or inspirational words can be formed by the beads. Facilitators can also comment that as they tie their jewelry, the string makes a circle that has not beginning or end, just like the relationships in our lives.

Ending the group meetings with a party or other form of celebration ends the sessions on a fun note. Not only does food and drink bring students together, the activity demonstrates that although loss is painful, there are still times of fun and celebration in life. There are opportunities to be grateful and thank the group members for their willingness to share their grief journey.

Some General Notes

Although these ideas, and the formal curricula, are useful and essential for a good group experience, that activities should be catered to the needs of each unique group. Participation is voluntary in both the activities and discussions. Facilitators should be sensitive to extreme reactions while recognizing that some level of heightened emotion is normal. Sessions merely offer support and do not replace professional counseling. This point should be made clear to parents and guardians. While any sensitive and empathetic educator can be a group facilitator, having a professional, such as a guidance counselor or school psychologist, as an available resource. Their support may be helpful not only in order to consult about the students' reactions but also as a safety net for a group leader's own need for positive coping. Being present for others' grief is often a trigger for one's own pain, and while sharing with the kids may be limited, expressing feelings to another adult can be cathartic.

Appendix H

Sample Nonprofit Outreach Letter

(Example only; consult other sources for specific legal advice.)

(Insert your organization's logo)

(Date)

Dear Partner in Education:

My name is (*director's name*), and I am writing to you to share the news about (*organization's name*), a new nonprofit incorporated and insured in the state of Pennsylvania. As the founder and director, I would like to take a quick opportunity to introduce myself and explain the mission of (*organization's name*).

(*Organization's name*) provides FREE support services to assist bereaved children and adults who love and work with them. The OMEGA Journal of Death and Dying indicates that 1 in 5 children will lose a loved one during their childhood. These children often report feeling alone and unsupported, especially at school. A nationwide survey conducted jointly by New York Life and the American Federation of Teachers found that bereaved students frequently withdraw from others and have difficulty in class; many exhibit behavior problems. This same study found that almost 70% of teachers reported having at least one grieving student in class each academic year. Clearly, grief is not a rare occurrence in today's schools. However, teachers, administrators, and even counselors are not always prepared to handle a child's grief. Methods to cope with this situation are rarely taught in educator preparation programs. In recent years, attention has been given to the effects of trauma on a young child's development, but often grief is not considered as a "trauma," especially when the loss involves someone who is not an immediate family member. However, young people often report that a grief experience is a major life event for them, regardless of the exact nature of the loss. For children who have lost a parent, the impact is specifically great; for example, in answers to the Childhood Bereavement Study completed by the Comfort Zone Camp, 56% of these children said they would trade a year of their own life for just one more day with the deceased parent. Since grief and bereavement may present differently from child to child, and may vary from the effects of trauma, it is important for adults to recognize the impact of a loss on a student and provide as much support as possible.

(*Organization's name*) can help in this process. We offer support group services in the school for children who are grieving. Groups follow a prescribed curriculum and meet for approximately 45 minutes per week, for a period of eight weeks, although there is flexibility to meet the needs of the students. (*Organization's name*) facilitators are volunteers with college degrees and experience in education or human services, and each has current clearances. Our services are designed to offer support, not counseling; however, (*organization's name*) has a clinical director who can be consulted if the need arises.

In addition, (*organization's name*) offers short presentations and in-service programs to provide educators with information about working with bereaved students. These are adaptable presentations to meet the needs of your organization.

If you believe your school has a need for any of (*organization's name*) services, please do not hesitate to contact me. You can also visit our website, (*website address*). There are grieving children in your school, even though many of them do not make their situation obvious. I would like the chance to help you reach these students and give them the support they need. Again, there is no charge for our services to these young people.

Thank you for your time and patience! I look forward to hearing from you at any time, with any questions. Together we can fill a void that is too often neglected, and we can help children who are hurting.

Sincerely,
(*Director's name and contact info*)

Appendix I

Sample Nonprofit Information Sheet for Stakeholders

About (Organization's Name)

Who: We are a small, local nonprofit incorporated in the state of *(your state)* and granted 501(c)(3) status. Our group consists of educators, counselors, and others who have an interest in or are trained in issues of grief.

What: (*Organization's name*) provides free grief support group services to students in local schools. We also offer educational materials and presentations for school personnel and other adults who work with grieving children. We strive to promote awareness of issues surrounding grief as they pertain to children and teens.

Where: Our services are available to schools and other interested organizations in the (*your town/city*) and surrounding areas.

Why: Despite increased awareness of the effects of childhood trauma, grief and bereavement are often overlooked as significant challenges. By educating others on how children grieve and the potential for multidirectional effects on children's development, we hope to focus the light on this common situation.

What can you do to help?

- (*Organization's name*) is always looking for individuals who might want to help with groups or with fundraising or advertising. We need all talents!
- Anyone interested in donating can do so through our Facebook page, (*organization's social media sites and web addresses*). We also plan on several fundraisers a year, so joining us for those is another way to help provide financial support.
- Each of us can be "grief ambassadors," spreading awareness about ways in which early loss can influence a child's development. Knowledge is power, and it is the first step on the path toward supporting grieving kids!

Appendix J

Sample Nonprofit Mission Statement

(Example only; consult other sources for specific legal advice.)

Mission Statement for (Organization's Name)

Mission Statement

To offer support and information to grieving children, families, and educators in the (your location's) area.

The Vision

Our goal is to provide the children in our community with ways in which to work through their grief journeys by offering bereavement support. By creating safe places to express themselves, we aim to empower our group attendees to find peace, comfort, joy, and meaning after a loss. Our vision also extends to providing information and resources to families, educators, and other adults who work with grieving children. We hope to encourage the formation of social "safety nets" in which children can learn to cope with their losses.

Specific Services

- Create and facilitate support groups in the schools for children who have been affected by grief. Participation is voluntary; groups run for 8–10 weeks. Goal of the group environment is to help students learn coping skills to process grief and provide social interaction. Groups offer support, not direct counseling services.
- Deliver trainings and information to educators who work with grieving students. This service can be offered as a professional development presentation or through consultation and informal support. Recommendations can be made for other services and materials via consultation services.
- Informational materials for parents and guardians are also available.

186   Appendices

Curriculum for Support Groups

Support groups follow the basic framework of the curriculum set forth in the books by Lehmann, Jimerson, and Gaasch entitled *Mourning Children Grief Support Curriculum*. The curriculum is age-graded and will be augmented by Alan Wolfelt's work, *Understanding Your Grief*. Additional activities will be incorporated from the attached list of references and contacts. Facilitators have a background in education and/or psychology.

Appendix K

Tips and Guidelines for Group Facilitators

(To be used with your volunteers; can be reprinted.)

- Review purpose and "safety" rules every session. Be sure to create a nonjudgmental environment.
- Emphasize the importance of confidentiality.
- Allow students to share or not share as they wish. Participation in all activities is voluntary. Remember that students may benefit just from attending and listening. Children's grief is often compounded by helplessness, so giving them a sense of control is helpful.
- Express tolerance and sensitivity for differing opinions, especially regarding spiritual beliefs.
- Be cognizant of the potential for trauma or grief triggers. Watch for body language and other nonverbal reactions.
- Remember that everyone grieves differently, so do not expect specific behaviors or feelings.
- Keep in mind that the goal of our organization is to offer support. Activities are not meant to be professional counseling or therapy, even though there may be therapeutic results!
- If you are concerned about a student, share with the director or a clinical point person.
- Do not be afraid to ask for help if you need it!
- Take care of yourself. Recognize that working with others' grief may remind you of your own issues and/or may be emotionally exhausting. Do something fun for yourself after each meeting.
- (*Your organization's name*) loves and appreciates you!!! You do great work!

© 2020, *The Grieving Child in the Classroom*, Sue Trace Lawrence, Routledge

Appendix L

Sample Letter to Send to Parents or Guardians

(Example only; consult other sources for specific legal advice.)

Dear Parent/Guardian,

(*Your organization's name*) is a local nonprofit organization that provides support group services within the schools for students who have lost a loved one. Your child has been identified by school personnel as a student who could benefit from our program.

The group offers peer support and is led by trained educators. While the purpose of the group is not to provide therapy or counseling, giving students the opportunity to talk about their feelings of grief with others who are going through similar experiences can be therapeutic. The students will also have the opportunity to share memories of the person who died. Other projects, such as crafts and journal writing, will be offered as well. Participation is completely voluntary, and the students share only when they are comfortable. Research has shown that bereaved children benefit from social support, especially from others who share and understand their feelings and concerns.

The group will meet 8 times over the course of a few months. All meetings will be held during the school day so no additional transportation will be required. While the meetings, approximately 45 minutes in duration, are held during the school day, every effort will be made to minimize disruption to your child's academic work.

Traces of Love Association is bringing this program to the school at no cost to the district or to you. If you would like more information, please visit our website (*your organization's website address*) or by contacting (*organization's contact person*) at (*email address*).

For your child to participate, you will need to complete the attached application and permission forms that are attached. Unfortunately, your child will not be able to participate unless the forms are signed. Once the group sessions begin, both you and your child will be asked to sign a confidentiality form as well. Once we have permission forms for all group members, we will schedule our first session and inform you of the details.

We hope that we can help your child cope with his or her loss. Thank you!

(Your organization's name)

(Organization's Logo)   *(Organization's name)*

Appendix M

Sample Application and Consent Form

(*Example only; consult other sources for specific legal advice.*)

Student's Name: _____ Birth Date: _____

Address: _____ Grade: _____

_____

Parent/Guardian's Name: _____

Phone: _____

Does the student have any food allergies? If so, please explain: _____

_____

_____

Has the student received any professional counseling regarding the loss? _____

For how long? _____ Are they in care currently? _____

Who is the deceased?

Mother _____ Father _____ Brother _____ Sister _____ Grandparent _____

Friend _____ Other (please specify): _____

Approximate date that death occurred: _____

How close was the student to this individual?

Not at all close _____ Somewhat close _____ Moderately close _____

Extremely close _____

What was the cause of the death?

Lengthy illness _____ Short-term illness _____ Accident _____ Overdose _____

Suicide _____ Homicide _____ Sudden death (stroke, heart attack) _____ Other (please specify): _____

Did the student witness the death? _____

What other losses has the student experienced? Please give approximate dates.

190 Appendices

Who is the student's primary emotional support person?

What activities or hobbies does the student currently enjoy?

Is there any special information we should know to help us better support this student? If so, please state and explain below.

I give consent for my child, (*child's name*), to participate in the (*your group's name*)'s grief support program. I have been informed of the group's purpose and understand that this service is meant to serve a supportive role, not provide professional counseling or therapy. I also give consent to (*child's school*) and (*your organization's name*) to share pertinent information to help my child. I understand that any information will be used only in conjunction with my child's participation in the group.

Signature of parent/guardian	Date

Printed name

Appendix N

Sample Confidentiality Pledge for Group Members

(Example only; consult other sources for specific legal advice.)

Confidentiality Promise

Confidentiality means that information shared during group sessions is private. In other words, please do not share others' personal stories or comments with anyone outside of the group. Other people may ask you what is discussed during our sessions, and you are free to share your own story. However, please do not repeat the information that other students have shared. Undoubtedly, you would not like them to share your personal remarks!

Information that should NOT be shared include names of other students or loved ones, details about the deaths, personal feelings shared by group members, or reactions of members during the sessions. If something seems private, it probably is! If you are not sure about what can and cannot be shared, do not be afraid to ask your group leader.

I understand what confidentiality means and I agree to uphold the confidentiality of people in our group.

_____   _____
(student's signature)   *(date)*

_____
(student's printed name)

Appendix O

Information Sheet on the Stages of Grief

(For parents or other stakeholders; may be reprinted.)

What Is Grieving?

Several psychologists and grief researchers have studied the grief process and attempted to describe stages of bereavement, primarily in adults (Kubler-Ross, 1969; Rando, 1991; Worden, 1996). No two individuals grieve in exactly the same way, however. This is especially true with young people, who are at varying levels of cognitive and emotional development. Regardless of the need to accept individual differences, there are some generalities that can be used as a framework for understanding dealing with a loss. TOLA considers four main tasks or stages in bereavement and uses these as guidelines in working with young people:

We Can Think of This as the 4 R's

Recognition: The griever needs to recognize the loss, and this process involves understanding. What exactly is death? Children may need specific information to face reality and comprehend what has happened in their lives. Many people are in denial after a loss occurs but recognizing and defining events is the crucial first step in bereavement.

Reaction: Grief elicits a variety of emotions, including sadness, anger, fear, and guilt. Bereaved people need a safe place in which to express these feelings. Children may need help to identify their conflicting reactions. Many young people are overwhelmed with the intensity of their emotions and are reluctant to express them for various reasons. The need for catharsis is real and vital to the healing process.

Re-experience: This process can take several forms depending on the individual. Much of re-experience means that the lost loved one is remembered and mourned. Recollections of time spent together, particularly positive memories, can reassure a young person that their person will live on their memory. Sometimes, if a child has dissociated emotionally after a loss, the child may naturally try to reenact the trauma of learning that a loved one died. Children may need to reprocess the loss in order to move forward.

Readjustment: The bereaved individual eventually needs to rebuild a life without the loved one. This process is highly individualized and depends on the

© 2020, *The Grieving Child in the Classroom*, Sue Trace Lawrence, Routledge

circumstances of the loss; however, at this point the griever will have some level of acceptance and will be on the path of reinvesting in life. This is not the end of the grieving process, but it is the first step in understanding that life goes on despite pain and loss.

Sources

Kubler-Ross, E. (1969). *On death and dying.* New York, NY: Macmillan Publishing Co., Inc.
Rando, T. A. (1991). *How to go on living when someone you love dies.* New York, NY: Bantam Books.
Worden, J. W. (1996). *Children and grief: When a parent dies.* New York, NY: Guilford Press.

Appendix P

Handout on Coping During the Holidays

(For parents or other stakeholders; can be reprinted.)

Tips for Helping a Grieving Child During the Holidays

Holidays can be especially difficult for someone who has lost a loved one, even if the loss is not recent. Reminders of the past and happier times are everywhere, and there is pressure to be happy, joyful, and grateful. Feelings of sadness are easily triggered. Here are some specific tips that can be useful in supporting bereaved kids during this time:

1. Acknowledge the feelings and don't add on pressure to "enjoy the season." Telling someone to "just be happy" is not helpful and only adds guilt to the equation.
2. Talk with the child about how some traditions might change, but new traditions can begin. Start this new tradition with the memory of the loved one in mind. Some specific ideas might be to make a special memorial ornament, light a designated candle, or create a holiday collage with pictures of the lost loved one.
3. Discuss holiday plans with the child. Depending on the specific circumstances, some families may prefer to stay home, while others may decide to travel somewhere completely new. Be open to new ideas and try to work together to find plans with which all are comfortable.
4. Don't over schedule or overcommit. During holidays or vacations, it is natural for people to have a busy schedule filled with activities and plans. This situation can create stress for all of us at times, but someone who is grieving may be particularly prone to fatigue and distraction. Pick some activities you all will enjoy but be reasonable and don't overburden someone who is grieving.
5. For at least part of the time, try to focus on helping others. Help your child choose a gift to donate to a charity or spend a couple of hours working at a soup kitchen. This activity refocuses perspective and can help a child feel good about him/herself.
6. Encourage the child to be kind to him/herself. If you are the child's caregiver, do the same for yourself. Pamper yourselves with a special meal or a small gift, or just spend time relaxing or doing something fun. Also remember to take

© 2020, *The Grieving Child in the Classroom*, Sue Trace Lawrence, Routledge

good physical care of yourselves. Grief is a process, and each little thing adds up to stronger resilience and coping skills.
7. Be aware of red flags that may indicate a child is having a hard time and may need more help. Feelings of depression, including suicidal ideation, may be intense during holiday times. Do not hesitate to ask a child how he/she is feeling and reach out for support if you think it is necessary.
8. Give yourselves time and space and realize that there are many "normal" ways to grieve. There is also no set timetable for grief. If the reactions are not destructive, be patient.

© 2020, *The Grieving Child in the Classroom*, Sue Trace Lawrence, Routledge

Appendix Q

Project Ideas for Grief Support Groups

(*Adjustable for use with any age group.*)

Ideas derived, suggested, and transformed from projects presented in Lehman (2000a, 2000b, 2000c, 2000d, 2000e), Lowenstein (2006), Morrissey (2013), and Wolfelt (1996).

- Design memory collages using magazines clipping or other items.
- Build dream catchers to snag bad dreams.
- Create "glass" designs using tissue paper or cellophane.
- Bead strings for necklaces, bracelets, or keyrings
- Paint to various styles of music to express emotions.
- Break plates to make mosaics.
- Create a "buddy" to use as security in the group, such as a painted pet rock or pom-pom animal.
- Write and illustrate a story about a grieving animal.
- Draw or paint a portrait of the loved one.
- Design remembrance tattoos (on paper only).
- Complete coloring pages.
- Decorate clay pots and plant a flower in them to nurture.
- Paint coffee filter and clothespin butterflies.
- Decorate inexpensive picture frames.
- Design and decorate luminary bags for the memorial ceremony.
- Construct a memory box that can be filled with special items.
- Write a fictional story or play including the loved one and/or the griever.
- Create a superhero that learns ways to cope with grief.
- Keep a journal of memories, dreams, and coping strategies.
- Write poems or songs to express feelings; share with the group in a "talent show."
- Create a collage of torn paper, on which were written thoughts and feelings about the loss.
- Write a letter to the deceased and read it aloud, either alone or to the group.
- Make snow globes by sealing a glass jar filled with colored water, glitter, and a special item.
- Decorate smooth rocks to use as "worry stones."
- Glue a "word collage" using cut words and phrases from magazines and newspapers.
- Create crossword puzzles or acrostics referring to the loved one.

Appendix R

Activities to Be Used With a Grief Support Group

(*Adjustable for use with any age group.*)

Ideas derived, suggested, and transformed from projects presented in Lehman (2000a, 2000b, 2000c, 2000d, 2000e), Lowenstein (2006), Morrissey (2013), and Wolfelt (1996).

- Provide distraction toys for use when students are sharing; squishy toys are excellent choices.
- To ensure that everyone gets a turn, pass a ball of yarn from child to child, making a spider web. Plastic spiders can be added to increase the fun!
- Allow kids to use clay or dough to make a desired figure, then alter it to demonstrate how while life changes, essential aspects stay the same.
- Ask kids to write letters to their support people, indicating what help they need.
- Put together a large jigsaw puzzle to demonstrate group cooperation and provide some distraction while kids are sharing. Kids may talk more when they do not feel like they are the center of attention.
- Use puppets with younger children to draw out responses. Kids may respond more readily to a character than to an adult.
- Provide group members with scraps of paper on which to write actions or thoughts about which they feel guilty. These can be kept private or shared if the child wishes. Then crumple them into a ball and throw into a makeshift basketball net or trashcan, thereby "throwing away" the sense of guilt.
- When discussing feelings, use a thumbs up, thumbs down activity so kids can acknowledge their emotions. Another idea is to make a paper plate emoji face with a mouth affixed with a paper fastener which can be turned around to indicate a smile or a frown.
- Do some research on how people in other cultures cope with death and grief. Students can learn about customs and beliefs, then share what they discover with the group. Members can then discuss their opinions while displaying tolerance for other ideas. Facilitators can focus on the positive aspects of each cultural perspective. What can be incorporated into our own grief practices?
- Provide a child-size punching bag with a villain character that members can take turns hitting to release anger.

198 Appendices

- To bolster self-esteem, have each child share positive comments with one other.
- Ask children to take a walk and photograph anything eye-catching that reminds them of their loved one, or grief in general. Print out the pictures and assemble them to make a story or a memory book. This activity can be done during group time if phones are allowed or can be assigned as homework.

Appendix S

Suggestions for Activities to Help Kids Cope With Grief

(For parents or other stakeholders; can be reprinted.)

Activities to Help Your Grieving Child

Here are some ideas for supporting your grieving son or daughter. While this is a short list, it might stimulate other ideas that would work for your child. These can easily be adapted to your particular situation. Pick and choose ones that might be beneficial to your family and remember that just spending time with a bereaved child can be reassuring.

- Write a letter to the deceased. Help your child express his or her feelings as well as discuss any regrets or unfinished business. The letter can then be saved or destroyed, depending on the needs of the child.
- Create a scrapbook with photos and other mementos of the loved one. Encourage your child to be creative, perhaps visiting a craft store to purchase stickers and other items to decorate the book. Not only is this an enjoyable project, it will serve as a cherished reminder of the relationship that was lost.
- Perform a random act of kindness. One of the most touching acts I have witnessed involved a very simple act. A stranger had attached a dollar bill onto a vending machine with a note stating that the money was offered in remembrance of a child who had died. Not only did this brighten up someone's day, but the deceased was given tribute, too. This is an example of an idea that can easily be done by a child.
- Visit places that remind the child of the loved one. While this activity may awaken painful feelings, good times can also be remembered. This option might be best undertaken after a little time has passed since the death.
- Use drama and play to express feelings that are difficult to put into words. Younger children may enjoy playing with stuffed animals and action figures along with pretend games. Older kids may appreciate improvisation or role-playing activities. Many times, a child's true thoughts and feelings emerge during playtime.
- Encourage physical and/or creative pursuits. Expending energy can be cathartic. Sometimes emotions can be expressed in direct ways, like smacking a punching bag or writing a sad song. Other times, the activity can be distracting,

© 2020, *The Grieving Child in the Classroom*, Sue Trace Lawrence, Routledge

giving the bereaved a few minutes in which attention is drawn to something other than grief.
- Participate in volunteer or charity work. Not only can these projects keep everyone busy but reaching out to others is also a great way to boost spirits.
- Learn and practice relaxation techniques. Progressive meditation tapes are widely available and can be used in the comfort of home. Taking yoga classes or getting a massage are other ways in which to lessen both physical and emotional stress.
- Encourage social interaction. While many of us withdraw when sad, preferring to lick our wounds in private, we all need to connect to other people sometimes. Suggest that your child visit with a close friend or participate in an activity out of the house. Do not pressure but urge your child to return to extracurricular activities like sports as soon as he or she seems ready. Creating and maintaining attachments to others is essential in the grieving process.
- Start a garden. Nourishing living organisms and watching them grow reinforces the miracle of life. Likewise, adopting and caring for a pet can be rewarding. In the case of an animal, however, there is always the possibility of losing the pet, so be cautious in moving too quickly to add a new family member after a loved one's death. The possibility of loss is always real when life is concerned, but being reminded of this lesson when grief is raw may not be the best timing.
- Celebrate the special occasions, both happy and sad. Bereaved people are usually aware of anniversaries and other holidays that remind them of the loved one. Many children may not mention the significance of these dates, in part to spare others in the family. They may wonder if anyone else remembers that the date of the deceased birthday and may hesitate to bring it up. Most likely, people remember, so it would be helpful to share thoughts and feelings. Have a family birthday dinner or do something else to remember the loved one. Grieving together is a good thing.
- Talk, talk, and talk some more. Keep the lines of communication open. It is unnecessary to talk specifically about the death; do so only when the child is ready. Often, a conversation may begin about a neutral, unrelated topic, only to wind its way around to topics related to the loss. Try not to be deliberate about starting a discussion. Spend time together and be available. Sometimes children will talk openly while busy or distracted, such as during car rides. It is often easier for them to broach an uncomfortable subject when all the attention is not aimed directly at them. This is fine. The point is to be present and accessible when a child wants to talk.

© 2020, *The Grieving Child in the Classroom*, Sue Trace Lawrence, Routledge

Appendix T

Grief Experiences Worksheet

(For use by students; adjust for age. Can be reprinted.)

3 Words that Describe
Me Before

3 Words that Describe
Me Now

What I Looked Liked
Before

What I Look Like
After

© 2020, *The Grieving Child in the Classroom*, Sue Trace Lawrence, Routledge

Appendix U

Grief Definitions Worksheet

(For use by students; adjust for age. Can be reprinted.)

What Is Grief?

Grief is the feeling we have after someone dies. It makes us feel bad. These feelings can include:

Sadness	Embarrassment
Fear	Uncertainty
Anxiety	Anguish
Anger	Worry
Guilt	Confusion
Shame	Loneliness

Circle the ones you have felt. Below, write any other emotions you have experienced. Draw an emoji to represent each of them.

© 2020, *The Grieving Child in the Classroom*, Sue Trace Lawrence, Routledge

Appendix V

Coping Strategies Worksheet

(For use by students; adjust for age. Can be reprinted.)

What Do I Do When I Feel Sad?

Circle the activities that help you feel better when you are missing your loved one.

Drawing or coloring	Reading	Watching TV or movies
Playing video games	Listening to music	Talking with a friend
Taking a walk	Exercising	Eating a favorite food
Playing a sport	Shopping	Writing in a journal or diary
Meditating or doing yoga	Sleeping	Spending time with a pet
Doing puzzles	Taking a hot bath	Participating in a hobby

Other things you do: _____

Are these activities positive or negative? Do they help? Why or why not?

What are some new activities you might try?

© 2020, *The Grieving Child in the Classroom*, Sue Trace Lawrence, Routledge

Appendix W

My Loved One Worksheet

(For use by students; adjust for age. Can be reprinted.)

My Loved One/Special Person

My special person's name is: _____

He/She is my (relationship to you): _____

My person died on (date): _____

My person died because: _____

My favorite thing about my special person is: _____

What I miss most about my special person is: _____

How I felt when I learned about the death: _____

How I feel right now when I think about my special person: _____

What I do to help me feel better: _____

What I would say to my special person if I could talk to him/her right now:

_____

_____

What I do to help me remember my special person: _____

_____

© 2020, *The Grieving Child in the Classroom,* Sue Trace Lawrence, Routledge

Appendix X

Dead or Alive Worksheet

(For use by students; adjust for age. Can be reprinted.)

Dead or Not? Worksheet

Can these things die? Mark the ones that can die with a check mark.

_____ 1. Dog		_____ 2. Car	
_____ 3. Pencil		_____ 4. Pizza	
_____ 5. Teddy bear		_____ 6. Rose	
_____ 7. Doctor		_____ 8. Cartoon characters	
_____ 9. Action figures		_____ 10. Goldfish	
_____ 11. Grandparents		_____ 12. Snake	
_____ 13. Police officer		_____ 14. Sea gull	
_____ 15. Television		_____ 16. Cell phone	
_____ 17. Cat		_____ 18. Christmas tree	
_____ 19. Rock		_____ 20. Ocean	

Which of these things can cause a death? Mark the ones that can with a check mark.

_____ 1. Gun		_____ 2. Mean thoughts	
_____ 3. Yelling		_____ 4. Knife	
_____ 5. Cancer		_____ 6. Car accident	
_____ 7. Drugs		_____ 8. Angry feelings	
_____ 9. Bad fall		_____ 10. Suicide	
_____ 11. Heart attack		_____ 12. Swearing	
_____ 13. Kissing		_____ 14. Plane crash	
_____ 15. Drowning		_____ 16. Severe illness	
_____ 17. Getting in trouble		_____ 18. Disobeying adults	
_____ 19. Wishing someone would go away		_____ 20. Telling someone to leave	

© 2020, *The Grieving Child in the Classroom*, Sue Trace Lawrence, Routledge

Appendix Y

Grief Scenarios Worksheet

(For use by students; adjust for age. Can be reprinted.)

Grief Problems and Solutions

Circle the best answer!

1. Sally yelled at her older sister and told her to "drop dead." She later died in an accident. What should Sally do?

    a. Understand that her angry comments did not kill her sister.
    b. Ask her parents to punish her since she killed her sister.
    c. Refuse to eat because she is guilty of killing her sister.

2. Mary's best friend drowned while away at summer camp. What should Mary do when school starts in the fall?

    a. Refuse to go to school since her friend will not be there.
    b. Get into trouble at school so her teachers will pay attention to her.
    c. Share her feelings with a trusted adult and other friends who are sad, too.

3. Johnny's dad recently died, and his mom is sad a lot of the time. He often feels that she is not paying much attention to him. What should Johnny do?

    a. Tell his mom to cheer up and make dinner.
    b. Yell at his mom and tell her that she is not being a good mom.
    c. Give his mom a hug and tell her that he understands since he is sad, too.

4. Tina's mother died of cancer. Her class is inviting moms to school for a special mother-child breakfast to celebrate Mother's Day. What should Tina do?

    a. Not go to school the day of the breakfast.
    b. Ask for permission to bring along another special person, like an aunt or grandmother.
    c. Yell at all the other girls who bring their mothers and stop being their friend.

© 2020, *The Grieving Child in the Classroom*, Sue Trace Lawrence, Routledge

5. One of the teachers in your school just died. You did not know this teacher well, but one of your friends did and is very sad. What should you do?
    a. Remind the friend that he/she should not be sad and that everything will be normal soon.
    b. Tell the friend that you are sorry about what happened and that you would be happy to talk about it.
    c. Ignore the friend until they he/she snaps out of his/her bad mood.

6. Jim's dog died over the weekend and he is having trouble concentrating in math class. He is very sad and just feels like crying. What should Jim do?
    a. Ignore his feelings and remember that it was just a dog.
    b. Accept his sad feelings and give himself time to feel better, maybe even privately explaining his sad mood to his teacher.
    c. Pretend to be sick or get into trouble so the teacher will send him home.

© 2020, *The Grieving Child in the Classroom*, Sue Trace Lawrence, Routledge

Appendix Z

Scavenger Hunt Worksheet

(For use by students; adjust for age. Can be reprinted.)

Scavenger Hunt

Find the objects (or pictures of objects) that relate to death, loss, and grief:

1. Something that can die.
2. Something that cannot die.
3. Something that makes me feel sad.
4. Something that makes me feel happy.
5. Something that reminds me of my loved one.
6. Something that helps me decrease my anger in a good way.
7. Something that reminds me of death.
8. Something that reminds me of life.
9. Something that reminds me of strength.
10. Something that reminds me that I am a good person who deserves happiness.
11. Something that reminds me of a loving person in my life who supports me.
12. Something that reminds me of a funeral or memorial service.
13. Something that reminds me of a good way to cope when I feel bad.
14. Something that represents my belief about what happens to us after we die.
15. Something that represents my future.

References

Adler, A. (1974). *Understanding human nature*. London: Rushin House.

Ainsworth, M. D., & Bell, S. M. (1970). Attachment, exploration, and separation: Illustrated by the behavior of one-year-olds in a strange situation. *Child Development, 41*(1), 49–67. doi:10.2307/1127388

Alisic, E. (2012). Teachers' perspectives on providing support to children after trauma: A qualitative study. *School Psychology Quarterly, 27*, 51–59. doi:10.1037/a0028590

Allender, S. A. (2015). Childhood and the impact of death of a loved one on behavioral functioning. *Dissertation Abstracts International DAI-B 77/01E.*

American Psychiatric Association. (2013). *Diagnostic and statistical manual of psychiatric disorders* (5th ed.). Arlington, VA: American Psychiatric Publishing.

American Psychological Association. (n.d.). *The road to resilience*. Retrieved 2019 from www.apa.org/helpcenter/road-resilience.

Archer, J. (1999). *The nature of grief: The evolution and psychology of reactions to loss*. New York: Routledge.

Archibald, H. C., Bell, D., Miller, C., & Tuddenham, R. D. (1962). Bereavement in childhood and adult psychiatric disturbance. *Psychosomatic Medicine, 24*(4), 343–351. doi:10.1097/00006842-196200700-00004

Arizmendi, B., Kaszniak, A. W., & O'Connor, M. F. (2016). Disrupted prefrontal activity during emotion processing in complicated grief: An fMRI investigation. *Neuroimage, 124*(Pt A), 968–976. doi:10.1016/j.neuroimage.2015.09.054

Arman, J. F. (2014). A grief counseling group design for Hispanic children. *Ideas and Research You Can Use, 69*, 1–14. Retrieved from www.counseling.org/knowledgecenter/vistas.

Atkinson, T. L. (1980). Teacher intervention with elementary school children in death-related situations. *Death Education, 4*(2), 149–163. doi:10.1080.07481188008252964

Attig, T. (2000). *The heart of grief: Death and the search for lasting love*. New York: Oxford University Press.

Attig, T. (2010). *How we grieve: Relearning the world* (2nd ed.). New York: Oxford University Press. doi:10.1093/acprof:oso/9780195074567.001.0001

Averill, J. R., & Nunley, E. P. (1993). Grief as an emotion and as a disease: A social-constructionist perspective. In M. S.Stroebe, W.Stroebe, & R. O. Hansson (Eds.), *Handbook of bereavement: Theory, research, and intervention*. New York: Cambridge University Press. doi:10.1017/cbo9780511664076.006

Baggerly, J., & Abugideiri, S. E. (2010). Grief counseling for Muslim preschool and elementary school children. *Journal of Multicultural Counseling and Development, 38*(2), 112–124. doi:10.1002/j.2161-1912.2010.tb00119.x

Bailis, L. A., & Kennedy, W. R. (1977). Effects of a death education program upon secondary school students. *The Journal of Educational Research, 71*(2), 63–66. doi:10.1080/00220671.1977.10885037

210 References

Baker, C. K., Norris, F. H., Jones, E. C., & Murphy, A. D. (2009). Childhood trauma and adulthood physical health in Mexico. *Journal of Behavior Modification, 32*, 255–269. doi:10.1007/s10865-009-9199-2

Baker, J. E., Sedney, M. A., & Gross, E. (1992). Psychological tasks for bereaved children. *American Journal of Orthopsychiatry, 62*(1), 105–116. doi:10.1037/h0079310

Bandura, A. (1986). *Social foundations of thought and action: A social cognitive theory.* Upper Saddle River, NJ: Prentice-Hall, Inc.

Barry, M., & McGovern, M. (2000). Death education: Knowledge, attitudes, and perspectives of Irish parents and teachers. *Death Studies, 24*(4), 325–333. doi:10.1080/074811800200487

Bazyk, S. (2007). Establishing a case for occupational therapy in meeting the needs of children with grief issues in school-based settings. *Occupational Therapy in Mental Health, 23*(2), 75–100.

Bendiksen, R. (1975). Death and the child: An anterospective test of the childhood bereavement and later behavior disorder hypothesis. *OMEGA: An International Journal for the Study of Dying, Death, Bereavement, Suicide, and Other Lethal Behaviors, 6*(1), 45–59.

Bharadwaj, R. A., Jaffe, A. E., Chen, Q., Deep-Soboslay, A., Goldman, A. L., Mighdoll, M. I. . . . Kleinman, J. E. (2016). Genetic risk mechanisms of posttraumatic stress disorder in the human brain. *Journal of Neuroscience Research, 96*, 21–30.

Biank, N. M., & Werner-Lin, A. (2011). Growing up with grief: Revisiting the death of a parent over the life course, *OMEGA, 63*(3), 271–290. doi:10.2190/OM.63.3.e

Birtchnell, J. (1969). The possible consequences of early parent death. *British Journal of Medical Psychology, 42*(1), 1–12. doi:10.1111/j.2044-8341.1969.tb02052.x

Black, D. (1998). Coping with loss: Bereavement in childhood. *BMJ (Clinical Research Edition), 316*(7135), 931–933. doi:10.111/j.1469-7610.1978.tb00471.x

Boelen, P. A., & Spuij, M. (2013). Symptoms of post-traumatic stress disorder in bereaved children and adolescents: Factor structure and correlates *Journal of Abnormal Child Psychology, 41*, 1097–1108. doi:10.1071.510802-013-9748-6

Boelen, P. A., van den Bout, J., & van den Hout, M. A. (2003). The role of cognitive variables in psychological functioning after the death of a first degree relative. *Behavioral Research Therapies, 41*(10), 1123–1136. doi:10:1016/S0005-7967(02)00259-0

Bonanno, G. A. (2009). *The other side of sadness: What the new science of bereavement tells us about life after loss.* New York: Basic Books.

Bonanno, G. A., & Mancini, A. D. (2008). The human capacity to thrive in the face of potential trauma. *Pediatrics, 121*(2), 369–375. doi:10.1542/peds.2007-1648

Boss, P. (1999). *Ambiguous loss: Learning to live with unresolved grief.* Cambridge, MA: Harvard University Press.

Bourne, C., Mackay, C. E., & Holmes, E. A. (2013). The neural basis of flashback formation: The impact of viewing trauma. *Psychological Medicine, 43*, 1521–1532. doi:10.1017/S0033291712002358

Bow, K. (2018). *The difference between grief, mourning, and bereavement.* Retrieved from www.nowilaymedowntosleep.org/articles/grief-mourning-bereavement/.

Bowlby, J. (1960). Grief and mourning in infancy and early childhood. *Psychoanalytic Study of the Child, 15*, 9–52.

Bowlby, J. (1969). *Attachment and loss volume 1: Attachment.* New York: Basic Books.

Bowlby, J. (1976). *Attachment and loss volume 2: Anxiety and anger.* New York: Basic Books.

Bowlby, J. (1980). *Attachment and loss volume 3: Sadness and depression.* New York: Basic Books.

Bowlby, J. (1982). Attachment and loss: Retrospect and prospect. *American Journal of Orthopsychiatry, 52*(4), 664–678. doi:10.1111/j.1939-0025.1982.tb01456.x

Breen, L. J., & O'Connor, M. (2007). The fundamental paradox in the grief literature: A critical reflection. *OMEGA, 55*(30), 199–218.

References 211

Breier, A., Kelsoe, J. R., Kirwin, P. D., Beller, S. A., Wolkowitz, O. M., & Pickar, D. (1988). Early parental loss and development of adult psychopathology. *Archives of General Psychiatry, 45*(11), 987–993. doi:10.1001/archpsyc.1988.01800350021003

Brent, D. A., Melhem, N. M., Donohoe, M. B., & Walker, M. (2009). The incidence and course of depression in bereaved youth 21 months after the loss of a parent to suicide, accident, or sudden natural death. *American Journal of Psychiatry, 166*(7), 786–794. doi:10.1176/appi.ajp.2009.08081244

Brent, D. A., Melhem, N. M., Masten, A. S., Porta, G., & Payne, M. W. (2012). Longitudinal effects of parental bereavement on adolescent developmental competence. *Journal of Clinical Child and Adolescent Psychology, 41*(6), 778–791. doi:10.1080/15374416.2012.717871

Briere, J. N., & Scott, C. (2014). *Principles of trauma therapy: A guide to symptoms, evaluation, and treatment (DSM-5 update)* (2nd ed.). Newbury Park, CA: Sage Publications, Inc.

Brohl, K. (2007.) *Working with traumatized children: A handbook for healing.* Arlington, VA: Child Welfare League of America, Inc.

Busch, T., & Kimble, C. S. (2001). Grieving children: Are we meeting the challenge? *Pediatric Nursing, 27*(4), 414–424.

Bush, A. D. (1997). *Transcending loss: Understanding the lifelong impact of grief and how to make it meaningful.* New York: Berkley Publishing.

Bybee, J., Merisca, R., & Velasco, R. (1998). The development of reactions of guilt-producing events. In J. Bybee (Ed.), *Guilt and children* (pp. 185–213). San Diego, CA: Academic Press. doi:10.1016/B978-012148610-5/50010-2

Cacciatore, J. (2017). *Bearing the unbearable: Love, loss, and the heartbreaking path of grief.* Beaumont, CA: Wisdom Press.

Cain, A. C., & LaFreniere, L. S. (2015). The taunting of parentally bereaved children: An exploratory study. *Death Studies, 39*, 219–225. doi:10.108/07481187.2014.975870

Carrion, V. G., & Wong, S. S. (2012). Can traumatic stress alter the brain? Understanding the implications of early trauma on brain development and learning. *Journal of Adolescent Health, 51*(2), S23–S28. doi:10.1016/j.jadohealth.2012.04.010

Cerniglia, L., Cimino, S., Ballarotto, G., & Monniello, G. (2014). Parental loss during childhood and outcomes on adolescents' psychological profiles: A longitudinal study. *Current Psychology: A Journal for Diverse Perspectives on Diverse Psychological Issues, 33*(4), 545–556. doi:10.1007/s12144-014-9228-3

Charles, R., & Ritz, D. (2004). *Brother Ray: Ray Charles' own story.* New York: DaCabo Press.

Cohen, J. A., Goodman, R. F., & Brown, E. J. (2004). Treatment of childhood traumatic grief: Contributing to a newly emerging condition in the wake of community trauma. *Harvard Review of Psychiatry, 12*(4), 213–216. doi:10.1080.10673220490509543

Cohen, J. A., & Mannarino, A. P. (2011). Supporting children with traumatic grief: What educators need to know. *School Psychology International, 32*(2), 117–131. doi:10.1177/0143034311400827

Conner, R. L., Vernikos-Danellis, J., & Levine, S. (1971). Stress, fighting, and neuroendocrine function. *Nature, 234*, 564–566.

Connolly, R. (2018). *Being John Lennon: A restless life.* Berkeley, CA: Pegasus Books.

Coplan, J. D., Andrews, M. W., Rosenblum, L. A., Owens, M. J., Friedman, S., Gorman, J. M., & Nemeroff, C. B. (1996). Persistent elevations of cerebrospinal fluid concentrations of corticotropin-releasing factor in adult nonhuman primates exposed to early-life stressors: Implications for the pathophysiology of mood and anxiety disorders. *Proceedings of the National Academy of Sciences USA, 93*(4), 1619–1623. doi:10.1073/pnas.93.4.1619

Cordaro, M. (2012). Pet loss and disenfranchised grief: Implications for mental health counseling practice. *Journal of Mental Health Counseling, 34*(4), 283–294.

212 References

Corr, C. A. (2010). Children, development, and encounters with death, bereavement, and coping. In C. A. Corr & D. E. Corr (Eds.), *Children's encounters with death, bereavement, and coping* (pp. 3–19). New York: Springer Publishing Company.

Corr, C. A., & Corr, D. M. (2007). Historical and contemporary perspectives on loss, grief, and mourning. In D. Balk, C. Wogrin, G. Thornton, & D. Meagher (Eds.), *Handbook of thanatology: The essential body of knowledge for the study, dying, and bereavement* (pp. 131–142). Northbrook, NY: Routledge/Taylor & Francis.

Courtois, C. A. (2014). *It's not you, it's what happened to you: Complex trauma and treatment.* Dublin, OH: Telemachus Press.

Cox, G. R. (2013). Religion, spirituality, and traumatic death. In D. K. Meagher & D. E. Balk (Eds.), *Handbook of thanatology* (2nd ed.). New York: Routledge.

Cox, M., Garrett, E., & Graham, J. A. (2004–5). Death in disney films: Implications for children's understanding of death. *Omega, 50*(4), 267–280. doi:10.2190/Q5VL-KLF7-060F-W69V

Cozolino, L. (2006). *The neuroscience of human relationships.* New York: W.W. Norton and Co., Inc.

Cronholm, P. F., Forke, C. M., Wade, R., Bair-Merritt, M. H., Davis, M., Harkins-Schwarz, M., . . . Fein, J. A. (2015). Adverse childhood experiences: Expanding the concept of adversity. *American Journal of Preventive Medicine, 49*(3), 354–361. doi:10.1016/j.amepre.2015.02.001

Currier, J. M., Holland, J. M., & Neimeyer, R. A. (2012). Prolonged grief symptoms and growth in the first 2 years of bereavement: Evidence for a nonlinear association. *Traumatology, 18*(4), 65–71. doi:10:1177/1534765612438948

Damasio, A. (1998). The somatic marker hypothesis and the possible functions of the prefrontal cortex. In A. C. Roberts, T. W. Robbins, & L. Weiskrantz (Eds.), *The prefrontal cortex: Executive and cognitive functions* (pp. 36–50). New York: Oxford University Press.

DeBellis, M. D., Hooper, S. R., & Sapia, J. L. (2005). Early trauma exposure and the brain. In J. J. Vasterling & C. R. Brewin (Eds.), *Neuropsychology of PTSD: Biological, cognitive, and clinical perspectives* (pp. 153–177). New York, NY: The Guilford Press.

Densen, A., Lansworth, T., & Siegel, L. (2012). *Grief in the classroom: Groundbreaking survey of educators shows overwhelming interest in helping grieving students and strong demand for training and more support.* Retrieved from www.aft.org.

Devine, M. (2017). *It's OK that you're not OK.* Boulder, CO: Sounds True Publishers.

DeYoung, P. A. (2015). *Understanding and treating chronic shame: A relational/neurobiological approach.* New York: Routledge Press.

DiCiacco, J. A. (2008). *The colors of grief: Understanding a child's journey through loss from birth to adulthood.* Philadelphia, PA: Jennifer Kingsley Publishers.

Dickens, N. (2014). Prevalence of complicated grief and posttraumatic stress disorder in children and adolescents following sibling death. *The Family Journal: Counseling and Therapy for Couples and Families, 22*(1), 119–126. doi:10.1177/1066480713505066

Dickinson, G. E., & Field, D. (2002). Teaching end-of-life issues: Current status in United Kingdom and United States medical schools. *American Journal of Hospice and Palliative Care, 19*, 181–186. doi:10.1177/104990910201900309

Dickinson, G. E., Sumner, E. D., & Frederick, L. M. (1992). Death education in selected health professions. *Death Studies, 16*, 281–289. doi:10.1080/07481189208252575

Did You Know? Children and Grief Statistics. (n.d.). Retrieved 2018 from www.childrensgriefawarenessday.org/cgad2/pdf/griefstatistics.pdf.

Dillon, N. J. (2012). *Children and grief: Information for school counselors.* Retrieved from www.2.uwstout.edu.

Dilworth, J. L., & Hildreth, G. J. (1997). Long-term unresolved grief: Applying Bowlby's variants to adult survivors of early parental death. *OMEGA, 36*(2), 147–159. doi:10.2190/66FT-3VPT-HT93-41H9

References   213

Doidge, N. (2007). *The brain that changes itself: Stories of personal triumph from the frontiers of brain science.* New York: Penguin Group.

Doka, K. J. (1989). *Disenfranchised grief: Recognizing hidden sorrow.* Lexington, MA and UK: Lexington Books/D. C. Heath and Com.

Doughty, C. (2014). *Smoke gets in your eyes and other lessons from the crematory.* New York: W.W. Norton & Company.

Dwinell, J. (2009, 11 September). Ted Kennedy, Jr. recalls fear for Dad. *Boston Herald.*

Dyregrov, A. (1991). *Grief in children: A handbook for adults* (1st ed.). Philadelphia, PA: Jessica Kingsley Publishers.

Dyregrov, A., bie Wikander, A. M., & Vigerust, S. (1999). Sudden death of a classmate and friend: Adolescents' perception of support from their school. *School Psychology International, 20*(2), 191–208. doi:10.1177.0143034399202003

Dyregrov, A., & Dyregrov, K. (2013). Complicated grief in children: The perspectives of experienced professionals. *OMEGA, 67*(3), 291–303. doi:10.2190/OM.67.3.c

Dyregrov, K. (2009). The important role of the school following suicide in Norway. What support do young people wish that school could provide? *OMEGA: Journal of Death and Dying, 59*(2), 147–161. doi:10.2190/OM.59.2.d

Edelman, H. (2014). *Motherless daughters: The legacy of loss* (20th anniversary ed.). Boston, MA: De Capo Lifelong Books.

Eilegard, A., Steineck, G., Nyberg, T., & Kreicbergs, U. (2013). Psychological health in siblings who lost a brother or sister to cancer 2 to 9 years earlier. *Psycho-Oncology, 22,* 683–691. doi:10.1002/pon.3053

Elizur, E., & Kaffman, M. (1983). Factors influencing the severity of childhood bereavement reactions. *American Journal of Orthopsychiatry, 53*(4), 668–676. doi:10.1111/j.1939-0025.1983.tb03410.x

Elkind, D. (1967). Egocentrism in adolescence. *Child Development, 38,* 1025–1033.

Ellis, J., Dowrick, C., & Lloyd-Williams, M. (2013). The long-term impact of early parental death: Lessons from a narrative study. *Journal of the Royal Society of Medicine, 106,* 57–67. doi:10.1177/0141076812472623

Engel, G. L. (1994). Is grief a disease? In R. Frankiel (Ed.), *Essential papers on object loss.* New York: New York University Press.

Epstein, M. (2013). *Trauma in everyday life.* New York: Penguin Books.

Erikson, E. (1963). *Childhood and society* (2nd ed.). New York: W.W. Norton and Co.

Fanos, J. H., & Nickerson, B. G. (1991). Long-term effects of sibling loss on adolescence. *Journal of Adolescent Research, 60*(1), 70–82. doi:10.1177/074355489161006

Felitti, V. J., Anda, R. F., Nordenberg, D., Williamson, D. F., Spitz, A. M., et al. (1998). Relationship of childhood abuse and household dysfunction to many of the leading causes of death in adults: The Adverse Childhood Experiences (ACE) study. *American Journal of Preventive Medicine, 14*(4), 245–258. doi:10.1016/S0749-3797(98)00017-8

Fenichel, O. (1943). Mourning and its relation to manic-depressive states. *Psychoanalytic Quarterly, 12,* 288–289.

Ferguson, T. J., & Stegge, H. (1998). Measuring guilt in children: A rose by any other name still has thorns. In J. Bybee (Ed.), *Guilt and children* (pp. 19–74). San Diego, CA: Academic Press. doi:10.1016/B978-012148610-5/50003-5

Ferguson, T. J., Stegge, H., & Damhuis, I. (1991). Children's understanding of guilt and shame. *Child Development, 62*(4), 827–839. doi:10.2307/1131180

Finkelhor, D., Shattuck, A., Turner, H., & Hamby, S. (2013). Improving the Adverse Childhood Experiences study scale. *JAMA Pediatrics, 167*(1), 70–75. doi:10.1001/jamapediatrics.2013.420

214   References

Fraley, C. R., & Bonanno, G. A. (2004). Attachment and loss: A test of three competing model on the association between attachment-related avoidance and adaptation to bereavement. *Personality and Social Psychology, 30*(7), 878–890. doi:10.1177/01461672 04264289

Frankl, V. (1984). *Man's search for meaning* (3rd ed.). New York: Simon and Schuster.

Freud, S. (1957). Mourning and melancholia. In *The standard edition of the complete psychological works of Sigmund Freud* (Vol. 14). London: The Hogarth Press.

Freud, S. (1961). *Civilization and its discontents* (Standard ed.) New York: W.W. Norton and Company.

Freud, S. (1986). *The complete psychological works of Sigmund Freud, Volume XVII: An infantile neurosis and other works.* London: The Hogarth Press.

Freud, S., & Breuer, J. (2004). *Studies in hysteria* (Lochurst, N., Trans.). New York: Penguin Group.

Gage, M. G., & Holcomb, R. (1991). Couples' perception of stressfulness of death of the family pet. *Family Relations: An Interdisciplinary Journal of Applied Family Studies, 40*(1), 103–105. doi:10.2307/585666

Galende, N. (2015). Death and its didactics in pre-school and primary school. *Procedia-Social and Behavioral Sciences, 185*, 91–97. doi:10:1016/j.sbspro.2015.03.403

Garber, B. (2008). Mourning in children: A theoretical synthesis and clinical application. *The Annual of Psychoanalysis, 36*, 174–188.

Glass, J. C. (1990). Death, loss, and grief in high school students. *The High School Journal, 73*(3), 154–160.

Glass, J. C. (1990). Death, loss, and grief among middle school children: Implications for the school counselor. *Elementary School Guidance and Counseling, 28*(2), 139–148.

Goldberg, D. (2019). *Serving the servant: Remembering Kurt Cobain.* New York: Ecco Press.

Golden, A. M. J., & Dalgleish, T. (2010). Is prolonged grief disorder distinct from bereavement- related posttraumatic stress? *Psychiatry Research, 178*, 336–341. doi:10.1016/j. psychres.2009.08.021

Golden, A. M. J., & Dalgleish, T. (2012). Facets of pejorative self-processing in complicated grief. *Journal of Consulting and Clinical Psychology, 80*(3), 512–524. doi:10.1037/a0027338

Golden, A. M., Dalgleish, T., & Mackintosh, B. (2007). Levels of specificity of autobiographical memories and of biographical memories of the deceased in bereaved individuals with and without complicated grief. *Journal of Abnormal Psychology, 116*(4), 786–795. doi:10.1037/0021-843X.116.4.786

Goldman, L. (2002). The assumptive world of children. In J. Kauffman (Ed.), *Loss of the assumptive world* (pp. 194–200). New York: Brunner-Routledge.

Gonzalez, C. L., & Bell, H. (2016). Child-centered play therapy for Hispanic children with traumatic grief: Cultural implications for treatment outcomes. *International Journal of Play Therapy, 25*(3), 146–153. doi:10.1037/pla0000023

Goodwin, R D., & Stein, M. B. (2004). Association between childhood trauma and physical disorders among adults in the United States. *Psychological Medicine, 34*(3), 509–520. doi:10.1300/j004v23n02_04

Graham, A. (2004). Life is like the seasons: Responding to change, loss, and grief through a peer-based education program. *Childhood Education, 80*(6), 317–321.

Graham, H. M. (1999). Help or hindrance? An examination of the effectiveness of children grief support groups. *Dissertation Abstracts International, 60*(6-A), 2227.

Granot, T. (2005). *Without you: Children and young people growing up with loss and its effects.* Philadelphia, PA: Jessica Kingsley Publishers.

Greene, J. (2019). *Once more we saw stars.* New York: Alfred A. Knopf, Publisher.

Hambrick, E. P., Brawner, T. W., Perry, B. D., Brandt, K., Hofmeister, C., & Collins, J. O. (2018). Beyond the ACE score: Examining relationships between timing of developmental adversity, relational health and development outcomes in children. *Archives of Psychiatric Nursing, 33*(3), 238–247. doi:10.1016/j.apnu.2018.11.001

Harris, M. A., Brett, C. E., Starr, J. M., Deary, I. J., & McIntosh, A. M. (2016). Early-life predictors of resilience and related outcomes up to 66 years later in the 6-day sample of the 1947 mental survey. *Social Psychiatry and Psychiatric Epidemiology: The International Journal for Research in Social and Genetic Epidemiology and Mental Health Services, 51*(5), 659–668.

Harrison, L., & Harrington, R. (2001). Adolescents' bereavement experiences. Prevalence, association with depressive symptoms, and use of services. *Journal of Adolescence, 24*(2), 159–169. doi:10.1006/jado.2001.0379

Hart, L. A., & Garza, Y. (2013). Teachers' perceptions of effects of a student's death: A phenomenological study. *OMEGA, 66*(4), 301–311.

Hart, L. A., Hart, B. L., & Mader, B. (1990). Humane euthanasia and companion animal death: Caring for the animal, the client, and the veterinarian. *Journal of the American Veterinary Medical Association, 197*(10), 1292–1299.

Hayes, J. (2016). Praising the dead: On the motivational tendency and psychological function of eulogizing the deceased. *Motivation & Emotion, 40*(3), 375–388. doi:10.1007/s11031-016-9545-y

Heim, C., Newport, D. J., Mletzko, T., Miller, A. H., & Nemeroff, C. B. (2008). The link between childhood trauma and depression: Insights from HPA axis studies in humans. *Psychoneuroendocrinology, 33*(6), 693–710. doi:10.1016/j.psyneuen.2008.03.008

Hensley, P. L., & Clayton, P. J. (2008). Bereavement: Signs, symptoms, and course. *Psychiatric Annals, 38*(10), 649–654.

Higgins, D. J. (2003). The relationship of childhood family characteristics and current attachment styles to depression and depressive vulnerability. *Australian Journal of Psychology, 55*(1), 9–14. doi:10.1080/0004953041233131814

Hilliard, R. E. (2001). The effects of music therapy-based bereavement groups on mood and behavior of grieving children: A pilot study. *Journal of Music Therapy, 38*(4), 291–306. doi:10.1093/jmt/38.4.291

Hirst, W., Phelps, E. A., Buckner, R. L., Budson, A. E., Cuc, A., Gabrieli, J.D., . . . Vaidya, C. J., (2009). Long-term memory for the terrorist attack of September 11: Flashbulb memories, event memories, and the factors that influence their retention. *Journal of Experimental Psychology: General, 138*(2), 161–176. doi:10.1037/a0015527

Hone, L. (2017) *Resilient grieving: Finding strength and embracing life after a loss that changes everything.* New York: The Experiment Publishing.

Hooyman, N. R., & Kramer, B. J. (2006). *Living through loss: Interventions across the life Span.* New York: Colombia University Press.

Horowitz, M. J., Siegel, B., Holen, A., Bonanno, G. A., Milbrath, C., & Stinson, C. H. (2003). Diagnostic criteria for complicated grief disorder. *FOCUS: The Journal of Lifelong Learning in Psychiatry, 1*, 290–298. doi:10.1176/ajp.154.7.904

Howarth, R. A. (2011). Concepts and controversies in grief and loss. *Journal of Mental Health and Counseling, 33*(1), 4–10. doi:10.17744/mehc.33.1.900m56162888u737

Hurd, R. C. (1999). Adults view their childhood bereavement experiences. *Death Studies, 23*, 17–41. doi:10.1080/074811899201172

Jacobs, J. R., & Bovasso, G. B. (2009). Re-examining the long-term effects of experiencing parental death in childhood on adult psychopathology. *The Journal of Nervous and Mental Disease, 197*(1), 24–27. doi:10.1097/NMD.0b013e318927723

Jacobs, S. (1999). *Traumatic grief: Diagnosis, treatment, and prevention.* New York: Bruner and Mazel.

James, J. W., & Friedman, R. (2001). *When children grieve: For adults to help children deal with death, divorce, pet loss, moving, and other losses.* New York: Harper Collins/Quill.

216 References

James, J. W., & Friedman, R. (2009). *The grief recovery handbook: 20th anniversary expanded edition.* New York: Harper Collins/Morrow.

Jamison, K. R. (1993). *Touched with fire: Manic-depressive illness and the artistic temperament.* New York: Simon & Schuster, Inc.

Jamison, K. R. (1995). *An unquiet mind.* New York: Vintage Books.

Jenkins, J., & Oatley, K. (1998). The development of emotion schemas in children: Processes that underlie psychopathology. In Jr. W. F. Flack & J. D. Laird (Eds.), *Emotions in psychopathology: Theory and research* (pp. 45–56). New York, NY: Oxford University Press.

Jenkins, M. A., Dunham, M., & Contreras-Bloomdahl, S. (2011). *The need for grief awareness and staff training in schools.* Retrieved from http://counselingoutfitters.com.

Johnson, K. (1998). *Trauma in the lives of children: Crisis and stress management techniques for counselors, teachers, and other professionals.* Alameda, CA: Hunter House, Inc.

Jonas-Simpson, C., Steele, R., Granek, L., Davies, B., & O'Leary, J. (2015). Always with me: Understanding experiences of bereaved children whose baby sibling died. *Death Studies, 39,* 242–251. doi:10.1080/07481187.2014.991954

Jones, C. H., Hodges, M., & Slate, J. R. (1995). Parental support for death education programs in the schools. *The School Counselor, 42,* 370–376.

Jones, J. D., Fraley, R. C., Ehrlich, K. B., Stern, J. A., Lejuez, C. W., Shaver, P.R., & Cassidy, J. (2018). Stability of attachment style in adolescence: An empirical test of alternative developmental processes. *Child Development, 89*(3), 871–880. doi:10.111/cdev.12775

Jung, C. G. (1963). *Memories, dreams, and reflections* (Jaffe, A., Ed., Winston, R., Trans., Winston, C. J., Author). New York: Pantheon Books.

Kagan, J. (1984). *The nature of the child.* New York: Basic Books, Inc.

Kaplow, J. B., Howell, K. H., & Layne, C. M. (2014). Do circumstances of the death matter? Identifying socioenvironmental risks for grief-related psychopathology in bereaved youth. *Journal of Traumatic Stress, 27,* 42–49. doi:10.1002/jts.21877

Kaplow, J. B., Layne, C. M., Pynoos, R. S., Cohen, J. A., & Lieberman, A. (2012). DSM-V diagnostic criteria for bereavement-related disorders in children and adolescents: Developmental considerations. *Psychiatry, 75*(3), 243–264. doi:1C.1177/07435548161006

Kaplow, J. B., Saunders, J., Angold, A., & Costello, E. J. (2010). Psychiatric symptoms in bereaved versus non-bereaved youth and young adults: A longitudinal epidemiological study. *Journal of the American Academy of Child and Adolescent Psychiatry, 49*(11), 1145–1154. doi:10.1016/j.jaac.2010.08.004

Kauffman, J. (2008). What is "no recovery?" *Death Studies, 32,* 74–83. doi:10.1080/07481180701741376

Kaufman, K. R., & Kaufman, N. D. (2006). And then the dog died. *Death Studies, 30,* 61–76. doi:10.1080/07481180500348811

Keppel-Benson, J. M., & Ollendick, T. H. (1993). Posttraumatic disorder in children and adolescents. In C. F. Saylor (Ed.), *Children and disasters.* New York: Plenum Press. doi:10.1007/978-1-4757-4766-9_3

King, B. (2013). *How animals grieve.* Chicago, IL: University of Chicago Press.

Klengel, T., & Binder, E. B. (2015). Epigenetics of stress-related psychiatric disorders and gene x environment interactions. *Neuron, 86*(6), 1343–1357. doi:10.1016/j.neuron.2015.05.036

Klingman, A. (1983). Simulation and simulation games as a strategy for death education. *Death Education, 7*(4), 339–352. doi:10.1080/07481188308251370

Klingman, A. (1987). A school-based emergency crisis intervention in a mass school disaster. *Professional Psychology: Research and Practice, 18*(6), 604–612. doi:10.1037//0735-7028.18.6.604

Klingman, A. (1988). School community in disaster: Planning for intervention. *Journal of Community Psychology, 16,* 205–240. doi:10.1002/1520-6629(198804)16:2<205::aid-jcop2290160210>3.0.co;2-0

References 217

Klingman, A. (1989). School-based emergency intervention following an adolescent's suicide. *Death Studies, 13*, 263–274. doi:10.1080/07481188908252303

Klingman, A., & Ben Ali, Z. (1981). A school community in disaster: Primary and secondary prevention in situational crisis. *Professional Psychology, 12*(4), 523–533. doi:10.1037//0735-7028.12.4.523

Kolb, B., & Whislaw, I. Q. (2003). *Fundamentals of human neuropsychology* (5th ed.). New York: Worth Publishers.

Kosminsky, P. S., & Jordan, J. R. (2016). *Attachment-informed grief therapy: The clinician's guide to foundations and applications.* New York: Routledge.

Kozlowska, K., Walker, P., McLean, L., Carrive, P. (2015). Fear and the defense cascade: Clinical implications and management. *Harvard Review of Psychiatry, 23*(4), 263–287. doi:10.1097/HRP.0000000000000065

Kubler-Ross, E. (1969). *On death and dying.* New York: MacMillen Publishing Co., Inc.

Ladd, C. O., Owens, M. J., & Nemeroff, C. B. (1996). Persistent changes in corticotropin-releasing factor neuronal systems induced by maternal deprivation. *Endocrinology, 137*(4), 1212–1218. doi:10.1210/endo.137.4.8625891

Lai, V. T. C. (2013). The inner world of bereaved children: A qualitative approach to understanding how children from three to seven-years-old experience the death of a parent. *Dissertation Abstracts International Section B: The Sciences and Engineering, 74*(6-B) (E).

Lawrence, S. T. (2015). *Turning the page: Helping a child cope with the loss of a sibling.* Morrisville, NC: Lulu Press.

Layne, C. M. (2014). Cumulative trauma exposure and high-risk behavior in adolescence: Findings from the National Child Trauma Stress Network core data set. *Psychological Trauma: Theory, Research, Practice, and Policy, 6*(S1), S40–S49. doi:10.1031.a0037799

LeBlanc, N. J., Unger, L. D., & McNally, R. J. (2016). Emotional and physiological reactivity in complicated grief. *Journal of Affective Disorders, 194*, 98–104. doi:10:10.1016/j.jad.2016.01.024

Lehman, L. (2000a). *Mourning child grief support curriculum* (Preschool ed.). New York: Routledge.

Lehman, L. (2000b). *Mourning child grief support curriculum* (Early Childhood ed.). New York: Routledge.

Lehman, L. (2000c). *Mourning child grief support curriculum* (Middle Childhood ed.). New York: Routledge.

Lehman, L. (2000d). *Teens together grief support curriculum.* New York: Routledge.

Lehman, L. (2000e). *Grief group support facilitator's handbook.* New York: Routledge.

Levi, P. (1988). *The drowned and the saved.* New York: Simon and Schuster, Inc.

Levine, P. A. (1997). *Waking the Tiger: Healing Trauma.* Berkeley, CA: North Atlantic Books.

Levine, P. A. (2010). *In an unspoken voice: How the body releases trauma and restores goodness.* Berkeley, CA: North Atlantic Books.

Levine, P. A. (2015). *Trauma and memory: Brain and body in a search for the living past.* Berkeley, CA: North Atlantic Books.

Levine, P. A., & Kline, M. (2007). *Trauma through a child's eyes.* Berkeley, CA: North Atlantic Books.

Lewis, C. S. (2001). *A grief observed.* New York: HarperOne.

Lewis, H. S. (1971). *Shame and guilt in neurosis.* Madison, CT: International Universities Press.

Lichtenthal, W. G., Cruess, D. G., & Prigerson, H. G. (2004). A case for establishing complicated grief as a distinct mental disorder in DSM-V. *Clinical Psychology Review, 24*(6), 637–662. doi:10.1016/j.cpr.2005.07.002

Life with Grief Research. (n.d.). Retrieved 2019 from www.childrensgriefawarenessday.org/cgad2/pdf/griefstatistics.pdf.

Lima, B. R., & Gittleman, M. (2004). Differential and long-term effects of disasters: The need for planning and preparation. *International Journal of Mental Health, 32*(4), 3–5.

218 References

Lindemann, E. (1944). Symptomatology and the management of acute grief. *The American Journal of Psychiatry, 101*, 186–201.

Lindsay-Hartz, J. (1984). Contrasting experiences of shame and guilt. *American Behavioral Scientist, 27*(6), 689–704. doi:10:1177/00027684027006003

Lowell, R. (1977). *Since 1939: Day by day first edition*. New York: Farrar, Straus, & Giroux.

Lowenstein, L. (2006). *Creative interventions for bereaved children*. Toronto, Canada: Champion Press.

Lowton, K., & Higginson, I. J. (2003). Managing bereavement in the classroom: A conspiracy of silence? *Death Studies, 27*, 717–741. doi:10.1080/713842340

Ludy-Dobson, C. R., & Perry, B. D. (2010). The role of healthy interactions in buffering the impact of childhood trauma. In E. Gil (Ed.), *Working with children to heal interpersonal trauma: The power of play* (pp. 26–43). New York: Guilford Press.

Maier, H., & Lachman, M. E. (2000). Consequences of early parental loss and separation for health and well-being in midlife. *International Journal of Behavioral Development, 24*(2), 183–189. doi:10.1080/016502500383304

Main, M., & Solomon, J. (1986). Discovery of an insecure-disorganized/disoriented attachment pattern. In T. Brazelton & M. W. Yogman (Eds.), *Affective development in infancy* (9th ed., pp. 5–124). Westport, CT: Ablex Publishing.

Mancini, A. D., & Bonanno, G. A. (2006). Resilience in the face of potential trauma: Clinical practices and illustrations. *Journal of Clinical Psychology: In Session, 62*(8), 971–985. doi:10.1002/jclp.20283

Mancini, A. D., & Bonanno, G. A. (2009). Predictors and parameters of resilience to loss: Toward an individual differences model. *Journal of Personality, 77*(6), 1805–1832. doi:10:1111/j.1467-6494.2009.00601.x

Mancuso, A. (2015). *How to form a nonprofit corporation: A step-by-step guide to forming a 501(c)(3) nonprofit in any state* (12th ed.). Berkeley, CA: NOLC.

Marino, R. C., Thornton, M. D., & Lange, T. (2015). *Professional school counselors address grief and loss: A creative group counseling intervention*. Retrieved from www.counseling.org.

Martin, J. D., & Ferris, F. D. (2013). *I can't stop crying: Grief and recovery, a compassionate guide*. Toronto, Canada: McClelland & Stewart.

Mash, H. B. H., Fullerton, C. S., & Ursano, R. J. (2013). Complicated grief and bereavement in young adults following close friend and sibling loss. *Depression and Anxiety, 30*, 1202–1210. doi:10.1002/da.22068

Maslow, A. H. (1943). A theory of human motivation. *Psychological Review, 50*(4), 370–396. doi:10.1037/h0054346

May, R. (1978). Foreword. In R. S. Valle & M. King (Eds.), *Existential-phenomenological alternatives for psychology*. New York: Oxford University Press.

McClatchey, I. S., & Peters, A. (2015). Can trauma focused grief education decrease acting-out behavior among bereaved children? A pilot study. *Journal of Human Services, 14*–27.

McClatchey, I. S., Vonk, M. E., & Palardy, G. (2009). The prevalence of childhood traumatic grief: A comparison of violent/sudden and expected loss. *OMEGA, 59*(4), 305–323. doi:10.1080/074811800200487

McCown, D. E., & Davies, B. (1995). Patterns of grief in young children following the death of a sibling. *Death Studies, 19*(1), 41–53. doi:10.1080/07481189508252712

McCoyd, J. L. M., & Walter, C. A. (2014). Developmental perspectives on death and dying, and maturational losses. In J. M. Stillion & T. Attig (Eds.), *Death, dying, and bereavement: Contemporary perspectives, institutions, and practices*. New York: Springer Publishing Company.

McCoyd, J. L. M., Walter, C. A., & Lopez-Levers, L. (2012). Issues of grief and loss. In L. Lopez Levers (Ed.), *Trauma counseling: Theories and interventions* (1st ed.). New York: Springer Publishing Company.

References 219

McLeod, J. D. (1991). Childhood parental loss and adult depression. *Journal of Health and Social Behavior, 32*(3), 205–220.

Melhem, N. M. (2011). Grief in children and adolescents bereaved by sudden parental death. *Archives of General Psychiatry, 68*(9), 911–919. doi:10.1001/archgenpsychiatry.2011.101.

Melhem, N. M., Day, N., Shear, M. K., Day, R., Reynolds, C. F., & Brent, D. (2004). Traumatic grief among adolescents exposed to a peer's suicide. *American Journal of Psychiatry, 161*(8), 1411–1416. doi:10.10.1176?appi.ajp.161.8.1411

Middleton-Moz, J. (1990). *Shame and guilt: The masters of disguise.* Deerfield Beach, FL: Health Communications, Inc.

Milgram, N. A., Toubiana, Y. H., Klingman, A., Raviv, A., & Goldstein, I. (1988). Situational exposure and personal loss in children's acute and chronic stress reactions to a school bus disaster. *Journal of Traumatic Stress, 1*(3), 339–352. doi:10.1007/bf00974769

Mitchell, L. M., Stephenson, P. H., Cadell, S., & MacDonald, M. E. (2012). Death and grief online: Virtual memorialization and changing concepts of childhood death and parental bereavement on the Internet. *Health Sociology Review, 21*(4), 413–431. doi:10.5172/hesr.2012.21.4.413

Molnar-Stickels, L. A. (1985). Effect of a brief instructional unit in death education on the death attitudes of prospective elementary school teachers. *Journal of School Health, 55*(6), 234–236. doi:10.1111/j.1746-1561.1985.tb04128.x

Morrissey, P. (2013). *The companioning the grieving child curriculum book.* Fort Collins, CO: Companion Press.

Nagy, M. H. (1959). The child's view of death. In H. Feifel (Ed.), *The meaning of death.* New York: McGraw-Hill Book Company.

National Institute of Mental Health. (n.d.). *Helping children and adolescents cope with disasters and other traumatic events: What parents, rescue workers, and the community can do.* Retrieved 25 May 2017 from www.nimh.nih.gov/health/publications/helping-children-and-adolescents-cope-with-disasters-and-other-traumatic-events/index.shtml#pub1.

Neimeyer, R. A., Baldwin, S. A., & Gillies, J. (2006). Continuing bonds and reconstructing meaning: Mitigating complications in bereavement. *Death Studies, 30*, 715–738. doi:10.1080/07481180600848322

Neimeyer, R. A., Botella, L., Herrero, O., Pacheco, M., Figeuras, S., & Werner-Wilder, L. A. (2002). The meaning of your absence: Traumatic loss and narrative reconstruction. In J. Kauffman (Ed.), *Loss of the assumptive world* (pp. 37–38). New York: Brunner-Routledge.

Nemeroff, C. B. (1996). The Corticotrophin-Releasing Factor (CRF) hypothesis of depression: New findings and new directions. *Molecular Psychiatry, 1*(4), 336–342.

Nemeroff, C. B., Widerlov, E., Bissette, G., Walleus, H., Karlsson, I., et al. (1984). Elevated concentrations of CSF corticotropin-releasing factor-like immunoreactivity in depressed patients. *Science, 226*(4680), 1342–1344. doi:10.1126/science.6334362

New York Life Foundation. (2017). *The New York Life Foundation's bereavement study: Key findings.* Retrieved 2018 from www.newyorklife.com/assets/foundation/docs/pdfs/survey_key_findings.pdf.

Nietzsche, F. (1997). *Untimely meditations* (2nd ed.). Cambridge: Cambridge University Press.

Noel, B., & Blair, P. (2008). *I wasn't ready to say goodbye: Surviving, coping, and healing after the sudden death of a loved one.* Naperville, IL: Sourcebooks.

O'Doherty, D. C. M., Chitty, K. M., Saddiqui, S., Bennett, M. R., & Lagopoulus, J. (2015). A systematic review and meta-analysis of magnetic resonance imaging measurement of structural volumes in posttraumatic stress disorder. *Psychiatry Research: Neuroimaging, 232*(1), 1–33. doi:10.1016/j.pscychresns.2015.01.002

Ober, A. M., Granello, D. H., & Wheaton, J. E. (2012). Grief counseling: An investigation of counselors' training, experience, and competencies. *Journal of Counseling & Development, 90*(2), 150–159. doi:10.1111/j.1556-6676.2012.00020.x

220 References

Oltjenbruns, K. A. (2013). Life span issues and loss, grief, and mourning: Childhood and adolescence. In *Handbook of thanatology* (2nd ed.). New York: Routledge.

Owens, D. (2008). Recognizing the needs of bereaved children in palliative care. *Journal of Hospice and Palliative Nursing, 10*(1), 14–16. doi:10.1097/01.njh.0000306709.20045.8f

Packman, W., Bussolari, C., Katz, R., Carmack, B. J., & Field, N. P. (2017). Posttraumatic growth following the loss of a pet. *OMEGA—Journal of Death and Dying, 75*(4), 337–359. doi:10.1177/0030222816663411

Packman, W., Field, N. P., Carmack, B. J., & Ronen, R. (2011). Continuing bonds and psychosocial adjustment in pet loss. *Journal of Loss and Trauma, 16*, 341–357. doi:10.1080/15 325024.2011.572046

Panagiotaki, G., Hopkins, M., Nobes, G., Ward, E., & Griffiths, D. (2018). Children's and adults' understanding of death: Cognitive, parental, and experiential influences. *Journal of Experimental Child Psychology, 166*, 96–115. doi.org/10.1016/j.jecp.2017.07.014

Parkes, C. M. (2011). Can individuals who are specialists in death, dying, and bereavement contribute to the prevention and/or mitigation of armed conflicts and cycles of violence? *Death Studies, 5*, 455–466.

Perez, H. C. S., Ikram, M. A., Direk, N., Prigerson, H. G., Freak-Poli, R., Verhaaren, B.F., . . . Tiemeier, H., (2015). Cognition, structural brain changes and complicated grief: A population-based study. *Psychological Medicine, 45*(7), 1389–1399. doi:10.1017/S0033291714002499

Perkins, H. W., & Harris, L. B. (1990). Familial bereavement and health in adult life course perspective. *Journal of Marriage and Family, 52*(1), 233–241. doi:10.2307/352853

Perry, B. D., & Pollard, R. A. (1998). Homeostasis, stress, trauma, and adaptation: A neuro-developmental view of childhood trauma. *Child and Adolescent Psychiatric Clinics of North America, 7*(1), 33–51. doi:10.1016/s1056-4993(18)30258-x

Perry, B. D., Pollard, R. A., Blaicley, T. L., Baker, W. L., & Vigilante, D. (1995). Childhood trauma, the neurobiology of adaptation, and "use-dependent" development of the brain: How "states" become "traits". *Infant Mental Health Journal, 16*(4), 271–291. doi:10.1002/1097-0335(199524)16:4<271

Perry, B. D., & Rosenfelt, J. L. (2013). *A child's loss: Helping children exposed to traumatic Death* (The Child Trauma Academy Press Caregiver Series Book 1). Houston, TX: Child Trauma Academy Press.

Pfeffer, C. R., Karus, D., Siegel, K., & Jiang, H. (2000). Child survivors of parental death from cancer or suicide: Depressive and behavioral outcomes. *Psycho-Oncology, 9*(1), 1–10. doi:10.1002/(SICI)1099-1611(200001/02)9:1 3.0.CO;2-5

Pfefferbaum, B., Nixon, S. J., Tucker, P. M., Tivis, R. D., Moore, V. L., Gurwitch, R.H., . . . Geis, H.K., (1999). Posttraumatic stress responses in bereaved children after the Oklahoma City bombing. *Journal of the American Academy of Child and Adolescent Psychiatry, 38*(11), 1372–1379. doi:10.1097/00004583-199911000-00011

Piaget, J. (1969). *Judgment and reasoning in the child* (Warden, M., Trans.). London: Routledge and Kegan Paul, Ltd.

Potts, S. (2013). Least said, soonest mended?: Responses of primary school teachers to the perceived support needs of bereaved children. *Journal of Early Childhood Research, 11*, 95–107. doi:10.1177/1476718X12466201

Prigerson, H. G., Bridge, J., Maciejewski, P. K., Beery, L. C., Rosenheck, R. A., et al. (1999). Influence of traumatic grief on suicidal ideation among young adults. *The American Journal of Psychiatry, 156*(12), 1994–1995.

Pynoos, R. S., Frederick, C., Nader, K., Arroyo, W., Steinberg, A., Eth, S. . . . Fairbanks, L. (1987). Life threat and posttraumatic stress in school-age children. *Archives of General Psychiatry, 44*, 1057–1063.

Quindlen, A. (2002). Young in a year of fear. *Newsweek, 140*(19), 68.

References 221

Rando, T. A. (1988). Anticipatory grief: The term is a misnomer but the phenomenon exists. *Journal of Palliative Care*, 4(1–2), 70–73. doi:10.1177/0825859788004001-223

Rando, T. A. (1991). *How to go on living when someone you love dies*. New York: Bantam Books.

Rando, T. A. (2012). On achieving clarity regarding complicated grief: Lessons from clinical perspective. In M. Stroebe, H. Schut, & J. van den Bout, ed., *Complicated grief: Scientific foundations for health care professionals* (Chapter 4, pp. 40–54). New York: Routledge/Taylor and Prentiss Group.

Range, L. (2013). Historical and contemporary perspectives on traumatic death. In *Handbook of thanatology*. New York: Routledge.

Rasmussen, C. (2019). *Second firsts: A step-by-step guide to life after loss*. Carlsbad, CA: Hay House, Inc.

Raveis, V. H., Siegel, K., & Karus, D. (1999). Children's psychological distress following the death of a friend. *Journal of Youth and Adolescence*, 28(2), 165–180. doi:0047-2891/99/0400-0165S16.00/0

Reid, J. K., & Dixon, W. A. (1999). Teacher attitudes on coping with grief in the public school classroom. *Psychology in the Schools*, 36(3), 219–229. doi:10.1002/(SICI)1520-6807(199905)36:3<219::AID-PITS5>3.0.CO;2-0

Richter, C. P. (1957). On the phenomenon of sudden death in animals in man. *Psychosomatic Medicine*, 19, 191–198. doi:10.1097/00006842-195705000-00004

Riely, M. (2003). Facilitating children's grief. *The Journal of School Nursing*, 19(4), 212–218. doi:10.1177/10598405030190040601

Roberts, J. E., & Gotlib, I. H. (1997). Lifetime episodes of dysphoria: Gender, early childhood loss and personality. *British Journal of Clinical Psychology*, 36(2), 195–208. doi:10.11111j2044-8260.1997.tb01407

Rosen, H., & Cohen, H. L. (1981). Children's reactions to sibling loss. *Clinical Social Work Journal*, 9(3), 211–219. doi:10.1007/BF00757179

Rosengren, K. S., Gutierrez, I. T., & Schein, S. S. (2014). Children's understanding of death: Toward a contextualized and integrated account: V. cognitive models of death. *Monographs of the Society for Research in Child Development*, 79(1), 83–96. doi:10.1111/mono.12080

Rosenthal, N. R. (1981). Attitudes toward death education and grief counseling. *Counselor Education and Supervision*, 20(3), 203–210. doi:10.1002/j.1556-6978.1981.tb01648.x

Rosenthal, N. R., & Terkelson, C. (1978). Death education and counseling: A survey. *Counselor Education and Supervision*, 18(2), 109–114. doi:10.1002/j.1556-6978.1978.tb01873.x

Rothschild, B. (2000). *The body remembers: The psychophysiology of trauma and trauma treatment*. New York: W.W. Norton and Co. Inc.

Saavedra Perez, H. C., Direk, N., Milic, J., Ikram, M. A., Hofman, A., Tiemeier, H. (2017). The impact of complicated grief on diurnal cortisol levels two years after loss: A population-based study. *Psychosomatic Medicine*, 79(4), 426–433. doi:10.1097/PSY.0000000000000422

Salloum, A., Garside, L. W., Irwin, C. L., Anderson, A. D., & Francois, A. H. (2009). Grief and trauma group therapy for children after Hurricane Katrina. *Social Work with Groups*, 32(1–2), 64–79. doi:10.1080/01609510802290958

Salloum, A., & Overstreet, S. (2008). Evaluation of individual and group grief and trauma interventions for children post disaster. *Journal of Clinical Child & Adolescent Psychology*, 37(3), 95–507. doi:10.1080/15374410802148194

Samuel, J. (2018). *Grief works: Stories of life, death, and surviving*. New York: Scribner.

Santrock, J. (2017). *Lifespan development* (17th ed.). New York: McGraw Hill.

Sapolsky, R. M. (2004). *Why zebras don't get ulcers* (3rd ed.). New York: Holt Paperbacks.

Scaer, R. (2001). *The body bears the burden: Trauma, dissociation, and disease*. Binghamton, NY: Haworth Medical Press.

Schimmenti, A., & Bifulco, A. (2015). Linking lack of care in childhood to anxiety disorders inemerging adulthood. The role of attachment styles. *Child and Adolescent MentalHealth*, 20(1), 41–48. doi:10.111/camh.12051

222 References

Schleifer, S. J., Keller, S. E., & Stein, M. (1985). Stress effects on immunity. *Psychiatric Journal of the University of Ottawa, 10*(3), 125–131.

Schore, A. N. (2001). The effects of early relational trauma on right brain development, affect regulation, and infant mental health. *Infant Mental Health Journal, 22*(1–2), 201–269. doi:10.1002/1097-0355(200101/04)22:1<201::aid-imhj8>3.0.co;2-9

Schupp, L. (2004). *Grief: Normal, complicated, traumatic.* Eau Claire, WI: PESI Healthcare, LLC.

Schwartz, J. M., & Begley, S. (2002). *The mind and the brain: Neuroplasticity and the power of mental force.* New York: Regan Books/Harper Collins Publishers.

Schwartz, R. F. (2000). "Peer support group": A program design aimed at helping adolescents deal with grief and loss issues. *Diissertation Abstracts International, 5-B*(61), 2781.

Schwarz, E. D., & Perry, B. D. (1994). The post-traumatic response in children and adolescents. *Psychiatric Clinics of North America, 17*(2), 311–326. doi.org/10.1016/s0193-953x(18)30117-5

Seadler, K. (2000). Death-related crisis intervention, grief counseling, grief consultation, and death education: A national survey of the role of school psychologists. *Dissertation Abstracts International, 60*(8-A), 2816.

Seligman, M. E. P., & Maier, S. F. (1967, May). Failure to escape traumatic shock. *Journal of Experimental Psychology, 74*(1), 1–9. doi:10.1037/h0024514

Shapiro, L. J., & Stewart, S. E. (2011). Pathological guilt: A persistent yet overlooked treatment factor in obsessive-compulsive disorder. *Annals of Clinical Psychiatry, 23*(1), 63–70.

Shear, K., Monk, T., Houck, P., Melhem, N., Frank, E., Reynolds, C., & Sillowash, R. (2007). An attachment-based model of complicated grief including the role of avoidance. *European Archives of Psychiatry and Clinical Neuroscience, 257*(8), 453–461. doi:10.1007/s00406-007-0745-z

Shonkoff, J. P., & Garner, A. S. (2012). The lifelong effects of early childhood adversity and toxic stress. *Pediatrics, 129*, 232–246. doi:10.1542/peds.2011-2663

Shonkoff, J. P., Garner, A. S., Siegel, B. S., Dobbins, M. I., Earls, M. F., McGuinn, L. P. . . . Wood, D. L. (2012). The lifelong effects of early childhood adversity and toxic stress. *Pediatrics, 129*(1), 232–246. doi:10.1542/peds.2011-2663

Siegel, D. J. (2001). Toward an interpersonal neurobiology of the developing mind: Attachment relationships, "mindsight," and neural integration. *Infant Mental Health Journal, Special Edition on Contributions of the Decade of the Brain to Infant Psychiatry, 22*, 67–94.

Skinner, B. F. (1958). Reinforcement today. *American Psychologist, 13*(3), 94–99. doi:10.1037/h0049039

Smith, C. B. (2018). *Anxiety: The missing stage of grief.* Boston, MA: Da Capo Books.

Smith, H. I. (2004). *Griefkeeping: Learning how long grief lasts.* New York: The Crossroad Publishing Company.

Sormanti, M., & Ballan, M. S. (2011). Strengthening grief support for children with developmental disabilities. *School Psychology International, 32*(2), 179–193. doi:10.1177/0143034311400831

Sprang, G., & McNeill, J. (1995). *The many faces of bereavement: The nature and treatment of natural, traumatic, and stigmatized grief.* New York: Brunner/Mazel, Inc.

Spuij, M., Dekovic, M., & Boelen, P. A. (2015). An open trial of "Grief-help": A cognitive-behavioral treatment for prolonged grief in children and adolescents. *Clinical Psychology and Psychotherapy, 22*, 185–192. doi:10.1002/cpp.1877

Spuij, M., Reitz, E., Prinzie, P., Stikkelbroek, Y., de Roos, C., & Boelen, P. A. (2012). Distinctiveness of symptoms of prolonged grief, depression, and post-traumatic stress in bereaved children and adolescents. *European Child and Adolescent Psychiatry, 21*, 673–679. doi:10.1007/s00787-012-0307-4

Sroufe, L. A. (2005). Attachment and development: A prospective, longitudinal study from birth to adulthood. *Attachment & Human Development, 7*(4), 349–367. doi:10.1080/14616730500365928

References 223

Standing, L. G., & Ringo, P. (2016). Parental loss and eminence: Is there a critical period for the phaeton effect? *North American Journal of Psychology, 18*(1), 147–157.

Stossel, S. (2013). *My age of anxiety.* New York: Alfred A. Knopf.

Stuber, M. L., & Mesrkhani, V. H. (2001). "What do we tell the children?": Understanding childhood grief. *Western Journal of Medicine, 174*(3), 187–191. doi:10.1136/ewjm.174.3.187

Supporting the Grieving Student. (n.d.). Retrieved 2018 from www.aft.org/childrenshealth/mental-health/supporting-grieving-student.

Szanto, K., Shear, K., Houck, P. R., Reynolds, III, C. F. Frank, E., Caroff, K., & Silowash, R. (2006). Indirect self-destructive behavior and overt suicidality in patients with complicated grief. *The Journal of Clinical Psychiatry, 67*(2), 233–239. doi:10.4088/JCP.v67n0209

Tangney, J. P. (1995). Recent advances in the empirical study of shame and guilt. *American Behavioral Scientist, 38*(8), 1132–1145. doi:10:1177/0002764295038008008

Tangney, J. P. (1998). How does guilt differ from shame? In J. Bybee (Ed.), *Guilt and children* (pp. 1–17). San Diego, CA: Academic Press. doi:10.1016/B978-012148610-5/50002-3

Tangney, J. P., & Dearing, R. L. (2002). *Shame and guilt.* New York: Guilford Press.

Tangney, J. P., Miller, R. S., Flicker, L., & Barlow, D. J. (1996). Are shame, guilt, and embarrassment distinct emotions? *Personality and Social Psychology, 70*(6), 1256–1269. doi:10.1037/0022-3514.70.6.1256

Tennant, C., Bebbington, P., & Hurry, J. (1980). Parental death in childhood and risk of adult depressive disorders: A review. *Psychological Medicine, 10,* 289–299. doi:10.1017/s0033291700044044

Tennant, C., & Bernardi, E. (1988). Childhood loss in alcoholics and narcotic addicts. *British Journal of Addiction, 83,* 695–703. doi:10.1111/j.1360-0443.1988tbo2600

Thorndike, E. L. (1933). A proof of the law of effect. *Science, 77,* 173–175. doi:10.1126/science.77.1989.173-a

Tillman, K. S., & Prazak, M. (2018). Kids supporting kids: A 10-week small group curriculum for grief and loss in schools. *Counseling and Psychotherapy Research, 18*(4), 395–401. doi:10.1002/capr.12190

Tonkins, S. A. M., & Lambert, M. J. (1996). A treatment outcome study of bereavement group for children. *Child and Adolescent Social Work Journal, 13*(1), 3–21. doi:10.1007/BF01876592

Torbic, H. (2011). Children and grief: but what about the children? *Home Healthcare Nurse, 29*(2), 67–79. doi:10.1097/nhh.0b013e31820861dd

Toubiana, Y. H., Milgram, N. A., Strich, Y., & Edelstein, A. (1988). Crisis intervention in a school community disaster: Principles and practices. *Journal of Community Psychology, 16,* 228–240. doi.org/10.1002/1520-6629(198804)16:2<228::aid-jcop2290160212>3.0.co;2-k

Toxic Stress: The Facts. (n.d.). Retrieved 2019 from http://developingchild.harvard.edu/topics/scienceofearlychildhood.

Ulin, R. O. (1977). *Death and dying in education.* Washington, DC: National Education Association of the United States.

Van der Kolk, B. A. (2014). *The body keeps the score: Brain, mind, and body in the healing of trauma.* New York: Viking Press.

Vernberg, E. M. (2002). Intervention approaches following disasters. In A. M. LaGreca, W. K. Silverman, E. M. Vernberg, & M. C. Roberts (Eds.), *Helping children cope with disasters and terrorism.* Washington, DC: American Psychological Association.

Virk, J., Ritz, B., Li, J., Obel, C., & Olsen, J. (2016). Childhood bereavement and Type 1 diabetes: A Danish national register study. *Paediatric and Perinatal Epidemiology, 30,* 86–92. doi:10.1111/ppe.12247

Volkan, V. D., & Zintl, E. (1993). *Life after loss.* New York: Charles Scribner's Sons, MacMillan Publishing Co.

224 References

Vonnegut, K. (1999). *Slapstick*. New York: Dial Press Trade Paperbacks.

Vythilingam, M., Heim, C., Newport, J., Miller, A. H., Anderson, E., Bronen, R., . . . Bremner, J.D. (2002). Childhood trauma associated with smaller hippocampal volume in women with major depression. *The American Journal of Psychiatry, 159*(12), 2072–2080. doi:10:1176/appi.ajp.159.12.2072

Walter, C. A., & McCoyd, J. L. M. (2015). *Grief and loss across the lifespan: A biopsychosocial perspective* (2nd ed.). New York: Springer Publishing.

Wass, H. (2000). Death education for children. In I. Corless, B. B. Germino, & M. A. Pittman (Eds.), *Dying, death, and bereavement* (2nd ed.). New York: Springer Publishing Company.

Wass, H. (2004). A perspective on the current state of death education. *Death Studies, 28,* 289–308. doi:10.1080?0748118/07481180490432315

Wass, H., Miller, M. D., & Thornton, G. (1990). Death education and grief/suicide intervention in the public schools. *Death Studies, 14*(3), 253–268. doi:10.1080/07481189008252366

Weiss, E. L., Longhurst, J. G., & Mazure, C. M. (1999). Childhood sexual abuse as a risk factor for depression in women: Psychosocial and neurobiological correlates. *The American Journal of Psychiatry, 156*(6), 816–828. doi:10.1176/ajp.156.6.816

Weymont, D., & Rae, T. (2006). *Supporting young people coping with grief, loss and death*. London: Paul Chapman Publishing.

Whitbourne, S. K., & Whitbourne, S. B. (2014). *Adult development and aging: Biopsychosocial perspectives* (5th ed.). Hoboken, NJ: Wiley Publishers.

White, P. G. (2008). *Sibling grief: Healing after the death of a brother or sister*. Bloomington, IN: iUniverse Publishing.

Wicker, F. W., Payne, G. C., & Morgan, R. D. (1983). Participant descriptions of guilt and shame. *Motivation and Emotion, 7*(1), 25–39. doi:10.1007/BF00992963

Wilcox, H. C., Kuramoto, S. J., Lichtenstein, P., Langstrom, N., Brent, D., & Runeson, B. (2010). Psychiatric morbidity, violent crime, and suicide among children and adolescents exposed to parental death. *Journal of the American Academy of Child & Adolescent Psychiatry, 49*(5), 514–523. doi:10.1097/00004583-201005000-00012

Williams, R. B., & Eichelman, B. (1971). Social setting: Influence on the physiological responseto electric shock in the rat. *Science, 174,* 613–614.

Wolfelt, A. D. (1996). *Healing the bereaved child*. Chicago, IL: Companion Press, Independent Publishers Group.

Wood, S. E., Wood, E. G., & Boyd, D. (2013). *Mastering the world of psychology* (5th ed.). Boston, MA: Pearson Publishing.

Worden, J. W. (1996). *Children and grief: When a parent dies*. New York: Guilford Press.

Wortman, C., & Silver, R. C. (1989). The myths of coping with loss. *Journal of Consulting and Clinical Psychology, 57*(3), 349–357. doi:10.1037/0022-006X.57.3.349

Zakreski, M. J. (2017). Treating complicated grief in a teenager with autism: When the client's limitations prevent engagement in therapy. *Clinical Practice in Pediatric Psychology, 5*(3), 272–281. doi:10.1037/cpp0000191

Zall, D. (1994). The long-term effects of childhood bereavement: Impact on role as mothers. *OMEGA: Journal of Death and Dying, 29*(3), 219–230. doi:10.2190/B93C-NDXK-5N6B-KFE6

Zonneblet-Smeenge, S. J., & DeVries, R. C. (2001). *The empty chair: Handling grief on holidays and special occasions*. Ada, MI: Baker Books.

Zonneblet-Smeenge, S. J., & DeVries, R. C. (2003). The effects of gender and age on grief work associated with grief support groups. *Illness, Crisis, & Loss, 11*(3), 226–241. doi:10.11n77/1054137303254313

Index

abnormal, definition 50–51, 97–99
abstract thought 28–29
acceptance 27–28, 46, 52, 62
accommodation 25
active listening 113–115
adjustment disorder 104
Adverse Childhood Experiences (ACE)
  study 43–44, 158
aggression 2, 72–75, 86, 93–94
alexithymia 94
altruism 86
ambiguous loss 52
American Psychiatric Association 99
American Psychological Association 154
amygdala 11–15, 21
anger 62–63, 72–75
anhedonia 68, 105
anniversary dates 149
antisocial personality disorder 107
anxiety 12–18, 44–47, 84, 103, 128–129,
  141–142
anxiety, death 100, 151
anxiety, separation 26, 42, 94–95, 104
anxiety disorders 105
articles of incorporation 136
assimilation 25
attachment 37–38, 41–42, 45, 144, 157
attributions 82–83
autonomy *vs.* shame and doubt 33, 36, 46

bargaining 62
bedwetting 94
bereavement leave 111
bibliotherapy 152
board of directors, nonprofit organization 136
Bowlby, J. 39, 45, 57
brief psychotic disorder 107
bullying 95–96, 125, 139, 149
bylaws, nonprofit organization 136

catharsis 72, 128–130
cerebral cortex 11
Children's Grief Awareness Day 16
Cobain, K. 129
Cocoanut Grove fire 51
competition, grief 140
complicated grief disorder *see* prolonged
  grief disorder
compulsions 87, 105
concrete operational stage 27–28
conduct disorders 2, 107
conscience development 31–34
copy-cat behaviors 140
cortisol 12, 48
counselors, grief 150–151
creativity 13
crying 66, 70, 85, 96, 112
cultural differences 153
curriculum, grief 126–127, 132–133, 140,
  150–152

Damasio, A. 16
death education 152–153
defense mechanisms 22, 57, 91, 128
delusional thought 107
denial 27, 53, 62–63, 100, 128
depression: agitated 51; biological
  vulnerability to 13; mental health
  disorder 44–48, 61–64, 69–70; 84, 91;
  rates 46–47; signs of 94–98, 105–106
Disney movies 29–30, 175
dissociation 16, 57, 103
distraction 94–95
diversity 132, 149, 153
donations, charitable 126, 137

egocentrism 26–28, 33, 58
Elkind, D. 36
endorphins 16, 129

226 Index

enmeshment 45
episodic memory 18
Erikson, E. 28, 31–37, 43, 49, 57, 82
euphemisms 120, 145
euthanasia 145
explicit memory 17–22, 48

false memories 21, 24
fantasy 26–28, 44, 60, 84, 107
fear 76–81
federal tax ID (EIN) 136–137
feelings, depressed 23, 46–48, 62–64, 84
fight or flight response 11–12, 21, 102
finding meaning 63, 101, 156
formal operational stage 28, 59
Frankl, V. 130
Freud, S.: defense mechanisms 22, 128;
    developmental theory 31–34, 43, 82;
    grief 79, 157; role of id 28
fundraising 126, 130, 137
funerals 122

gender differences 46
generalized anxiety disorder (GAD)105
grants, charitable 136
gratitude 147, 157, 179
grief: acute 51; anticipatory 52–53;
    complicated 14, 46, 53, 102;
    disenfranchised 46, 52, 144; morbid
    51; pathological 102; traumatic 44–47,
    53, 156
guilt 21, 51–54, 63–68, 72–74, 80–89

hippocampus 11–13, 17–19, 21, 48
humor 115
hygiene, poor 94
hyperactivity 94
hypervigilance 104
hypochondria 58, 77, 106, 155
hypothalamus-pituitary-adrenal (HPA) axis
    12–13

id 28
identity 28, 64–65, 83–84, 121, 155
identity vs. role confusion 36, 59, 100–101
illness, in griever 45, 47, 58, 77, 94, 97
imaginary audience 36
implicit memory 11, 18, 21
impulsivity 94
industry vs. inferiority 35
informed consent 133
initiative vs. guilt 33–34
in-service training 136, 150–152
Israeli bus accident 138–139

Jung, C. xii

Kubler-Ross. E. 62–63, 72

lateralization 11, 13–14, 41
law of effect 90
learned helplessness 33, 69, 73, 90–91, 112
Lennon, J. 129
Levi, P. 22, 130
Lewis, C.S. 76

magical thinking 26–27, 34, 53, 62, 84, 87
major depressive disorder 44–48, 61–64,
    69–70, 91, 140, 156
Maslow, A.H. 93
May, R. 154
media, role of 21, 103, 141
media, social 29, 103, 117, 124, 153
meditation 11, 124, 129
mindfulness 11, 129
Mozart, W. A. 129

National Institute of Mental Health
    (NIMH) 44
natural disasters 140, 151
neuropsychology 9
New York Life Foundation 2, 95
Nietzsche, F. 23–24, 130
nightmares 58, 64, 86, 103, 105
nonprofit status, 501(c)3 137
nostalgia 147–149

object permanence 26
obsessions 84, 87, 98, 105
obsessive-compulsive disorder (OCD) 87,
    105–106
Oedipal complex 31
Oklahoma City bombing 141
oppositional defiant disorder (ODD) 107
ostracism 96

panic attacks 86, 89, 95, 104, 106
persistent complex bereavement disorder
    100–103
personal fable 36
pessimism 12, 46, 91–92
pet loss 117, 144–146
Phaeton effect 48
phobias: in early development 42, 58, 77;
    mental health diagnosis 61, 79–80, 86,
    95, 106
physical activity 129
physiological responses 14–15, 80, 104,
    155, 121
Piaget, J. 25–28, 34, 57
plasticity 9–10
play, role in grief 123
Poe, E.A. 129

post-traumatic stress disorder (PTSD):
flashbacks 15, 53; genetic basis 15;
memory issues 21–22; mental health
disorder 61, 103–104, 156; symptoms 13,
44, 47, 141
powerlessness 69, 79, 90–91, 105
prefrontal cortex 13, 48–49
preoperational stage 26–27
professional development 151–152
prolonged grief disorder 102
psychological "crisis" 31
psychosexual stages 31
psychosocial stages 31

reactions, grief 51
reconstructive memory 20–21
recovery, grief 154
registration, state 136–137
regression 58, 64, 128
re-grieving 59
religion 95, 156
religiosity 95
repressed memories 22, 24
repression 33, 68, 74, 84–85, 119
resilience 66, 92, 128, 145, 154–157
responses, grief 51
reversibility 27
risk-taking 36
rituals, grief 66, 139, 145–146
rituals, OCD 87, 106–107
role diffusion 36
role play 149, 153
Rousseau, J.J. 31

sadness: emotional reaction 14, 57, 62,
68–71, 83, 129; after pet death 144–146;
signs of 94, 105
safety, sense of 93, 121, 129, 140–143

schema 17–18, 25–26, 42, 82
school shootings 143
secondary losses 64, 66, 68
self-esteem 2, 33–35, 44, 69, 84
self-harm 70, 86, 94, 102, 140, 172
sensorimotor stage 25–26
shame 33–34, 43, 74, 82–87
sleep 58
sleep disturbances 64
social and emotional learning 152–153
somatic markers 16, 19
somatic symptoms 46, 58
strange situation 39–40
stress relief 129
sublimation 128, 130
substance use 155
suicide 23, 47, 130, 140
survivor guilt 84–85
symbolic thought 27
sympathetic nervous system 12, 104

toxic stress 12–15
Traces of Love Association xii
trauma: definition 44; triggers 14, 125
traumatic bereavement 101
traumatic deaths 66
trust *vs.* mistrust 32–33
*Turning the Page: Helping a Child Cope with
the Loss of a Sibling* 4

unfinished business 40, 53, 119
Ursinus College traumatic loss study 3–5,
123, 155

Van Gogh, V. 129
violence 141
volunteering 130
Vonnegut, K. 24, 74

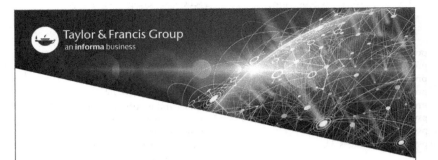